Partisan Nation

Partisan Nation

The Dangerous New Logic of American Politics in a Nationalized Era

PAUL PIERSON AND
ERIC SCHICKLER

The University of Chicago Press
Chicago and London

The University of Chicago Press, Chicago 60637
The University of Chicago Press, Ltd., London
© 2024 by The University of Chicago
Published 2024
Printed in the United States of America

33 32 31 30 29 28 27 26 25 24   1 2 3 4 5

ISBN-13: 978-0-226-83643-0 (cloth)
ISBN-13: 978-0-226-83644-7 (e-book)
DOI: https://doi.org/10.7208/chicago/9780226836447.001.0001

Library of Congress Cataloging-in-Publication Data

Names: Pierson, Paul, author. | Schickler, Eric, 1969– author.
Title: Partisan nation : the dangerous new logic of American politics in a
    nationalized era / Paul Pierson and Eric Schickler.
Description: Chicago : The University of Chicago Press, 2024. | Includes
    bibliographical references and index.
Identifiers: LCCN 2024007655 | ISBN 9780226836430 (cloth) |
    ISBN 9780226836447 (ebook)
Subjects: LCSH: Political parties—United States. | Polarization (Social sciences)—
    United States. | Constitutional history—United States. | United States—Politics
    and government—21st century.
Classification: LCC JK2265 .P54 2024 | DDC 324.273—dc23/eng/20240320
LC record available at https://lccn.loc.gov/2024007655

♾ This paper meets the requirements of ANSI/NISO Z39.48-1992 (Permanence of Paper).

Contents

Contents

The Dangerous New Logic of American Politics

Democrats and Republicans may not agree on much, but for the past two decades, they have regularly shared one very important assumption: a victory by the other party's candidates would constitute a grave threat to the future of their country. Some Republicans called 2016 the "Flight 93" election—implying that terrorists were flying the plane and it was time to storm the cockpit. Many Democrats viewed Donald Trump's 2020 bid for reelection in similar terms. There have been elections in earlier eras where much the same could be said—but never before has there been such a long—and intensifying—run of presidential contests in which so many participants regarded the stakes as existential. This book aims to understand this critical transformation—and its implications for the future of the American political system.

Partisan rancor has become a defining feature of American politics. Growing numbers regard the other party with hostility and fear. Party elites are more polarized still. In Washington and many state capitals, politics has devolved into a zero-sum conflict increasingly detached from long-standing norms and increasingly focused on sustaining partisan advantage. Moreover, party polarization has not simply endured; it has deepened. Aside from a brief post-9/11 interlude, the intensity of these divisions has been building for more than four decades. Even such massive crises as the Great Recession of 2008–9 and the COVID-19 pandemic of 2020–22 failed to disrupt it.

Political scientists and journalists have devoted enormous effort to understanding both the sources of partisan polarization and the many ways in which it shapes the day-to-day behavior of ordinary citizens, election outcomes, and governance. But the intensity and durability of current divisions raise deeper questions. America's constitutional system was not built for this. The Framers clearly hoped that the institutions they designed would prevent intense and durable partisan divisions, and political analysts long believed the Constitution had in fact become a solid bulwark against it. Today, however, we need to ask: Can our constitutional order function effectively amid this polarized politics? Can it even survive?

Polarization itself is not necessarily a threat to America's constitutional democracy. American politics has been polarized in earlier periods, and core institutions emerged largely unscathed, or even strengthened, in its aftermath. Indeed, many commentators have drawn solace from these precedents.

But today's polarization is quite distinctive. Precisely because it is different it has become self-reinforcing—increasingly difficult to dislodge and tending toward even greater intensification. Because today's polarization is so different, it represents an unprecedented challenge to our constitutional system.

The nationalization of political conflict is at the heart of today's dynamics. In past polarized eras, national parties operated within an altogether different political context. Key features—the character of state parties, the nature of group organizations and demands, and the structure of the press—acted as effective countervailing mechanisms against the risk of fierce and sustained polarization. Within a decentralized federal polity, these features created openings for major factional divisions, ultimately disrupting party lines. Repeatedly, the precise dynamic that James Madison famously expected the nation's fragmented institutional structure to encourage emerged. Crosscutting cleavages limited both the intensity and durability of polarizing forces.

Today's polarization, by contrast, has followed a different path. It emerged within a polity that was rapidly nationalizing, giving rise to new organizations and transforming existing ones. Nationalization created new relationships, balances of political power, and incentives. These changes, in turn, have further intensified divisions between the parties, their supporting coalitions, and voters. And the consolidation of this nationalized and polarized polity undercut many of the traditional sources of de-polarization that worked in the past.

While we use the language of polarization it has an unfortunate limitation; it elicits images of symmetry. Speaking of polarization can be taken to imply that the two parties are mirror images of each other, that they have both moved equally—and in similar ways—away from centrism and moderation. Such a depiction may seem a useful simplification (and one that helpfully casts the observer in a seemingly neutral position). But it is simply false. Yes, the new context of nationalization has transformed both parties in some respects that are similar. Both coalitions have become more internally homogeneous and distinct from each other. Each faces growing incentives to operate as a team, both within and across the many venues of our politics. Both parties feel an increasing pull from their electoral base.

Yet the parties are not mirror images. They are *different* coalitions. They have different political aspirations. They have different political strengths and weaknesses—many of them powerfully shaped by the nation's peculiar Constitution. Broad changes in American society, including dramatic changes in media and equally dramatic changes in the nation's demographics, affect the two party coalitions very differently.

The self-reinforcing dynamics we describe are particularly intense in the Republican Party, and these developments in the GOP are particularly damaging to the prospects for effective governance and democratic stability. They have encouraged Republican Party members and constituencies to support actions that escalate perceptions of partisan threat and endanger prior shared understandings of democratic governance. While the forces that would previously have counseled compromise and forbearance have weakened on the left, they have been eviscerated on the right.

In the chapters that follow, we elaborate on the sources of the stark asymmetry between the parties, focusing on differences in their coalitions, agendas, and media environments. A combination of unfavorable demographic change and a favorable skew of American political institutions (the Senate, the Supreme Court, and state legislative maps) present Republican elites with a particularly volatile combination of threat and opportunity.[1] Republican politicians now face strong incentives to behave in ways that both impede governance and threaten the stability of American democracy. Critically, nationalized polarization has severely weakened the traditional institutional and electoral checks on such behavior. The Constitution was simply not designed to meet the challenges we now face. In fact, in many respects it magnifies vulnerabilities to dysfunctional governance and democratic backsliding.

As this brief synopsis suggests, we ground our analysis in historical inquiry. We are by no means the first to use historical evidence to analyze contemporary polarization.[2] Indeed, many studies of polarization begin with a simple graph charting congressional roll-call voting patterns over time to show that Democrats and Republicans have grown much further apart in their voting behavior in recent decades. These data demonstrate that contemporary divisions exceed even those in the late nineteenth century, which had until recently been viewed as the era with the deepest party polarization in American history.[3] Many analysts concerned about the high level of polarization evident today have drawn comfort from their observation that polarization between the two parties, at least when it comes to voting in Congress, has been common in American history. If anything, the period of low polarization from the 1930s–70s was the anomaly.[4] From this standpoint, worry about the intense divisions we observe today is overstated.

Yet these measures of polarization levels only take us so far. They reveal how differently Democrats and Republicans vote in Congress, but that does not tell us whether the parties are fighting about big or small policy issues, how far disagreement extends beyond the subjects of those roll-call votes, or the degree of animus between the parties. Democrats and Republicans can vote in diametrically opposed ways without viewing the other side as fundamentally illegitimate. Ideological "scores" do not tell us whether the strategies used by one or both parties seek to undermine basic democratic values. Put simply, these measures offer a picture of just one form of behavioral differences.[5]

Others have turned to history as a source of analogies for today's politics. The pitched battles between Jeffersonians and Federalists in the early years of the republic, the violent confrontations of the Civil War era, and the conflicts over industrial development and financial policy in the 1890s and early 1900s provide valuable lessons for what polarized politics looks like in practice. Yet these comparisons are also limited in important ways. In particular, historical analogies tend to rely on the assumption that the political context was sufficiently similar across time. If, say, the emergence of a new, crosscutting issue undermined polarization in the past, one might expect something similar to happen now. In fact, we argue, the contexts are so different that these analogies are forced and misleading. Unfortunately, like measures of roll-call votes, simple reliance on historical analogies runs the risk of normalizing today's political dynamics.

Our approach is different. We look at considerable stretches of time during periods identified as highly polarized, laying out the development of both polarization and subsequent de-polarization. Adopting a "thicker" view of the relevant institutions that incorporates mass media, the organization of interests, and the structure of parties, we pay particular attention to the political mechanisms that have generally limited the scope and durability of polarization in these eras. These mechanisms, we argue, were based upon both the Constitution itself *and* a broader institutional context which once allowed decentralizing forces to flourish but no longer does. We draw a crucial distinction between the Constitution—the formal institutions of American government—and constitutional *orders*, which include both the Constitution and the nature of key mediating institutions.

We turn to history, in short, both to consider the rise and fall of polarization in prior eras and to make clear how different the contemporary challenge is from its predecessors. It is different because the constitutional order is different, even as the Constitution itself has remained essentially unchanged.

Our "thicker" view allows us to explore crucial differences between the contemporary parties, to deepen our understanding of the relationship between elite- and mass-level politics, to clarify why contemporary polarization is so durable and intense, and to highlight poorly understood fragilities of the American political system.

How "Madisonian" Institutions Channeled Conflict

While historical analogies have generally offered reassurance,[6] confidence in the durability of American institutions has rested on a deeply rooted conventional understanding that the "Madisonian" system—a design far from the mainstream of constitutions in long-lasting democracies—promises to be a consistent source of compromise and stability.

The Framers were, of course, preoccupied with the question of how to create a stable republic. It is important, however, to emphasize that the Constitution written in 1787 was the product of compromise rather than an overarching, widely shared view of good governance. The formula for dividing authority across levels of government—federalism—was a political necessity given that those seeking a stronger national government had to accommodate thirteen preexisting state governments that jealously protected their power. The specific system of separation of powers and checks and balances enacted differed dramatically from James Madison's original Virginia Plan, which contemplated a much stronger, population-based Congress at the center of American government. Madison's own words defending the proposed Constitution in *The Federalist Papers* include arguments that are inconsistent with the Virginia Plan. Perhaps ironically, given Madison's own disappointment with the final text approved at the Philadelphia convention, progressive historians and pluralist political scientists would, more than a century later, look back to those same essays for inspiration. They articulated a "Madisonian" theory as both an explanation for how the Constitution was intended to work and as a model for good democratic government.[7]

For our purposes, the "Madisonian" construct is useful, even as we acknowledge the danger of reading too much coherence and design into a document that resulted from multiple, problematic compromises, as well as the deep disappointment the "father of the Constitution" felt about the final product, and the fundamental moral limitations of the bargains that were struck. *Federalist,* nos. 10 and 51 were lawyer's briefs intended to defend a painful compromise, but what extraordinarily perceptive briefs they were. Viewing the Constitution through a "Madisonian" lens provides insight into how the constitutional framework gave rise to incentives for compromise and accommodation—at times at great cost—while reducing the potential for intense polarization. Even more, however, thinking seriously about the design and operations of these institutions illuminates why, in practice, they are prone to very specific dangers in today's changed context.

Most obviously, separation of powers, checks and balances, and federalism divide up power, making it less likely that any single group will gain control of the entire government. This, in turn, has meant that governance would routinely require accommodating a range of group interests. The rules structuring elections have also required building different kinds of coalitions for different offices, discouraging the emergence of a single coherent and dominant cleavage. And the geographic foundation of representation—with officials elected to represent specific slices of territory—further bolstered the expression of diverse interests.

Reinforcing the role of geography was the nation's size. When the Constitution was drafted many assumed that a stable republic was only possible on a small scale, such as a city-state. In *Federalist*, no. 10, Madison turned the then-conventional understanding of the relationship between scale and representative government on its head, arguing that the nation's vastness ensured a greatly increased diversity of viewpoints, which would prevent an oppressive majority from gaining control.[8] While a small republic might succumb to a single intense cleavage—over religion, wealth, or some other characteristic—the sprawling new republic would give rise to a much greater variety of issues and interests. Politicians seeking to create a majority would need to make broad appeals to widely shared interests rather than narrow, parochial appeals to a particular faction. Social pluralism, when combined with America's fragmented constitutional structure, forces bargaining and compromise among diverse groups to achieve policy success.[9]

Federalism, from this perspective, is a crucial constitutional feature, interacting with the scale of the republic and the separation of powers to foster pluralism. It is not just that the national government shares power with fifty separate state governments. The diversity of state circumstances, combined with the relative autonomy of state political institutions, makes it highly likely that diverse concerns will not only be commonplace but will gain political expression. A system of geographically based electoral representation further ensures that a wide range of concerns will be funneled up from varied localities into national politics. This pluralism in turn promotes carefully brokered compromises that are mindful of an array of distinctive interests.[10]

Of course, the Constitution had acute moral shortcomings from the start. Most important, the patterns of exclusion built into the document itself—particularly with regard to race and slavery—continue to leave a heavy mark on American politics. And the concessions necessary to gain the acceptance of several smaller states entrenched a system of severe malapportionment that is inconsistent with modern understandings of equal representation. When the great scholar of democracy Robert Dahl—who decades earlier offered one of the most incisive elaborations of the "Madisonian" system—asked in 2001, "How Democratic is the American Constitution?" his answer was that it fell decidedly short of the mark.[11]

The largely celebratory account of the American political system derived from this understanding of the Madisonian framework always had critical blind spots. Most glaringly, it tended to overlook the systematic biases in representation and inequalities in social and economic resources that ensured that, even if power waxed and waned among contending groups and parties, there were plenty of near-permanent losers. Institutionalized white supremacy is the most obvious example. The weakness of organized labor is another—giving rise to E. E. Schattschneider's famous quip that "the flaw in the pluralist heaven is that the heavenly chorus sings with a strong upper-class accent."[12] Madisonian depictions also did not easily accommodate social movements that, in important moments, challenged the legitimacy and stability of the American political system. The political violence of southern "redeemers" during Reconstruction, the rise and suppression of labor militance in the late nineteenth century, and the civil rights—and later, Black Power and anti-war—movements of the 1960s each presupposed a kind of politics that is not comfortably categorized in terms of "pluralist stability." And, of course, there is the Civil War: a rupture when the Madisonian system failed to contain conflict, and a single, overarching division broke the polity apart.

Yet, for all of its blind spots, this conventional understanding of "Madisonian" democracy captured important aspects of how the US system worked. For almost a quarter of a millennium, the operation of American government tended to frustrate the efforts of a particular coalition or individual to consolidate power, dispersing political authority and encouraging pluralism. The operations of the constitutional system might be remade on the ground over time by assertive presidents or new ideological formations (e.g., Franklin Roosevelt and the New Deal), but the core features that gave rise to pluralism and fragmented power remained: separation of powers, checks and balances, territorially grounded representation, federalism, and the extended republic.

The Vital (and Underappreciated) Role of Intermediary Institutions

As we have noted, the formal Constitution operates within a broader constitutional order, which includes critical elements of civil society like political parties, powerful organized interests, and media. These arrangements affect how citizens interpret the political world and how, and how effectively, they act collectively. In turn, they also structure the incentives and resources of political elites. As a consequence, they exert a powerful influence on the way the formal rules embodied in the Constitution operate.

We argue that one cannot understand how American politics "works" without careful attention to the nature of these intermediary institutions and their "fit" with the rules embedded in the Constitution. The failure to appreciate these mediating institutions leads to the mistaken belief that if the formal institutions of American government remain unaltered, we continue to operate within an essentially Madisonian framework. On the contrary, the recent path of polarization—in particular its intensity and durability—can only be understood if we recognize the dramatic changes that have occurred in these mediating institutions and consider how their transformation influences ordinary citizens, political elites, and relationships between the two.

Famously, political parties were not part of the Constitution. Many leading figures at the time expressed a fervent hope that parties could be avoided. Had parties been anticipated, the Framers might well have made quite different choices. Nonetheless, for over two centuries, the unusual American party structure functioned in a manner broadly consistent with Madison's vision.

Indeed, the decentralized parties that developed were essential to making the Madisonian system work, providing much-needed glue across institutions and levels of government, and channels for voters to participate meaningfully in politics. Key here is the unusual organization of American political parties at both the national level and the state and local level. By creating a stronger national government, the Constitution paved the way for national parties, rather than a system of independent state parties. Nonetheless, federalism and the geographic basis of representation, operating in the context of a highly decentralized political system, ensured that state parties would be important players. For politicians, the pathways to power within a state party required a local orientation and focus.[13]

For most of the nation's history, these decentralizing tendencies rendered American parties unlikely vessels for intensely and durably polarized politics. Each state party remained a site of relatively autonomous political power. A critical source of that power and independence was their role in shaping career opportunities for ambitious politicians. David Truman observed that "the basic political fact of federalism is that it creates separate, self-sustaining centers of power, privilege, and profit . . . [and] bases from which individuals may move to places of greater influence and prestige in and out of government."[14]

The diversity of the states themselves reinforced these decentralizing tendencies. States, or clusters of states, were distinctive parts of a nation that spanned a continent. The national economy rested on a complex, geographically structured division of labor. This diversity encouraged strong regional economic ties, along with the development of powerful local elites who energetically protected their interests. Thus, in addition to the formal leverage stemming from state parties' control of nominations, the need to compete for power across a wide span of very different states forced American national parties to take the form of catchall organizations that accommodated a range of ideologies and social groups.

All of this explains why political scientist Nelson Polsby—echoing an earlier comment from Dwight Eisenhower—could argue that "one may be justified in referring to the American two-party system as masking something more like a hundred-party system."[15] A Massachusetts Democrat and an Alabama Democrat might belong to the same formal organization at the national level, but they need not agree on much of anything when it came to policy. It was this arrangement that provided the underpinnings for the famous Will Rogers joke: "I'm a member of no organized political party; I'm a Democrat."

It bears emphasis that scholars who study political systems comparatively—long concerned about the stability of democracy and that of presidential systems in particular—have noted this unusual political fragmentation. The political sociologist Juan Linz, who had witnessed the 1930s breakdown of Spanish democracy as a child, feared that presidential systems tend to be less stable due to dueling bases of legitimacy.[16] Linz viewed the United States as an exception, noting that its weak and fragmented parties prevented this kind of all-or-nothing showdown between an executive and a legislature under the control of competing parties. In short, as Marjorie Hershey put it in her textbook on American parties, federalism and separation of powers has meant that American legislative parties "can rarely achieve the degree of party discipline that is common in parliamentary systems."[17]

These features of party politics lowered the stakes of political conflict—something that scholars of democratic breakdown have long stressed is conducive to stability.[18] Elections were hard fought, but the system constrained winners and offered solace to losers. If one party won power, it was forced to accommodate a diverse array of interests that likely would make its ultimate policies broadly acceptable. Furthermore, the crosscutting cleavages and fluidity of alliances ensured that even if one's side lost today, the outcome could easily change soon.[19]

In the analysis to come, we stress the significance of how parties are organized along with two other critical mediating institutions: the system of organized interests and the structure of mass media. While mistaken about parties, Madison actually had an acute sense of the significance of organized interests, such as wealthy landowners and merchants. In fact, he argued that political mobilization (the emergence of "factions") would naturally flow from perceptions of shared interests, which he saw as grounded largely in economics. The Madisonian framework rested in no small part on the expectation that fracturing authority, especially along geographic lines, would nurture the diversity of these interests and thus anchor political pluralism. Writing in a sprawling and largely agrarian society, where travel and communication were necessarily cumbersome, Madison may have taken this decentralized structure of economic interests for granted. And for much of American political history it generally played its part in supporting the Madisonian vision. But no more. The nationalization of the interest group system has had a profound impact on the constitutional order.

Media is an equally important structure operating between citizens and government. Most of the time, citizens do not experience politics directly, but through various pathways (including family, social contacts, schools, and churches) that inform their views of politics. In modern societies operating on a vast scale, media is arguably the dominant pathway through which citizens make sense of the political world, either directly or indirectly (since family, social contacts, and leaders in institutions like schools and churches also draw on the media to fashion *their* understandings of politics). As Benedict Anderson famously argued, modern polities are "imagined communities." The emergence of "printing-press capitalism," in which reading a daily newspaper becomes "a mass ceremony," played an integral role in fashioning these imagined communities.[20]

Madison appears to have thought less about the role of the press than he did about organized interests. Here again, however, it is easy to see how in an eighteenth-century agrarian context one could anticipate that news media would also reinforce decentralization and thus diversity. Most news would be firmly local. Even where it was partisan, its partisanship would carry a strong local inflection. Again, as we shall see, this basic dynamic held true for most of American political history, with highly localized media joining localized interest groups and highly decentralized parties in reinforcing pluralism. But here again, no more.

In short, the capacity of the Madisonian framework to manage political divisions did not rest on the famous rules of the Constitution alone. It rested as well on a set of decentralized intermediary arrangements—encouraged in key respects by the Constitution itself—that fostered political diversity. The crucial role of these mediating institutions would not be apparent until they underwent a dramatic transformation.

The Rise of Nationalized Polarization

For all its limitations, the Madisonian framework was, for much of American history, a robust obstacle to narrow and durable consolidations of power. But the Madisonian system no longer operates as it once did.

What happened? As with so much in American politics, battles over racial equality were the starting point, though additional factors would also come to play a critical role as a much more nationalized form of polarization developed and became entrenched.

Questions surrounding racial justice have been polarizing in American politics from the founding era. But national *partisan* polarization on questions of racial equality has been rare, and when it has occurred, it has not previously proven durable. This was no accident. The Constitution itself protected slavery from political challenges until the Civil War, while federalism and the fragmentation of power at the national level enabled white supremacy to be institutionalized throughout much of the US for generations after 1865. By creating incentives for a two-party system in which both parties appeal to voters across regions, the Madisonian framework nurtured a national political elite that would generally seek to suppress racial justice claims. This was the case, for example, under the Whigs and Democrats in the party system of the 1830s–50s, as both parties sought to suppress the slavery issue to preserve their north–south coalitions. In the brief moments when one party did embrace racial justice claims, party leaders soon determined it in their interest to back off. After the Civil War, nineteenth-century Republicans saw that a forceful, egalitarian stance on race threatened their national electoral ambitions. Their retreat from the issue—the so-called Southern Compromise— combined with federalism to allow durable, one-party authoritarian enclaves to take hold throughout the South.[21]

Nonetheless, in the 1930s–50s, the same fragmentation of political authority that had enabled the entrenchment of white supremacy also provided openings for the civil rights movement to gain a foothold at the state and local level, and, over time, to overcome the gatekeeping of national party leaders. Here, as in the past, a decentralized structure promoted shifts in party coalitions.

The racial realignment that began in the 1930s, however, was different; it turned out to be the critical first step in the creation of ideologically cohesive parties that offer voters dramatically different visions for the country's future. Prior to this realignment, the Democratic Party was an unwieldy coalition of southern white supremacists and urban ethnic voters. The entry of Black Americans into the New Deal coalition, alongside the rise of racially liberal industrial labor unions, gradually transformed the Democratic Party from below, displacing its uneasy north–south coalition. When civil rights movement mobilization finally forced the issue to the top of the legislative agenda, national Democratic leaders, such as Lyndon Johnson, found themselves leading a party in which critical coalition partners and core party voters had years ago chosen the pro–civil rights side. At the same time Johnson pushed for the landmark Civil Rights Act of 1964 and the Voting Rights Act of 1965 (VRA), Republicans—under the leadership of Barry Goldwater and then, more successfully, Richard Nixon—embraced a "Southern strategy." The two national parties had clearly placed themselves on the conservative and liberal sides of racial issues.[22]

The civil rights movement created a new political environment in which this emerging alignment could endure. Black political organizations, activists, elected officials, and primary voters came to occupy an important place in the national Democratic network, making it less likely that the party would return to its earlier straddle. Meanwhile, changes in demography—as white voters constitute a declining share of the electorate—and changes in racial attitudes in response to decades of civil rights movement activism, have made it possible to win elections by appealing to a coalition composed of people of color and racially liberal and moderate white voters. These same changes in demography and attitudes have, however, also sparked a reaction that has made white identity an even more potent force for many voters, ensuring that Republicans are able to win a substantial share of votes by making explicit appeals to racial resentment.[23] An unprecedented feature of today's politics is that the two "sides" on questions of racial justice and multiracial democracy are closely balanced. For the first time, both political parties have durable incentives to mobilize around racial identities.

Racial realignment was the essential first trigger in the development of contemporary polarization. It made the Republicans and Democrats, respectively, more clearly "conservative" and "liberal" parties and set them apart on a deep and enduring societal divide.

Nonetheless, a second "trigger"—the expanded scope of the national government and of policy battles over that expansion—has also played a key role, propelling the transformation in mediating institutions that has made polarization self-reinforcing. Civil rights played a significant part in this second process as well, though it soon came to encompass many other group interests and policy areas. Given America's political geography and history, enforcing civil rights would inevitably require a major expansion in national authority.[24] The landmark civil rights legislation of 1964–65 empowered the national government to use its fiscal, regulatory, and judicial tools to intervene forcefully in education, employment, public accommodations, and the conduct of elections.

This vigorous expansion helped launch what Theda Skocpol has termed the "Long 1960s," a period spanning the 1960s and early 1970s, which featured a dramatic expansion and centralization of public policy.[25] Liberal Congresses enacted, usually on a bipartisan basis, major new domestic spending programs, such as Medicare and Medicaid. They created powerful new regulatory agencies, establishing extensive rules covering environmental and consumer protection, and workplace safety. Finally, federal courts embarked on a "rights revolution," introducing or expanding a range of rights (most dramatically, reproductive rights enshrined in *Roe v. Wade*). These rulings essentially nationalized policymaking on a host of controversial social issues that had previously been considered state-by-state.

By the late 1970s, Washington had become a much more prominent force, across a much wider range of issues, than it had been two decades earlier. In turn, the expanded role of Washington became a critical issue dividing the parties. It contributed to polarization both directly and indirectly.[26] Directly, it reinforced the process of sorting between the consolidating "liberal" and "conservative" parties. Increasingly, the two parties diverged around fundamental questions regarding this emerging activist federal state.

Indirectly, the growing stakes in national-level politics encouraged the mobilization and nationalization of interest groups.[27] As expanded national authority extended to new environmental and social regulations, an increasingly organized business community fought back. Christian conservatives mobilized in opposition to the policy victories won by social movements on the left during the Long 1960s. Feminists, civil rights advocates and others redoubled their organizational efforts to build upon—and defend—these gains. The conservative Christian reaction featured an enormously consequential change as evangelical Protestants shifted from viewing Catholics as a primary "out-group" to focusing their anger and fears on "secularists."[28] This fostered the development of "Christian" identity as a focal point for political mobilization on the right, one that would over time give rise to dangerous forms of Christian nationalism.

As we shall see, over time these two dynamics—party sorting and the intense mobilization of interest groups—merged. These extensive and now nationalized groups—such as the National Rifle Association (NRA), Christian conservatives, the US Chamber of Commerce, environmental, women's and civil rights groups—faced growing incentives to align themselves with one party or the other.

In some cases, such as organized business, responding to the incentives of the new political context meant tightening an alliance with one party—the Republicans—that dated back generations. For non-economic groups, however, the racial realignment had a decisive impact on the nature of the alliances that formed. By starting the process of sorting southern white conservatives into the GOP, the realignment on race clarified each party's reputation, for the first time making the Democrats an unambiguously "liberal" party and the Republicans a more sharply defined conservative party. The voters predisposed to back conservative positions on gender, sexuality, guns, and a range of other issues were already moving into the GOP due to racial issues.[29] This created the conditions for a stacking of cleavages as each emergent "social" or "cultural" issue mapped onto this earlier racial cleavage. As a result, the two parties do not simply offer different renditions of America's future with respect to racial politics; instead, the sorting around race became intertwined with deep divisions regarding the future of gender relations, the family, and religion in public life.

As the perceived stakes of victory and defeat grew for the groups on each side, they fought more intensely, and their fortunes in those fights became ever more tightly connected to the fortunes of the two political parties. Reinforcing the sharpness of the partisan division was the extraordinarily close political balance between the two parties, which has persisted for decades.[30] Every election has become a high-stakes battle for political supremacy between two evenly matched opponents.

This brief description of interest group evolution is just one example of a broader phenomenon: the transformation of mediating institutions. The initial polarization of the parties interacted with the increasingly national focus of political conflicts to generate major changes in all three sets of mediating institutions. It wasn't only interest group structures that became much more nationalized and partisan. State parties, too, became far more tightly linked to national networks, including the increasingly national system of party-aligned interest groups just described. This didn't just diminish the considerable autonomy that they had possessed through most of American history. State parties faced new incentives to sharpen partisan divisions, in part by bringing national political divisions into local politics.[31] Rather than playing the braking role that had been common in earlier eras, state political parties became engines of polarization.

The vital realm of political media has also nationalized and polarized, although in this case the primary catalyst has been technological change. Indeed, sweeping changes in technology, along with economic globalization, were undoubtedly important drivers of the broad nationalizing dynamics we analyze. Local sources of political news have severely eroded. That has deprived citizens of sites of information that in prior eras had encouraged diverse local concerns to flow into politics and had often led voters to have more nuanced views of the political parties and their candidates. National outlets have become more influential. Fox News exemplifies a shift toward increasingly partisan media, especially on the right. As with the decline of local news, media technology played a central role in this transformation. The developing markets for talk radio, cable, and social media encouraged niche strategies based on the mobilization of outrage. The parties' divide on explosive racial and cultural issues became fodder for partisan media—a source of ratings that in turn focused voters' attention on issues that exacerbate these divisions. There is considerable evidence to suggest that the decline of local media and the rise of partisan national outlets has made polarization at both the mass and elite levels more intense and more durable.

This transformation of vital mediating institutions—all three becoming both more nationalized and more tightly linked to partisan networks—constitutes an unprecedented alteration in how the pieces of the complex American polity fit together. The Constitution has been stable, but the profound shifts in mediating institutions created a new constitutional order.[32] As a result, the Madisonian framework no longer functions. It is because of these changes that contemporary polarization raises distinctive challenges to the American polity.

Voters and Partisan Attachments

A focus on mediating institutions helps to clarify the sources of the nation's increasingly partisan political mindsets. No facet of polarization has been studied in greater detail than changes in the attitudes and behavior of ordinary citizens. Recent work has emphasized that even if most ordinary voters are not consistent liberals or conservatives with sharply polarized policy views, a large share of the electorate is now tied firmly to one party or the other. Moreover, they view the other party more negatively than in the past.[33] There is now extensive research on the psychological processes that make us prone to adopt sectarian attitudes. This account captures part of the story, but it also leaves much out. The psychological mechanisms that induce sectarian thinking are not unique to any one time period. Moreover, the era we live in is by no means the first in which a large number of voters viewed the opposing party and its leaders as enemies. In the decades following the Civil War, for example, Democrats were dismissed as disloyal rebels in large swaths of the North, while just as many white southerners associated Republican identity with race treason, financial exploitation, and military occupation.[34]

Recognizing that voters are susceptible to us versus them partisanship is not enough. It is a bit like noting that mice like cheese (although it turns out that they do not particularly like cheese). We also need to know why there is so much more cheese around. Even if something in human psychology makes us prone to partisan thinking, we show in chapters 2 and 3 that in the past, intense partisan polarization has tended to be relatively short-lived, giving way as other identities and values came into conflict with existing partisan cleavages. A focus on mediating institutions encourages us to push beyond a simple bottom-up (voter-driven) or top-down (national elite-driven) view of how polarization is sustained and intensifies.

The emergence of a more nationalized and polarized system of mediating institutions has powerful effects on political elites, voters, and the interplay between them. The structure of mediating institutions shapes the incentives facing individual politicians. When politicians' career paths ran through diverse state and local parties and depended on courting locally rooted interests and press outlets, they often had good reason to take stands that departed from their national party—and to actively work with opposition party members. Centralized mediating institutions reverse the incentives, encouraging elites to stick with their national party.

This changed behavior of elites in turn has had big effects on voters. Cues that voters receive from political elites, interest groups, and media play a very important role in shaping voters' priorities, directing their attention to some matters rather than others, and encouraging them to identify particular figures as friends and others as foes.[35] In earlier eras many of these cue givers were firmly embedded in diverse local environments. They were at least partly independent of national party leaders and networks and thus could serve as distinctive sources of information for voters.

A common denominator across the recent changes in state parties, interest groups, and the press is that they have fostered a decline in credible, alternative cue givers that in the past created pathways for voters to embrace policies or issues that cut across existing partisan lines. This loss of diversity is crucial, because as the political scientist Jenna Bednar has noted, "in a democracy diversity substitutes for neutrality."[36] When voters draw their cues from a far less diverse set of actors their sectarian tendencies are reinforced. As these sentiments are strengthened among voters it further increases the incentives of politicians to stay with their national team, or even double down on sectarian appeals. Polarization becomes a feeding cycle between elites and voters, with mediating institutions increasing the acceleration.

To highlight how much this change matters, consider briefly the contrast with nineteenth-century parties' reliance on ethnoreligious bonds to win over voters. Then as now, cultural issues were powerful mobilizers and dividers. Yet there was no simple national "cultural" cleavage. In the late nineteenth and early twentieth centuries, for instance, northern Republicans did tend to appeal to native-born, Protestant, and older immigrant groups, while Democrats did better with more recent immigrants and Catholics. However, these ethnoreligious ties structured opinion on a relatively narrow set of issues, such as Prohibition and education (e.g., the use of German in public schools). An individual voter often belonged to multiple groups—ethnic, religious, economic, and geographic—that crosscut rather than reinforced one another. Furthermore, the decentralization of traditional party structures meant that state Republicans or Democrats might tailor their approach to win over—or at least defuse the opposition of—an ethnoreligious group that ordinarily sided with the other party.

Today, cleavages have "stacked" in a manner that promotes partisan animosity. Stark divisions among voters—race, ideology, geography, religion, education—align with party. Political scientist Lilliana Mason argues persuasively that this alignment—and the associated degradation of crosscutting social ties—has turned partisanship into a kind of "mega identity."[37] Mason further suggests that social sorting is self-reinforcing. When a range of social identities all push in a single direction it becomes much easier to see one's opponents as socially distant and perhaps deserving of hatred. Numerous studies have documented the increase in "negative partisanship" and "affective polarization" that is evident as more voters associate the other party's adherents with social groups that they dislike. The stacking of cleavages and growth in negative partisanship make it harder to move individual partisans, generating a dynamic that John Sides, Chris Tausanovitch, and Lynn Vavreck refer to as "calcification."[38]

What becomes clearer when one considers the role of mediating institutions, however, is that neither "stacking" nor "calcification" are automatic processes, resting on voters' naturally occurring political understandings.[39] They are not just a reflection of psychological traits of individual voters, but grounded in the ways mediating institutions promote partisanship in the electorate.

Today's cue givers in state parties, the press, and interest groups are more likely to line up along national party lines than in the past. As a result, they generally intensify, rather than retard, these processes. Local elites are less important, less distinctive, and less autonomous than they once were. They face powerful incentives to align their rhetoric and behavior with that of their national party. Across the country, Republican voters hear consistent messages about the latest threat to America—in the summer of 2021, the outrage of the moment was critical race theory (depicted as the position that whites are inherently evil); two years later, trans Americans became the target, as legislators in Republican states across the US put forward restrictive legislation. Rather than facilitating the emergence of crosscutting issues in American political life, the increasingly nationalized arrangements of party, media and organized interests now typically block that emergence. Instead, even issues like the coronavirus pandemic, which has no obvious partisan valence, are funneled into the ever-hardening lines of partisan enmity.

Of course, a significant share of voters are not hard-core partisans. Many hold moderate views in between the two national parties, even on the hot-button social and cultural issues that lend much of the intensity to today's politics. This leads to the question of why one or both parties does not follow the "median voter" in the electorate, moderating its position on these issues to maximize its vote share. The changes in mediating institutions discussed above help explain why this has not happened. Federalism in earlier eras created space for state parties to do quite a lot to accommodate local preferences, even on hot-button issues. Facing a nationalized network of allied interest groups and media outlets—and a primary electorate that receives a common set of messages from these sources—state and national candidates now face strong incentives to cater to the party base, particularly on identity-laden issues in which the penalties for perceived disloyalty are likely to be most severe.

Immigration politics in the late nineteenth century provides a useful point of comparison. At that time, Republican leaders sidelined hard-core nativists in their coalition by nominating William McKinley for president in 1896. This was part of an effort to compete in urban, immigrant-heavy constituencies. McKinley's success built upon earlier adaptations at the state level, in which Republican organizations turned their backs on several nativist policies that their own core constituents had pushed in previous years.[40] Such moderating adaptations are far more difficult to pull off in contemporary politics. The authors of the post-2012 Republican National Committee (RNC) "autopsy"—which advocated moderating on immigration to compete for Latino and Asian American voters–tried something similar to McKinley's strategy. But it turned out that the RNC did not have the kind of autonomy from allied groups and base party voters that might have allowed such a maneuver to succeed. The rise of Donald Trump—fueled in part by a nationalized partisan media environment that rewards the loudest voices with the greatest resonance among base voters—is in many ways the polar opposite of McKinley's success more than a century ago. In a context where partisan media and nationalized networks of intense policy demanders dominate, the strategy of doubling down on, rather than tempering, nativist appeals won out. Similarly, even in states like California, where demographic change and a culturally liberal electorate scream out to local Republicans to distance themselves from the unpopular positions of the national party, the state GOP has embraced the national agenda favored by its narrowing base. In doing so, it has effectively ceded control of all statewide offices to Democrats, along with supermajorities in the state legislature.

Partisan polarization on race and other so-called "cultural" issues is not itself necessarily problematic. What is problematic is the overlay of these cleavages on each other and on an institutional environment that systematically intensifies the divide and largely blocks the emergence of alternative lines of division that might moderate their impact. Aligned with party, supercharged by other stacking forms of identity, and amplified by media, party and interest group forces, it is hardly surprising that racial division has become a fundamental part of a partisan politics in which members of both parties increasingly perceive the other as an immediate danger to core values.

Dysfunctional Governance and Democratic Backsliding

At the heart of the contemporary crisis is a mismatch between our institutions and the new world of more centralized politics. Put bluntly, the emergent constitutional order is an unstable one. The peculiar nature of the US Constitution makes it poorly suited to handle a highly nationalized system of calcified polarization.

In assessing what this mismatch entails it is essential to remember again the differences between the two parties. These show up in governance, where Republican ambitions—often related to shrinking government and stopping challenges to well-entrenched interests—are much more compatible with a politics of legislative obstruction (especially when backed by an increasingly radical and partisan Supreme Court with the capacity and will to remake policy along conservative lines). The result has been a decline in the capacity of Congress to address pressing national problems, and the rising prospect of unpopular policy initiatives emanating from sites (like the Supreme Court and many state legislatures) where a minority of the electorate has been able to capture political authority.

Even more ominously, a growing partisan gulf dividing urban and rural areas intersects with American political institutions in ways that threaten democratic resilience. On the one hand, the Republican Party base is shrink-ing. On the other hand, features of the US electoral system tilt sharply to-ward the rural-based party—especially in the powerful Senate, but carrying over to most other sites of political authority, including state legislatures, the courts, and (at least prior to 2022) the House of Representatives.[41] Within an increasingly homogeneous party these biases may become cumulative and self-reinforcing (as when a Republican-tilted Senate yields a Republican-dominated Supreme Court, which protects the extreme GOP gerrymander-ing of state legislatures).

This means Republicans may have both motive and opportunity to en-gage in behaviors that undermine democracy. The GOP's conservative, ru-rally grounded coalition possesses a greater sense of existential threat, fueled by both the nation's shifting demographics and a right-wing media ecosystem that is far more extensive, more extreme, and more successful in insulating its audience from diverse viewpoints than anything operating on the left. With many Republicans viewing Democratic successes as a threat to their core identity as white Christian Americans, the willingness to engage in tactics that undermine democratic values will likely continue to grow.

Ironically, the same forces that generate these dangers has also given rise to serious Republican Party factionalism. With a self-contained media envi-ronment that rewards extreme voices and a grassroots base that sees com-promise with Democrats as treasonous, party leaders have repeatedly found themselves beset by challenges from within. Crucially, and in contrast to the generally moderating tendencies of factionalism in more decentralized times, these challenges have come from the far right—from insurgents claiming to be the true voices of conservatism—rather than from moderates from swing districts.

Instead of responding to local demands that differentiate them from most other Republicans, these rank-and-file insurgents tap into a national media and online ecosystem in which the most extreme voices find great rewards. These machinations have pulled the party's leaders further to the right as they seek to keep up with the so-called base, in a process of "outbidding" in which the fear of being labeled a "Republican in Name Only" (RINO) is far more salient than worries about appealing to centrist swing voters.[42]

Republican factionalism has, at times, prevented the party from maximiz-ing achievement of its short-term policy goals. But because it also contributes to a sense of ungovernability, the erosion in trust that follows is not neces-sarily a drawback for Republicans. It weakens faith in the same institutions that Republicans' democracy-eroding initiatives target. If the government is chaotic and ineffectual, defending existing institutions becomes a harder sell.

The ability of Republicans to capture control of national governing institutions (and state governments) while winning a minority of votes creates ample opportunities to enact such democracy-eroding policies. A critical question, which we turn to in chapter 8, is whether it is possible to change the party's incentive structure so that competing to win majorities, rather than aiming to entrench minority rule, will be in its interest. Stepping back, the alarming rise of dysfunction is not inherent in the institutional rules themselves; it is contingent on the strategies of political elites, responding to a specific set of electoral, organizational, and institutional incentives. Change these incentives and you will change the results.

Today's intense polarization thus opens two doors. One leads to the achievement of a genuine multiracial democracy in the United States, the other to serious democratic backsliding. It is no wonder that both sides see the stakes of each election as so momentous.

IS THE UNITED STATES EXCEPTIONAL?

The threats to US democracy are specific, not general. Of course, the US is not the only country to face the threat of democratic erosion. The list of countries that have undergone democratic backsliding, or face increasingly clear threats of it, is distressingly long. The international order as a whole is experiencing what Tom Ginsburg and Aziz Huq call "a democratic recession."[43] These trends have coincided with the rise of (mostly right-wing) populism and ethnonationalism, a rhetorical turn against elites, and an increasingly virulent rejection of shifting gender relations, growing racial and ethnic diversity, and cultural cosmopolitanism. Many of these cases, in short, display at least superficial similarities to recent political dynamics within the United States.

One might ask: Do we need to look for specifically *American* political dynamics to explain our precarious situation? Some relevant trends are doubtless global in scope: shifts in culture and the information environment that fuel grievance and a sense of loss and threat; demographic changes that bolster those fears and give them a focus for political outrage; the loss of manufacturing jobs in industrialized economies that once provided income and opportunity for those without an advanced education. An account of democratic erosion needs to recognize that these trends are widely shared, and that important elements of the rise of right-wing populism involve transnational processes of diffusion. We thus find it unsurprising that scholars who draw on their knowledge of a much wider set of countries figured prominently in the first wave of political scientists raising the alarm about political trends in the United States.[44] The rich comparative literature on democratic erosion contains essential insights for contemporary students of American democracy.

However, there are also very good reasons to see the American case as highly distinctive, with dynamics strongly shaped by internal features. First, on key dimensions, the US is a huge outlier among instances of democratic backsliding. The major cases discussed—Hungary, Poland, Turkey, the Philippines, Venezuela, Brazil, India—are typically middle-income countries with relatively short (and often volatile) histories of continuous democratic governance.[45] Indeed, Ginsburg and Huq note that "the most important insulating factors" protecting against democratic erosion are "wealth and length of democratic experience."[46] On both measures, of course, the United States is very far from the cluster of countries within which it is now increasingly being grouped. The case for considering transnational explanations sufficient would be more convincing if other long-enduring and wealthy democracies were experiencing events like January 6. Instead, we need to discover why the US finds itself sharing the challenges of countries that differ so dramatically on these supposedly crucial structural conditions.

Second, the particular *mechanisms* through which democratic backsliding is emerging as a threat in the United States are not only quite distinctive, but distinctive in ways that are closely tied to the features of the contemporary American constitutional order. Ginsburg and Huq, drawing on a review of a wide range of countries that have undergone democratic erosion, identify the typical mechanisms through which erosion occurs. The specific mechanisms they highlight include: (1) the use of constitutional amendments to alter basic governance; (2) the elimination of checks between branches; (3) the centralization and politicization of executive power; (4) the contraction of a shared public sphere with rights to speech and association; and (5) the elimination or contraction of effective electoral competition.

This list, culled from commonalities across many instances of democratic backsliding in moderate-income countries with short democratic histories, meshes poorly with the dynamics of the United States. There is some overlap, of course, as for instance with President Trump's efforts to weaken the administrative state and place loyalists unconcerned about the rule of law in key positions (mechanism #3).

Yet what is striking in the United States is the extent to which threats of democratic backsliding operate through mechanisms that exploit the constitutional order's *dispersion* of political authority. Among the points of vulnerability are local (and partisan) control of election administration; massive (and partisan) judicial power to determine unilaterally what will be considered a "level" playing field; and heightened (and partisan) capacity to induce gridlock and thus erode the legitimacy of core institutions while avoiding effective oversight over malfeasance.

We will argue that what is critical, and distinctively American, is the combination of this "Madisonian" dispersion of authority with the presence of a nationalized and highly motivated partisan team operating across these dispersed sites. Moreover, two unusual features of our Constitution amplify the potential of these mechanisms to generate democratic backsliding. The first is the prominence of minoritarian elements of the American system: the grossly malapportioned Senate and its judicial offspring, along with acute gerrymandering at the national and, especially, state levels. The second is electoral arrangements that reliably generate two parties and, in the context of intense nationalized polarization, make it possible for a powerful faction within a party to capture the party as a whole.

The structure of the American constitutional order is not the only factor pushing the United States unexpectedly into a backsliding club otherwise populated exclusively by far less wealthy and less institutionalized democracies. Other important factors include the unusual strength of conservative religiosity in the US, the weakness of supports for social mobility for those without a college education, and the nation's ongoing trauma of racial divisions. Yet the capacity of all these factors to generate such profound threats, in an enormously wealthy country with extremely durable institutions of constitutional democracy, cannot be understood absent serious attention to the acute failings of that Constitution itself and, in particular, its poor fit for a political order characterized by nationalized partisan polarization.

The rest of this book proceeds in three parts. In part 1, we look to the past to address the common claim that polarization is the "normal" state of affairs in American politics. Considering the 1790s, the Civil War period, and the turn of the twentieth century, we argue that, while partisan polarization has been a recurrent feature of American political development, periods of intense and truly nationalized polarization have been short-lived and vulnerable to disruption by crosscutting issues and cleavages. In a less nationalized polity, relatively autonomous state parties (at times responding to regionally based third-party threats), the interest group structure, and the press provided critical openings for party dissidents to disrupt the polarized battle lines in Washington.

Part 2 charts the transition to a much more nationalized and deeply polarized era. We explore the developments that initiated the emergence of a deeper and more nationalized form of polarization (namely, racial realignment, ideological sorting, and the great expansion of the federal government from the mid-1960s to the late 1970s). Next, we examine how state parties,

interest groups, and media have all been transformed and pulled into this nationalizing system, such that these dynamics are now self-reinforcing. What
were once brakes have become engines of polarization.

In part 3, we analyze the implications of nationalized polarization for governance and the durability of American democracy. We emphasize that the
impact of this shift is not symmetrical between the parties. The legislative
gridlock induced by polarization results in a shift in power to the executive,
the courts, and state legislatures that has advantaged conservatives. While
nationalized polarization encourages legislative gridlock, it also makes the
Constitution itself vulnerable. A conservative alliance spanning the three
branches—capitalizing on rural overrepresentation in the Senate and the
resulting entrenched Supreme Court majority—has the potential to short-
circuit the process of "ambition checking ambition" that has been a foundation of constitutional governance in the US.

Finally, we close by assessing the depth of contemporary challenges and
considering potential pathways out of the current crisis. The contemporary
political configuration raises deep questions about the future of multiracial
democracy—which itself dates only to the 1960s. Where cleavages stack rather
than crosscut, and partisan media reward the most strident voices, the pluralist
faith that elites will accommodate potential opponents grows shaky. One cannot assume that Republicans will choose to adapt to growing racial diversity by
moderating their approach. Rather, the GOP may double down on strategies
that limit the ability of popular majorities to rule, allowing the party to cling
to power despite demographic headwinds. Addressing this threat will require
reforms that encourage moderation, but achieving this within the contours of
the contemporary constitutional order will be extraordinarily challenging.

PART I

Polarization in Historical Perspective

Conflict and Faction in the
Early Republic and Civil War Era

We begin our history in the late eighteenth century, when the two-party system was emerging but looked very different than it does today. Parties appeared, splintered, and disappeared. They took on highly varied, regional forms. Over the next century, there would be multiple transformations in party politics, including the rise of the mass-based Jacksonian Democratic Party and their Whig opponents in the 1820s–30s, the dissolution of the Whigs in the 1850s, and the onset of a long period of competition between Democrats and Republicans. Yet throughout this long time span, the structure of state parties, group demands, and the press remained decentralized.

In this chapter, we consider the 1790s and the Civil War and Reconstruction era—periods in US history that are often highlighted as deeply polarized along party lines. Chapter 3 considers a third such period, the 1890s–1900s, in greater depth. We selected these periods because they are the ones most often compared to the highly polarized politics of today.[1] We acknowledge that it is possible to specify the boundaries of these periods in a variety of ways, and we do not mean to suggest a sharp dichotomy between "polarized" and "non-polarized" eras.[2] Rather, our goal is to probe the *mechanisms* through which intense polarization developed and then gradually gave way in the face of new policy demands and coalitions.

The 1790s and Civil War era are the periods in US history in which polarized politics came closest to generating a complete breakdown in the constitutional order. The young republic could have collapsed during the confrontations that peaked during the 1800 presidential election contest between Thomas Jefferson and John Adams. The Civil War was the culmination of a decades-long crisis that temporarily dissolved the Union, resulting in hundreds of thousands of deaths before the North's military victory would finally stamp out the crime of slavery. Later, the end of Reconstruction allowed the destruction of the biracial governments that had briefly taken hold in much of the South; it brought about a prolonged era of democratic backsliding and authoritarian rule.

These periods, therefore, clearly demonstrate that polarized politics *can* generate systemic breakdowns. They also show that polarization may, at times, be necessary to achieve social justice, and that de-polarization can be deeply destructive (as it was when Republicans gradually abandoned their commitment to Reconstruction).[3]

Nonetheless, we believe that a critical lesson for the contemporary period is just how *different* the processes surrounding polarization were in these earlier eras. What stands out in each of these periods, especially compared with our own era, is that despite deep antagonisms partisan polarization did not prove durable. Disparate local voices demanded a say. New issues emerged. Coalitions were reshuffled. As we will see, it was rare for societal polarization to map neatly onto the two-party system for an extended period. Instead, party polarization was vulnerable to disruption. Locally rooted party factions, organized interests, and media all played key roles in shaping and limiting nationalized interparty conflict.

Indeed, these new political dynamics typically grew out of intraparty tensions resting on geographic location. Rather than polarization intensifying and "stacking" on issue after issue, divisions in the polity on many matters continued to cut across party lines. Over and over, the parties had to adapt to these pressures. And as they adapted, they further diminished the scope and intensity of polarization.

The Early Republic

The new republic did not have to wait long to experience its first bout of partisan rancor. Almost from the moment they formed, the Federalists and Jeffersonian Republicans denied the very legitimacy of their opponents, each aspiring to be a "party to end all parties."[4] Describing the early parties' deep differences over the character of the new republic, historian Richard L. McCormick claims that no other major parties in American history match their ideological intensity.[5]

Several features of the 1790s find an echo in recent American politics. Eric Foner, writing in the *Nation* in 2021, observes that "if you think our current moment of hyperpartisanship [and] political polarization . . . is unprecedented, think again. As far back as the 1790s, opponents called George Washington a British agent and Thomas Jefferson a lackey of revolutionary

France."[6] Jeffersonians and Federalists viewed one another as bitter enemies, believing that their opponents were traitors bent on destroying the Constitution. Party competition in the late 1790s took on the character of America's "first culture war," with Federalists depicting Jefferson as an atheistic radical who would bring Jacobinism to America, just as John Adams, in the eyes of Jeffersonians, was an aspiring tyrant.[7] Policy conflicts repeatedly spilled over into violent confrontations in the streets.

In 1794, President Washington responded to the anti-tax Whiskey rebellion with a force of more than twelve thousand soldiers, and six years later President Adams sent federal troops back into Pennsylvania to quash Fries's tax rebellion. The fight over ratification of the Jay Treaty with Great Britain featured violence and disorder in several cities, most notably when Alexander Hamilton was reportedly dragged from his platform by a hostile New York City debate audience. As Joanne Freeman notes, "national crises occurred almost annually . . . each one raising serious questions about the survival and character of the national government."[8] Just as the 2020 election aftermath left many wondering about the durability of American institutions, the peaceful transfer of power was very much up in the air in the 1790s and early 1800s.

But in a growing and diversifying polity, the Federalists were soon at a disadvantage because of their pro-British policies, their aversion to newer immigrant groups (such as Germans, French, and Irish), and their identification with wealthy merchants and financial interests. The party might have responded to these growing electoral vulnerabilities by shifting its policies toward citizens' demands. Instead, Federalists passed the Alien and Sedition Acts of 1798 to stifle dissent, limit the naturalization of immigrant groups supportive of the Jeffersonians, and make deportation easier. Their Jeffersonian opponents responded with the Kentucky and Virginia Resolutions, asserting that states had the power to declare federal laws unconstitutional.

It should be no surprise, then, that the future of the republic was widely understood to be at stake in the presidential election of 1800.[9] With neither side believing that the other would uphold basic constitutional rules, many assumed that an opposition victory would destroy the Union. Jeffersonians and Federalists each sought to change Electoral College rules in their favor. Federalist leader Alexander Hamilton went so far as to lobby (unsuccessfully) for Governor John Jay to have New York's lame duck legislature choose electors early, rather than allow the newly elected Republican majority to do so. Hamilton defended the maneuver as essential to block Jefferson—"an *atheist* in religion and a *fanatic* in politics"—from winning the presidency.[10]

When the contest resulted in an Electoral College tie between Jefferson and his running mate, Aaron Burr, it was by no means a foregone conclusion that a peaceful transition of power would take place. Prominent Federalists contemplated ways to block Jefferson's path, while the governors of Pennsylvania and Virginia put their state militias on alert to fight back in case the Federalists were successful. Although enough Federalists eventually voted in the House of Representatives to break the tie in Jefferson's favor, their party by no means gave up on efforts to entrench its power.[11] The Judiciary Act of 1801, which reduced the size of the Supreme Court and created several last-minute Federalist judgeships, was a last gasp effort to frustrate the Jeffersonian takeover.

With these repeated crises and battles over fundamental rules of political competition, the 1790s offer a vivid illustration of the kind of democratic crisis that many fear has started to develop in the contemporary US. When one drills below the surface, though, the sharp contrast to the present era becomes clear. Most notably, the period of polarized two-party competition proved brief, undermined by some of the same mediating institutions that today reinforce polarization.

According to most accounts, the Jeffersonians and Federalists did not congeal into readily identifiable parties at the national level until the fight over the Jay Treaty in 1794–95.[12] Soon thereafter, Federalist influence eroded greatly, starting in 1801 as President Jefferson's moderate approach to policy and personnel co-opted parts of the opposition. Jefferson's success inaugurated two decades of national dominance for his party. After 1803, the Federalists were largely confined to New England and the mid-Atlantic, and never held more than 37 percent of the seats in the US House or 32 percent of Senate seats. Although their New England base would allow hard-core Federalists to remain a threat to national unity—culminating with calls for secession during the War of 1812—the party could not compete on its own for national power.[13]

Equally important, developments within each party transformed their respective stances on key economic issues; many Republicans embraced policies initially put forward by the arch-Federalist Hamilton, and the remaining Federalists moved away from their pro-tariff roots to support free trade. Serious divisions emerged among the overwhelming Republican majorities that controlled the national government after 1800, as pro-manufacturing interests contended with agrarian "Old Republicans." As Federalist power declined nationally, the differences among Jeffersonians generally became more consequential than the battle between the two parties.[14] In contrast to today's intensification of polarization, the overall trajectory in the 1790s–1800s was one of growing factionalism.

Crucially, decentralized mediating institutions—state parties, the structure of group demands, and the press—fostered the development of these factional divisions. The interplay of state parties and group interests was particularly important. In a far more decentralized polity, state and local parties were highly responsive to local political–economic interests even when those interests cut against their national party's purported ideology.

Traditional historical accounts often depict the Jeffersonian Republicans as an agrarian party opposed to the developmental, pro-manufacturing agenda of the Federalists.[15] In fact, the Jeffersonians crafted their eventual majority by absorbing an urban constituency of artisans and mechanics (workers who used machines and tools) in northern and mid-Atlantic cities who favored a stronger national government that would promote manufacturing through tariffs and infrastructure investments.

Urban artisans and mechanics were initially a solid Federalist constituency, hopeful that the Washington administration's developmental program would provide tariffs and other supports for manufacturing. By the mid-1790s, however, the pro-British tilt of Federalist policy frustrated mechanics who were seeking greater protection from British imports, while also alienating those sympathetic to the French Revolution as conflict in Europe grew.[16]

Locally rooted Democratic-Republican societies brought these potential new constituents into their own incipient party's camp by advocating for domestic policies that better fit these groups' interests. New York City Republicans began to style themselves as "spokesmen for productive capital," borrowing the language of Federalist mechanics from 1789 in advocating for tariffs.[17] Philadelphia Democratic-Republican societies capitalized on mechanic opposition to the Federalist-passed Revenue Act of 1794, recruiting congressional candidates who ran on an anti–excise tax, pro-tariff platform.[18] Jeffersonian-controlled northern state legislatures undertook economic development policies, such as chartering corporations to build bridges and turnpikes, and banks to provide finance. The historian Alan Peskin concludes that by 1800, "many, if not most urban advocates of manufacturing had flocked to the party of Jefferson, an ironic development considering the Virginian's well-known pronouncement that his countrymen should 'let our workshops remain in Europe.'"[19] Because of the considerable autonomy of state and local organizations the doors had opened to incorporate these new interests at the local level despite the tension with Jefferson's own stated ideology.

The entry of urban, pro-manufacturing interests not only broadened the base of the emergent party, it fostered an ongoing conflict with agrarians. The historian John Brooke notes that by the early 1800s, "in each state a mosaic of factions emerged, pitting more developmentally inclined Federalists and moderate Republicans against agrarian 'Old Republicans.'"[20] In this fragmented polity, Federalists could continue to maintain a foothold in New

England, even as the party faded away nationally. The remaining Federalists, however, primarily represented a commercial constituency of merchants reliant on trade, rather than aspiring manufacturers. In the 1790s and early 1800s, Federalists moved away from Hamilton's mercantilism, instead pushing for increased overseas trade. Even in Boston, where the Federalists retained a large constituency of mechanics, party members emphasized how free trade promoted manufacturing in the long run. As a result, it is ironic but not surprising that it was a Jeffersonian Republican, Adam Seybert of Pennsylvania, who in 1809 proposed on the House floor that Hamilton's Report on Manufactures be reprinted, as it could serve as "the basis on which an important superstructure might be raised."[21] Seybert's proposal reflected a prominent but by no means consensus viewpoint among the Jeffersonians, as many other party members continued to uphold the ideal of an agrarian republic.

Critically, the competition primarily occurred within the Republican Party, with different coalitions dominating in different states. These dueling groups were locally based rather than deeply embedded in national organizations. As such, there was little pressure for a reckoning. Instead, the Jeffersonian Republicans could thrive as a catchall coalition, in Peskin's words, "divided over the details of the producer economy" and disagreeing about "what role government should play in its realization."[22] The relationship of group demands to the party system in this era bears little relationship to the current durable "stacking" of cleavages.

Southern slaveholders, of course, were a foundational constituency for the Jeffersonians throughout this period. But the party coalition also depended heavily on northern artisans and mechanics who supported economic development policies that, at a minimum, made many of these slaveholders nervous at the prospect of uneven regional development. The northerners, in turn, repeatedly chafed at the southerners' sway over the party. Padraig Riley observes that "as the national power of Federalism declined [after 1800], the differences between the two wings of the Jeffersonian coalition, one tied to democracy and one tied to slavery, became more apparent."[23] A faction of northern Republicans in the House repeatedly angered their southern counterparts, voting for proposals to tax the slave trade and to emancipate enslaved people in the nation's capital.[24]

More generally, antislavery movements in northern states gained support from both Federalists and Republicans, rather than polarizing the parties.[25] David Bateman's study of legislative voting on Black suffrage shows that 45 percent of Federalists and 40 percent of Jeffersonians supported continued free Black voting rights in their states prior to 1821.[26] This small overall partisan difference reflected tremendous regional variability in both parties, with southern Federalists among the most strident in their opposition to rights for free Black residents. Battles over Black suffrage in states such as Ohio and New York reflected the particular coalitional dynamics among competing Jeffersonian factions in those states. Concerns about offending southern slaveholders were part of the mix, but of varying importance to the contending forces within the party. From this perspective, slavery was a critical factor shaping the politics of the era, but it did not cleave the parties into opposing camps as it would decades later.

Like local parties, the partisan press both reflected and reinforced the co-alitional diversity within the Jeffersonian party. Jeffrey Pasley documents the central role newspapers played in forging the first party system, emphasizing that newspaper editors were "the face and voice" of their party in many cities and towns. This voice, however, varied across geographic units. Rather than centrally directed messaging outlets, party newspapers operated as decentralized networks, with great flexibility to "show different faces in different localities."[27]

Local editors were free to choose aspects of the national campaign that fit locally. For example, William Duane's Philadelphia Aurora—arguably the leading Republican paper at the time—portrayed Thomas Jefferson as anti-slavery in the lead-up to the 1800 election, while southern papers claimed Jefferson as proslavery. A few years later, Duane would argue that the Louisiana Territory would ultimately not have slavery. The Aurora, along with other northern Republican papers, celebrated the abolition of the slave trade in 1808 as a first step toward national abolition. The Republicans thus could present their party as a friend of slavery to southern audiences, while appealing to abolitionists in the North.[28]

A decentralized press also facilitated the incorporation of new manufacturing interests and former Federalists into the Republican fold. In his study of Jeffersonian politics, Peskin highlights the role of mid-Atlantic newspapers, such as the Baltimore American, in giving voice to manufacturers within the Republican Party. Rather than echoing a single national line, the local party press expressed a range of competing views. For example, "old-school" Republicans who were more skeptical of manufacturing were represented by New York's American Citizen, while "new-school" pro-manufacturing views were reflected in the American, along with the Aurora.[29] Pasley similarly traces the rise of Republican newspapers in former Federalist strongholds, underscoring how decentralization helped "tailor party messages to suit local audiences." The Worcester, Massachusetts Aegis, an important Republican paper, "exploited the decentralization of the Republican newspaper network to present the party in a form that was far more acceptable to New England sensibilities than the one appearing in the *Aurora* or even Jefferson's Washington mouthpiece, the *National Intelligencer.*" In the pages of the *Aegis* and other New England papers, "the Republican cause was cast in as conservative light as possible" and the focus was placed on issues—such as the Louisiana Purchase—that were broadly popular in the region.[30] Republican voters in Massachusetts, Pennsylvania, Maryland, or Virginia would thus find a range of perspectives on how to balance the priorities of new manufacturing and traditional agrarian interests in the party, as well as on the extent to which the party stood for egalitarian reforms.

Although newspapers would come together at critical moments—such as the 1800 election—to push for the election of their party's standard-bearer, their decentralization also made them potent channels for factional divisions to flourish. Soon after Jefferson's inauguration, Philadelphia radicals and moderates engaged in a heated power struggle, each side deploying its newspaper in an effort to read the other faction out of the party. As Republicans gained national dominance, the party became increasingly factionalized, with each wing of a local party requiring its own newspaper to stay competitive.[31]

Within a few years, there were multiple competing party papers, not just in Philadelphia, but in New York, Baltimore, and Pittsburgh, among other cities. This launched a pattern that would hold for decades; party factions battled to control key newspapers through most of the nineteenth century.

The net result was an inchoate ideological politics rather than a sharp polarization into two competing camps. Today, few observers of our polarized politics would have much trouble identifying the main ideological commitments of the two parties, yet when it comes to this early era of much more limited and short-lived party polarization, historians have put forward "wildly conflicting interpretations" of what Federalists and Jeffersonians stood for. As Brooke puts it, "Were the Federalists self-seeking capitalist speculators or order-seeking conservative gentry? Were the Jeffersonians liberal capitalists or republicans ever fearful of the consolidation of power?" These conflicting understandings can be reconciled by recognizing "regional political cultures . . . the most coherent 'classical republicanism' could be found among country Calvinist Federalists in New England and southern planter 'Old Republicans'; urban northern Jeffersonians were by far the most liberal in outlook."[32]

In short, the earliest American parties competed nationally (if only briefly) for power, but they were embedded in a fragmented political system that allowed each party's label to hold a different meaning for voters in different regions and, at times, within a given state.[33] Far from doubling down on a single set of commitments as the Federalist Party gave way as a national force,[34] the

Jeffersonian Republicans quickly incorporated such a broad range of views and interests that they could be readily identified as the ideological forerunner of both the Jacksonian Democrats and Whigs of the second party system.

The Civil War

The Civil War stands out as the most dramatic moment of institutional breakdown since the founding—one that sets it apart from all subsequent polarized eras. Nonetheless, there are striking similarities between the polarization process that took place in the 1850s and recent developments: Intense societal polarization became aligned with partisanship as cleavages increasingly stacked, politics acquired a greater national focus as the slavery issue became explicitly connected to a range of other policy battles, and changes in the press furthered the nationalization of conflict. Together, these shifts fostered the belief that the opposing party's victory posed an existential threat to the country.

A critical difference, however, is that a single issue about the very nature of the republic—slavery—underwrote both societal and party polarization. This issue divided the nation into clearly defined regional camps, each with the will and capacity to mobilize massive numbers of soldiers to fight. The constitutional system's failure to withstand deep societal and partisan division on an issue of existential importance makes plain the limits of institutional "solutions" to formative divides.[35]

A crucial feature of the lead-up to the Civil War is that societal polarization *preceded* intense partisan polarization. The second party system, forged in the 1830s as the Whig Party formed in opposition to Andrew Jackson's Democrats, had been premised on the suppression of slavery as a political issue. The Whigs and Democrats each sought to appeal to white voters in both the North and the South. This gave national party leaders an incentive to avoid discussing slavery, fearing it would divide their coalition.[36]

When advocates on either side forced the future of slavery onto the political agenda, these leaders moved to enact compromises that would avert an open confrontation. In this context, candidates—continuing the Jeffersonians' 1800 campaign strategy—presented very different party messages about slavery to their northern and southern constituents. In 1836 the Whigs went so far as to run multiple presidential candidates, each representing a different region. As late as 1852, both major party nominees for president—Democrat Franklin Pierce and Whig Winfield Scott—were attacked by the opposing party as either instruments of slaveholders or as abolitionists, depending on whether the audience was in the South or North. Joanne Freeman writes that "banking on the limited reach of some local papers . . . neither party had a single Frank Pierce running for president; they had Northern and Southern Pierces of opposing politics."[37]

Abolitionist movement activism, enslaved people's resistance, third-party insurgencies, westward expansion, and southern extremism brought slavery to the top of the political agenda in the 1850s. Soon, these strategies of obfuscation collapsed, and the two major parties broke apart.

Locally rooted Whig and Democratic politicians played a significant role in this process, responding to bottom-up pressure by repeatedly forcing slavery onto the legislative agenda through such initiatives as the Wilmot Proviso barring slavery in the territories acquired in the Mexican War. The Proviso, proposed by a Pennsylvania Democrat and supported by New England Conscience Whigs, inspired the formation of the Free-Soil Party ahead of the 1848 election. While top party leaders sought to suppress these antislavery forces, individual politicians' career paths mainly went through their state and local communities, giving them ample incentive and opportunity to resist leadership pressure. As the single issue of slavery came to dominate public debate and sharply divide North from South it became impossible for a party to succeed by refusing to take a clear stand.

The polarization process bore important parallels to recent developments in the US. Just as technological changes have transformed the media environment in recent decades, the growth of the penny press and a more diverse print market in the 1830s, followed by the spread of the telegraph in the mid to late 1840s, connected the nation in new ways, making it harder for the parties to tell entirely different stories to different regions on a highly salient issue. By the 1850s, when southern slaveholders attacked northerners (or vice versa) in Congress, the conflict was more likely to be relayed across the country, regardless of Whig or Democratic leaders' hopes of submerging the debate.[38] As the historian Ariel Ron observes, "the explosion of print-based formats . . . disrupted a political system that, for about thirty years, gave party leaders the power to position the issues of the day."[39]

New communication technologies also facilitated the growth of social movements, policy-demanding groups, and third parties that further undermined the major parties' agenda control and contributed to the sharpening north–south divide. Starting in the 1830s, Black and white abolitionists took advantage of declining print costs, launching newspapers and distributing pamphlets that spread their message to a national audience. They also coordinated a mass petition drive to Congress calling for an end to slavery in the District of Columbia. Southerners' furious response—particularly their successful push to pass a "gag rule" barring such petitions—dramatized the Slave Power's hold on the government, providing a further boost to antislavery organizing.[40]

Although the Liberty Party, which formed in 1839–40, had only limited electoral success, its leaders and allied newspaper editors actively lobbied for the abolitionist cause in Washington. The historian Corey Brooks credits the party with "channeling grassroots abolitionist activism into national politics," pressuring northern representatives to stand up to the South.[41] Its successor, the Free-Soil Party, was able to win enough House seats to control the balance of power following the 1848 elections. It capitalized on its leverage to force an extended fight over electing the Speaker in 1849, highlighting Slave Power influence. The chaotic party competition of the 1850s—in which the Whigs disintegrated and the Democrats divided along regional lines—reflected movement activists' success in forcing slavery to the top of the agenda, along with southerners' extreme response to this challenge.[42]

Ariel Ron's analysis of agricultural interests offers a telling example of the stacking of cleavages that took hold "as political abolitionism succeeded in making slavery the one inescapable issue, [and] other movements were driven into sectional alignment."[43] Exploiting new communication channels, a vibrant and politically powerful agricultural reform movement developed in the 1830s–50s that, in principle, could have appealed to both southern and northern farm audiences. However, the movement's policy goals—the promotion of scientific agriculture through the creation of a Department of Agriculture and land grant colleges—ran aground of southern slaveholder hostility to forms of national governmental power that might ultimately threaten slavery. Although the agricultural reformers sought to steer clear of the north–south divide on slavery, southern opposition repeatedly stymied their policy proposals. The nascent Republican Party quickly embraced the agricultural movement, pushing its legislation, and bolstering the support of northern rural voters in the process.

A range of other societal groups also staked out opposing stances as slavery came to dominate the agenda. For example, religious and fraternal organizations that had crosscut region and party split into northern and southern branches in the 1840s–50s, as advocates on either side pushed for a clear stance on abolition.[44] Ron aptly summarizes how more issues and groups were drawn into the slavery conflict: "A run of binaries now stacked up in ordered columns: national versus state sovereignty, active versus limited government, domestic versus overseas markets, sectoral diversification versus concentration, free versus slave labor, and, finally, North versus South."[45] The South's effort to use the national government's power to enforce slavery throughout the US—through such moves as the Fugitive Slave Act and the *Dred Scott* decision—only heightened the focus on the contest for national control.

Sectional polarization on a single overriding issue destroyed a party system that had not been highly polarized, and served as the basis for a new, polarized system in which the Republicans represented northerners opposed to the extension of slavery and Democrats were the party of southern enslavers.[46] This overlay of sectional and partisan polarization very quickly sparked the Civil War, as southern Democrats concluded that Republican victory constituted a mortal threat to slavery.[47]

There is a rich debate concerning the extent to which the war itself was "partisan," with some emphasizing the extent to which the Republican Party served as an essential organizational and mobilizing agent for the battle, and others instead pointing to Lincoln's efforts to win over pro-war northern Democrats through creation of the Union Party and (initially) downplaying the antislavery purposes of the war.[48]

One way to synthesize these views is to note that while partisanship was potent, the new party alignment forged in the late 1850s was, from the perspective of actors on the ground at the time, far from secure. Signaling the unsettled status of party lines, only one of the four presidential elections from 1860–72 featured clear-cut Democratic versus Republican tickets. In 1860, Democrats split into northern and southern wings, competing with Constitutional Unionists and Republicans. Lincoln ran for reelection in 1864 under the Union Party banner, fatefully including Democrat Andrew Johnson on the ticket in a bid to win over border state voters.[49] After the more traditional 1868 contest, Liberal Republicans bolted from the party in 1872, fusing with Democrats to nominate former Republican Horace Greeley to face off against Republican incumbent Ulysses Grant.

The shifting party labels and fusion efforts were rooted in the sharp geographic cleavage underpinning the new party system, which left both parties vulnerable. Republicans were able to build a northern majority on a platform of no further extension of slavery, but the issues that flowed downstream from this commitment—the questions of immediate abolition, equal rights for Black Americans, and the terms of Reconstruction for the South—divided the party's potential supporters in the North. These divisions help make sense of the observation that, for all of their free-soil advocacy, Republicans tended to avoid talking about race.[50]

For Democrats, the divide between "war" and "peace" camps made plain the problem that association with secession posed in many northern states. In the postwar era, regaining power would require that Democrats recreate a co-alition of white southerners with parts of the North—such as New York—that occupied a very different position in America's political economy.[51]

Today, there is no single issue that defines the party system in a manner analogous to slavery. Nor are party lines so sharply delineated by region, so that an all-out war is on the table. Instead, as we show in parts 2 and 3, con-temporary polarization is self-reinforcing precisely because each new issue or policy demand can readily be folded into the partisan divide. So far, at least, no single, uncompromisable issue has forced an ultimate reckoning. It is pos-sible that the deepening of authoritarian impulses of the Republican Party is doing so—an issue that we will take up in chapters 7 and 8.

Republican Factionalism and Reconstruction

The development of the party system in the immediate postwar years offers a telling example for how the operations of mediating institutions provided space for factional divisions to work their way into the party system, under-mining the intense polarization that had brought about the Civil War. One might argue that the outcome of the Civil War, on its own, did away with polarization; after all, with the slavery issue settled, Republicans had lost the one issue that had unified their ranks. But the war itself, with its hundreds of thousands of casualties, forged very strong partisan identities—and hatred of the opposing party—that rival or exceed the partisan animus in any other period. The stacked cleavages that emerged in the lead-up to the war did not automatically evaporate with the end of fighting. Nor did political elites' in-centive to remind their fellow partisans of the death and destruction that they attributed to the other party's decisions. But national leaders' efforts to keep their respective sides unified as the US confronted the question of postwar Reconstruction faltered as rank-and-file politicians faced strong incentives to respond to local interests and demands.[52]

As new questions reached the agenda, they were not absorbed into the existing sectional cleavage over slavery and race. Instead, crosscutting inter-ests emerged that undermined polarization. Conflicting economic interests within the GOP coalition weakened the party's commitment to racial equal-ity, helping to lead to a dramatic narrowing of the interparty conflict on the issue at the heart of the Civil War and Reconstruction. We first consider the role of growing Republican factionalism in undermining Reconstruction, and then focus in on the crosscutting economic cleavages that came to domi-nate politics by the mid to late 1870s.

From the start, Republicans had dueling visions of Reconstruction. So-called "radicals" and "moderates" disagreed on the extent to which Black rights should be expanded through federal legislation and on the scope of federal authority over states and individuals. President Andrew Johnson's explicit identification with southern white supremacists momentarily unified his Republican opponents behind radical Reconstruction in 1866–68, but this unity quickly broke down. Amid mounting southern white violence against Black voters, "radicals" battled with more conservative Republicans over legislation to protect civil rights. Increasingly, the latter argued that the party should essentially declare victory and move on from Reconstruction.

Republicans faced bitter divisions over a series of enforcement and civil rights acts in the early to mid-1870s. This ended with the failure, in early March 1875, to enact President Grant's proposed measure to fight back against white southerners' violent repression of Black voters. Grant himself refused to deploy troops to suppress the wave of Mississippi violence that same year. Republicans' waning commitment to intervention in the South meant that by the time of the 1876 election, Reconstruction was "nearly moribund."[53] The Republican *Chicago Tribune*, turning a blind eye to the violent voter suppression, argued in April 1877 that "peace prevails between the whites and the Blacks" in the South, declaring that "the colored men have nothing more to ask; there is nothing which national politics can give them as a class."[54]

The Republican factionalism on Reconstruction reflected an institutional context in which locally rooted members of Congress remained free to adapt to the diverse constituent demands and interests they faced. A series of election setbacks starting in 1867 signaled to many northern Republicans that their voters simply did not favor aggressive action on civil rights. The *Nation*, founded by antislavery activists, criticized Radical Republicans for "preaching equal suffrage with as lofty an indifference to the prejudices or opinions or traditions of the mass of the public as if they had been offering the gospel to a set of heathens," concluding that "it would not now be a bad plan for the advanced Republicans to come down off the theological platform and bring [Black] suffrage down with them."[55] This appalling judgment would become increasingly common among Republican politicians over the next several years. Speaker James Blaine (R-ME) told a Black Republican colleague that he was relieved the Senate had failed to approve legislation responding to southern white violence in the 1874 elections, noting "it was better to lose the South and save the North."[56]

The prospect of relying on southern votes to maintain their national majorities had become less appealing to many northern leaders and rank-and-file politicians as they came to believe that Reconstruction was costing them votes in the North. The drive to solidify the party's hold in their northern and western base increasingly took precedence over deploying the resources necessary to defend southern Black rights.

Changes in the interest group environment also mattered. Financed by debt, the Civil War created a new constituency of finance capitalists. Richard Bensel argues that representatives of finance capital became the Republican faction most hostile to continued Reconstruction due to their interest in financial stability and the resumption of the gold standard. With spending on Reconstruction accounting for roughly 25 percent of the federal budget, finance capitalists urged retrenchment. Rather than continued military occupation, their economic interests called for speedy reincorporation of the old southern planter elite, and with it, a restoration of cotton exports.[57]

The Liberal Republican bolt from the GOP in 1872 clearly signaled that the terrain was shifting. The new party was led by former Republicans who favored reining in Reconstruction, a rapid return to the gold standard, and low tariffs.[58]

Once again, news organizations played a major role. The editors of several traditionally Republican newspapers helped to launch the third-party movement.[59] The fragmented nineteenth-century political system created considerable space for party newspapers to take positions with local appeal that nonetheless undercut their national party's stance. For Liberal Republican editors, the goal of shifting the Republican Party away from both Reconstruction and Grant trumped any loyalty to the legacy of the Civil War. The idea of a Liberal Republican alliance with Democrats first took hold at the state level, when liberal Missouri Republicans defeated the Radicals by forming an alliance with Democrats, persuading liberals that they could achieve similar success with this strategy at the national level.[60]

Although the Liberal Republican–Democratic fusion ticket for president was defeated at the polls, it highlighted the ongoing potential for third-party challenges to put pressure on existing party lines. Indeed, Foner observes that the fear of the liberal insurgency "sent Republicans scurrying to solidify a moderate image in relation to Reconstruction," leading, among other retreats, to the passage of the Amnesty Act restoring the right to hold office to nearly all former Confederates. Black Republicans in Congress accurately feared the act "presaged the complete abandonment of Reconstruction."[61]

The official positions of Republican state parties signaled the fracturing of the party's commitment to Reconstruction. Amid violent southern repression of Black voters in the mid-1870s, New York's 1876 platform coupled a vague call for safeguarding the equal rights of all with a paean to "earnestly seeking the true harmony of the Union." Reflecting New York's status as a financial center, the platform was much more detailed and straightforward in urging the reestablishment of the gold standard, devoting about four times as much text to that subject as to securing citizen rights. Similarly, neighboring New Jersey's platform offered no condemnation of ongoing southern violence or call to action to bolster protection for Black voting rights. It instead emphasized the need for "the earliest possible resumption of specie [gold] payments."[62]

More generally, state Republican Party platforms were split about equally between those—such as Pennsylvania, Illinois, and Mississippi—calling for strong action against southern violence, and those—such as Iowa, Michigan, and New Hampshire—that took credit for the Civil War and the successful passage of the Reconstruction amendments, but were silent on the need to respond to the threats engulfing southern Black voters.[63] Although there were Republicans who continued to push for Black voting rights after 1876—culminating in the drive to pass a Federal Elections Bill in 1890–91 (see discussion in chapter 3)—ensuring Black rights in the South was no longer a priority for the party. Instead, economic issues that brought about new divisions took on increased prominence.

It is important to note that even amid Republican factionalism, the possibility of a violent partisan conflict over national power loomed as late as the 1876 presidential election, which pitted Republican Rutherford B. Hayes against Democrat Samuel Tilden. In the days following the election, it became clear that the winner would be determined by the resolution of disputed results from Florida, Louisiana, and South Carolina, in which the violent suppression of Black voters and extensive fraud gave rise to dueling slates of electors. As the stalemate dragged on, it sparked fears of a "two governments" problem in Washington, DC. Historians have long debated whether there was a "Compromise of 1877" that resolved the election contest through an agreement to end Reconstruction. Gregory Downs argues persuasively that the narrow focus on whether there was an explicit "compromise" has distracted from the deeper questions about the nature and limits of democratic consolidation in the US, concluding that "stabilization" ultimately was "tied to the retraction of democracy . . . through violent Democratic domination of southern freedpeople."[64]

A key point is that Republicans' willingness to embrace "stabilization" on these terms reflected a shift in GOP commitments and priorities that had been unfolding for several years amid mounting intraparty divisions. Given southern Democrats' refusal to accept democratic rules of the game for the region, it would have required continued national polarization to afford any possibility of achieving a degree of racial justice. Instead, the interests of northern Republican politicians competing for power in their home states—in the context of continued racism along with emergent economic demands—cut against sustaining the national commitment necessary to turn back white southern violence.

THE "UNSTACKING" OF CLEAVAGES AFTER THE WAR

The shift away from Reconstruction reflected a broader "unstacking" of cleavages, as a diverse set of group demands displaced the north–south divide that had previously absorbed so many other issues. Changes in the agricultural reform movement were an important contributor. The end of slavery transformed the political calculus for agrarians, who soon shifted from their exclusive connection to the Republican Party. It was now feasible to link the interests of southern and northern farmers behind shared policy goals.[65]

From the Department of Agriculture's standpoint, promoting farmers' organizations across the US could bolster the agency's support and insulate the agency from fluctuations in party power. The Grange, which was founded in 1867 and grew dramatically in the 1870s as the leading farmer lobby, deliberately positioned itself as a nonpartisan organization and courted southern planters with a promise of sectional reconciliation that upheld white supremacy.[66] Charles Postel observes that the Grange combined large membership numbers, disciplined organization, a network of influential farm journals, and strong ties to politicians in both the states and Washington. Drawing on support from both Democrats and Republicans, it "pioneered a new politics of the mass interest group."[67]

Cleavages around economic issues emerged in the Republican Party well before the collapse of Reconstruction. The tension between agrarian interests and eastern Republicans was evident by the late 1860s, as midwestern farmers began to chafe against the hard money position promoted by eastern financial interests. Ohio Democrat George Pendleton was the first to capitalize on the division, putting forward the "Ohio Idea" opposing the withdrawal of greenbacks—paper dollars not backed by gold—from circulation.[68] Ohio Democrats' stance put pressure on midwestern Republicans to respond. Nicolas Barreyre notes that "by taking a subject that divided Republicans sectionally and making it an issue in a state election, [Pendleton] gave it political legitimacy and lifted it to national prominence." Several midwestern Republican state parties endorsed the Ohio Idea in their platforms, underscoring how "the federal structure of the party facilitated the expression of geographical differences."[69]

The Panic of 1873—a financial crisis that triggered a depression in Europe and North America—greatly heightened the salience of economic issues that crosscut party lines. The panic fueled labor-capital tensions and exacerbated the Republican split on railroad regulation, corporate regulation, and the currency.[70] The latter issues increasingly divided Republicans representing industrial and finance interests in the North from agrarians in the plains and western states. While conservatives generally enjoyed the upper hand in the GOP, agrarians were a continual source of pressure for regulatory action and against resumption of the gold standard, a pattern that would recur at the turn of the century. Democrats, meanwhile, faced their own divisions on these economic issues, with the party's southern base often at odds with Democrats from key northern urban battlegrounds. Indeed, Pendleton's 1868 bid for the Democratic presidential nomination was derailed by opposition from New York financiers angered by his soft money stance.[71]

With neither national party fully responding to agrarian or labor discontent—not to mention movement demands for temperance—a series of third-party insurgencies, starting with the Greenback Party and continuing with the Farmers' Alliance and Prohibition Party, kept the pressure on both Democrats and Republicans.[72] Even if the two major parties might have preferred to confine competition to issues where they were better able to maintain unity—such as the tariff—there was substantial space for third parties and insurgent movements to force their concerns onto the agenda.

Perhaps no issue better illustrates the shift away from polarized politics than railroad regulation. With railroads swiftly becoming a dominant economic force after the Civil War, farmers and small-town merchants, in particular, demanded regulation that would protect them from discriminatory rates that favored shippers in big cities that were connected by competing rail lines.[73] But corporate-oriented national Republican leaders had no interest in railroad regulation, and Democratic leaders initially showed little inclination to push policies that threatened to divide their urban northern constituents from southern agrarians. The parties were forced to take a stand, however, by the Grange, which by the 1870s had considerable strength in both the Midwest and South.[74] In contrast to the silence on railroad rate regulation in both parties' national platforms from 1868–80, midwestern and plains state Republican and Democratic parties responded to the grassroots pressure from agrarians, endorsing rail regulation in many of their platforms and adopting regulatory laws in Illinois, Wisconsin, Iowa, and Minnesota.[75] The historian Mark Summers concludes that maintaining two-party control in a world of third-party challengers depended on Democratic and Republican state parties' responding to the demands of their local constituents.[76]

The threat of third-party challenges also focused the attention of members of Congress. As the Greenback Party expanded its influence in Texas,

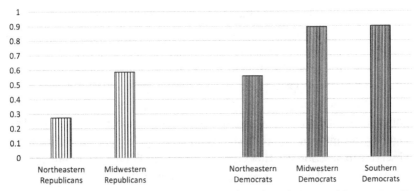

FIGURE 2.1. House Member Support for Strong Railroad Regulation by Party and Region, 1878–1887 (Average across Series of Key Roll Call Votes)
Note: The roll call votes were selected because they were final passage, conference reports, or the most consequential substitute amendments for what became the Interstate Commerce Act. These votes were identified based on the coding in David A. Bateman, Ira Katznelson, and John S. Lapinski, *Southern Nation: Congress and White Supremacy after Reconstruction* (Princeton: Princeton University Press, 2018). We thank the authors for sharing their roll-call codes. The votes were: roll call #266 in the Forty-Fifth Congress (pass Reagan substitute); roll calls #199 (pass revised Reagan substitute) and #225 (passage of Reagan bill) in the Forty-Eighth Congress; and roll calls #191 (Reagan amendment to eliminate commission), #192 (Republican-sponsored recommit with instructions), #193 (initial passage in the House), and #239 (passage of conference report) in the Forty-Ninth Congress. Roll call #192 would have effectively amended the bill to substitute a less stringent version; it was sponsored by New York Republican Charles Baker. For that vote, a "no" vote is coded as pro-regulation.

conservative John Reagan (D-TX) became a key advocate for rail regulation in the House. Stephen Skowronek notes Reagan's strategy was "informed at every step by his position in local party politics. As a southern conservative, he faced an ever-present threat from the waves of agrarian radicalism that were sweeping the Southwest."[77] Although final enactment of rail regulation took twenty years from the formation of the Grange, from the mid-1870s forward the two parties repeatedly needed to grapple with the issue in Congress. Votes on rail regulation generally split both parties along regional lines, with midwestern Republicans and southern Democrats supporting strong legislation that most northeastern Republicans and roughly half the northeastern Democrats opposed.

Figure 2.1 summarizes the partisan and regional alignment across a series of key House votes from 1878–87. On average, Republicans from the Northeast were 31 percentage points less likely to vote in favor of the pro-regulatory side than were midwestern Republicans. Among Democrats, northeastern representatives were 34 percentage points less likely to vote in favor of strong regulation than were both midwestern and southern Democrats.

In sum, with memories of the Civil War still very much alive, partisanship continued to be a major force in American politics in the 1870s and 1880s. But the sharp sectional and partisan polarization that led to the war gave way to a more factionalized politics in which the two parties represented a diverse set of overlapping policy demanders. To gain a majority, each party needed to craft a complicated coalition that bridged very different sectional political economies and accommodated a range of sociocultural groups. This regularly meant avoiding clear stands on major policy issues, leading some observers to question whether Gilded Age parties differed at all in their ideological visions.[78] The sharp party polarization of the Civil War had dissipated by the mid-1870s.

Conclusion

The 1790s and the Civil War experience make plain that deep partisan polarization is by no means anomalous in American history. These periods also demonstrate some of the pathways through which polarization can pose a deep challenge even within a decentralized constitutional order. In the case of the 1790s, the legitimacy of political opposition remained hotly contested and the peaceful transfer of power nearly broke down as Jeffersonian Republicans and Federalists struggled for power. Decades later, the violent rupture of the Civil War posed the gravest threat to the survival of the republic in its long history.

Yet fundamentally, these periods underscore the ways in which decentralized mediating institutions created multiple openings for intraparty factional divisions to disrupt polarization and loosen partisan lines. The dominant Jeffersonian Republicans gained their hold on power in large part by welcoming in, at the state level, new coalition partners who were out of step with the party's original core constituents. Neither side was read out of the party; instead, multiple factions continually jockeyed for influence through a decentralized structure of press outlets, state parties, and associations.

Similarly, while the Civil War represented an all-encompassing division that has not been duplicated, party lines came under severe challenge in the war's aftermath. The prevalence of white racism even among northern Republicans meant that the racial justice issues that came to the fore following abolition could not reliably polarize the two parties. Instead, the structure of mediating institutions created openings for new cleavages and coalitions to take hold in the states, disrupting the existing national alignment. Geographically based interests that diverged from national Republicans' policy vision on Reconstruction, the currency, and railroad regulation found expression through state parties and locally rooted representatives.

By the 1870s, these dynamics brought the era of intense party polarization to a close. Democrats and Republicans continued to harbor considerable animus toward each other, and the parties often voted in opposition to one another on many issues on the legislative agenda. But intraparty factional divisions on emergent economic issues, as well as on "cultural issues"—such as Prohibition and immigration—created space for cross-party coalitions to shape many important policies at both the state and national level. The growth in factionalism so soon after the end of the war is shocking given the scope and destructiveness of the conflict. The war had sharpened partisan enmity to new levels, but it had not changed the decentralized structure of parties and policy-demanding groups, allowing the pluralism-generating dynamics we identify in chapter 1 to once again come to the fore.

The result of this de-polarization process was itself destructive, leaving in its wake a repressive political and economic system in the South that displaced the nascent multiracial democracy that had begun to take shape. As noted in chapter 1—and taken up in greater depth in chapter 8—pathways out of polarization have their own characteristic dangers. In particular, de-polarization can undermine democracy when it involves one party sacrificing a commitment to equal rights and justice to blur distinctions with its opponent.

The intraparty, sectional divisions that came to the fore by the 1870s did partially give way in the 1890s, as party competition came to focus on issues—such as the tariff—where the two parties were more cohesive. As we will see in the next chapter, however, the ensuing period of party polarization, while enduring longer than the earlier ones, faded by the early 1900s as geographically rooted interests that did not fit neatly into either national party's camp fostered renewed internal divisions.

Constrained Polarization at the Turn of the Century

By the Gilded Age, the political landscape looked closer to today's. Democratic and Republican Parties had assumed their current status as America's two durable and nationally competitive parties. Political contestation took place within a dramatically changed economic and social context that also looks much more familiar than that of the mid-nineteenth century. The rise of massive, national corporations and the dramatic expansion of industrial production was remaking the American economy, provoking a heated response from farmers and small proprietors who often found it harder to compete. These economic changes created vast constellations of wealth—and poverty—that ramped up inequality to new levels. Waves of immigration from southern and eastern Europe threatened the dominance of groups that had been accustomed to monopolizing power, and, alongside industrialization, contributed to rapid urbanization—which exacerbated the sense of cultural and political threat experienced in many rural areas.

The turn of the twentieth century offers arguably the closest parallel to the contemporary era of polarization. Where the two-party polarization of both the 1790s and the Civil War was soon disrupted by serious intraparty factionalism, one can reasonably view the twenty-year period from 1890 to 1910 as comprising a long, coherent span of polarized politics. Political scientists Julia Azari and Marc Hetherington, for example, liken the turn-of-the-century party system to today's politics, noting "the level of partisanship apparent in voting behavior in both periods stands out as particular strong" and "congressional roll-call voting behavior was highly partisan then as it is now." Eric Foner concurs that the "high point of . . . acrimonious politics came in the Gilded Age."[1]

Yet, while the period may superficially appear similar to the present, there are profound structural differences, as we shall see. Sharp party divisions notwithstanding, the decentralized political and economic system provided critical openings for crosscutting issues and interests to challenge party lines. Regionally based economic interests were a particularly important force shaping party politics in this era. The belt of states running from the Northeast through the mid-Atlantic and upper Midwest featured unprecedented agglomerations of corporate power and wealth, while the South remained relatively underdeveloped—in part due to local elites' determination to maintain strict control over a heavily exploited agricultural labor force. The west and plains states, meanwhile, played the role of a swing region, more closely integrated with the eastern economy than the South, yet also chafing at the dominance of those same eastern interests.[2]

One can date the initial onset of high polarization in a variety of ways. Furthermore, the decline in the first decades of the twentieth century was gradual rather than sudden. There was considerable continuity in coalitions from the 1870s–80s into the 1890s, as well as in the aftermath of the 1910 revolt against House Speaker Joe Cannon, which we mark as the end of our period of focus.

Although our analysis attends to developments both before 1890 and after 1910, we concentrate on the narrower twenty-year window because it offers the strongest case for intense, durable polarization. When one tracks the difference between the two major parties' average scores using the first-dimension NOMINATE measure—the preeminent indicator of polarization used by Congress scholars—the four decades with the greatest party separation are the 1890s, 1900s, 2000s, and 2010s.[3] Figure 3.1 makes plain that the only sustained period approaching today's polarization, at least when it comes to NOMINATE-based measures, spans the late nineteenth and early twentieth centuries. Historical accounts indicate that party leadership strength peaked in 1890–1910, reaching a level not matched until the contemporary era.[4] In this way, the period is a "hard test" for our argument that the prominence of localized interests diminished polarization in earlier eras.

Standard accounts identify the Fifty-First Congress of 1889–91 as a key moment marking the intensification of late nineteenth–century polarization. Indeed, we see evidence of heightened party unity and a turn to hardball tactics. It was in January 1890 that the new Republican majority in the House banded together to enact Reed's Rules, which eliminated the main gambits that the minority had used to block action in the lower chamber.[5] These rules changes enabled the majority party to pass an ambitious program over fiery Democratic opposition. House Republicans then proceeded to approve, on party-line votes, a major tariff increase; a Federal Elections Bill intended to halt the violent disenfranchisement of southern Black voters by providing for court-appointed federal supervisors of elections; the Sherman Silver

FIGURE 3.1. Difference in Party Means (NOMINATE Scores), 1867–2023

Purchase Act; and the admission of two new (sparsely populated) Republican states, Idaho and Wyoming. The percentage of party votes in the House soared from just over half (54 percent) in the Fiftieth Congress (1887–89) to more than four-fifths (81 percent) in the Fifty-First Congress. Republicans achieved near-perfect (94 percent) unity on those votes, the highest rate of majority party loyalty since the Seventh Congress (1801–3).

Looking beyond the roll-call record, we also see evidence of intensifying polarization in the ways that party elites and news organizations spoke of opposing partisans and understood the stakes of conflict. Democratic leader Charles Crisp declared that Reed's Rules violated the Constitution and were "the foundation for [the] greatest legislative frauds ever committed in this country."[6] Charges that Reed was a dictatorial "czar" became common in 1890 and persisted throughout his tenure. The future of democratic elections was at stake in the fight over the elections bill, with Democrats depicting the legislation in apocalyptic terms, given their fear of what free and fair elections in the South might portend. Democrat Wilkinson Call of Florida condemned the bill as a "foul ... attempt to subvert the fundamental laws of the country."[7] Southern Democratic newspapers threatened a boycott of northern goods and industry, and several Democratic-controlled legislatures promised to withhold participation in the Chicago World's Fair if the bill were enacted.

The Senate battle over the legislation—which culminated in Republicans' failure (by a single vote) to defeat a Democratic filibuster through a version of today's "nuclear option"—featured Democratic charges of a "parliamentary revolution" that would eviscerate freedom of debate.[8] The ultimate failure of the elections bill was a key moment sealing Republicans' momentous retreat from the civil rights cause. But the removal of civil rights from Congress's agenda coincided with continuing party polarization on major economic issues, such as the tariff, and aggressive partisan use of the House rules. It should be no surprise, then, that scholars have repeatedly turned to these decades as a point of comparison for today's polarization.

We focus our discussion on the issues historians and political scientists have identified as the most salient during this era. With respect to economic policy, these issues were the tariff, the currency, and corporate regulation, while immigration, temperance, and race were commonly identified as central "cultural" or "social" issues.[9] The tariff best fits the characterization of this period as highly polarized, with the two parties generally taking sharply opposed positions. But the picture is very different when it comes to the currency and corporate regulation, each of which for a time dominated the economic policy agenda. In the early 1890s, silver Republicans gained the upper hand in western state parties, taking on national party leaders, and allying with disgruntled agrarians in the South and plains states. While Democrats absorbed the silverites in 1894–96, briefly reestablishing firm party lines, just a few years later midwestern progressive Republicans forced corporate regulation to the top of the agenda. The progressives launched an insurgency that undermined GOP unity.

The two parties also incorporated considerable diversity on highly salient ethnocultural issues, such as temperance and immigration, with cleavages crosscutting one another rather than stacking. Instead of serving as focal points for intense interparty battles, these cultural debates divided American society more sharply than they distinguished the two major parties.[10]

On both economic and social-cultural issues we see that the looser party-group ties of the era gave state and national parties the opportunity and incentive to compete by moving toward the (perceived) center of voter opinion, often by adopting a vague position or straddling a controversial question.

We conclude by examining Republican efforts to entrench their power through aggressive deck-stacking strategies, particularly the admission of sparsely populated western states.[11] These efforts are worthy of particular attention because they raise questions about the potential for one party, operating in a polarized context, to lock in advantages through manipulating the structure of political competition. But the decentralized party system and configuration of group demands greatly limited the long-term success of state admissions as a deck-stacking strategy. Amid today's closer party-group alliances, stacked cleavages, and nationalized partisan media, we are far less confident that efforts to entrench power through hardball strategies would again prove self-limiting (see chapter 7).

Polarization and Economic Policy

The late nineteenth century was a period of tremendous economic growth and wealth accumulation—alongside substantial dislocations that grew out of uneven regional development and recurrent financial crises. As a result, economic debates often dominated the political agenda.

Sharp party polarization showed up most obviously in battles over the tariff, which—more than any other economic issue—attracted sustained attention from Congress throughout the second half of the nineteenth century. The two parties had long taken opposing positions on the tariff, with Republicans backing protection and Democrats favoring lower rates.

These positions were rooted in the distinct economic interests of the two parties' coalitions. Republicans generally represented industrial areas that were believed to benefit from tariffs. Democrats more often represented export-reliant agricultural districts that viewed protection as harmful—both due to retaliatory rates put on their exports and the increased costs of the manufactured goods that they needed to purchase.

Yet notwithstanding this general interparty divide, both parties had to grapple with serious dissent on the tariff in the 1870s and 1880s, which stemmed from the diversity of local economic interests within their respective coalitions. Republicans faced ongoing pressure from their own farm members to lower the exorbitant rates set during the Civil War. Democrats faced even deeper divisions. They were repeatedly hampered by a faction representing industrial districts—led by House Appropriations Chair (and former Speaker) Samuel Randall of Pennsylvania—who refused to go along with tariff cuts, foiling several Democratic legislative drives.[12] Based on roll-call voting on tariff policy, more than 10 percent of House Democrats were closer to the GOP than to their own party during the 1879–89 period (see panel 1 of figure 3.2, which displays the distribution of member tariff preferences by party).

Party lines on the tariff tightened substantially starting in 1888 when President Grover Cleveland made rate reductions the centerpiece of his program and reelection campaign. Moving swiftly to capitalize on Cleveland's election defeat, Republicans passed the McKinley Tariff of 1890, which dramatically

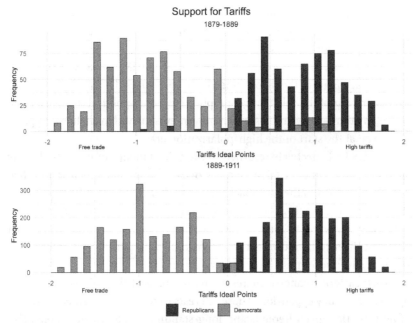

FIGURE 3.2. Tariff Ideal Points by Party. Top Panel: 1879–1889; Bottom Panel: 1889–1911
Note: Scores calculated by David Bateman based on roll call coding in Bateman et al., *Southern Nation*.

increased rates on industrial products, while also attempting to solidify farm belt support by extending protection to more agricultural staples. The increased tariff on raw wool was a priority given the need to attract western wool farmers to the protectionist coalition.[13] Voting on the McKinley bill and its many proposed amendments was nearly always along party lines, and this sharp party division proved durable. From 1889–1911, the share of House Democrats closer to the GOP than their own party fell to just 2 percent, and just three of 865 Republicans serving during these years were closer to the Democrats than to their own party (see panel 2 of figure 3.2).[14] Party polarization on the tariff can be viewed as a defining feature of the politics of these decades.

Even so, the high level of roll-call unity obscures some significant intraparty divisions on the tariff. Cleveland's bid for major reductions when he returned to the White House in 1893 was thwarted by a handful of protectionist Democrats, including Senate leader Arthur Pue Gorman of Maryland. While the Wilson–Gorman Tariff of 1894 did, on balance, reduce rates, it fell far short of Cleveland's goals and the president condemned those who forced the compromises for "party perfidy and party dishonor."[15] Less than a decade later, Republicans experienced their own serious divisions on the tariff, with midwestern progressive members demanding reduced rates. Their pressure forced the party to consider tariff revisions in 1909, though the resulting Payne–Aldrich Act mostly kept the prevailing high rates in place, further alienating the progressives.

Nonetheless, the intraparty disputes over the tariff pale in comparison to the currency issue of the 1890s. Indeed, the battle over the currency is a critical illustration of the role that geographically rooted political diversity, often carried by third-party and insurgent movements, played in challenging party lines even at the start of the high-polarization era.

The US had effectively returned to the gold standard in 1873 after having abandoned it during the Civil War. Advocates of currency expansion pushed either for a return to the greenbacks (paper dollars not backed by gold) of the 1860s or for "bimetallism"—the use of silver as a currency at a fixed ratio with gold. As silver prices fell on the world market, though, it became evident that allowing silver to be redeemed at a fixed ratio with gold would, in practice, result in silver becoming the currency standard.[16]

Northeastern financial interests strongly backed the gold standard and opposed currency expansion. These interests were well represented at the top of both parties, given Republicans' long-standing ties to finance capital and Democrats' need to win New York state in order to have a reasonable chance of winning the presidency.[17] At the same time, both parties also included a substantial, regionally based faction of agrarian interests, which favored currency expansion. In addition, silver mining interests in western states increasingly gained influence, particularly as new states entered the Union.

With the currency question crosscutting the prevailing partisan line of division, the national parties attempted to keep the peace internally by avoiding a clear stand. Republicans' 1888 national platform sidestepped the inconvenient reality that their party's members had taken a more pro-gold position than the Democrats in nearly every roll-call vote on the currency in the past decade. Instead, the party disingenuously claimed to support "use of both gold and silver as money" while blaming the Cleveland administration for its "efforts to demonetize silver." The Democrats, torn between President Cleveland's pro-gold stance and rank-and-file members' support for currency expansion, offered generic praise for Cleveland's leadership in their platform, while keeping silent about whether the status of silver should change.[18]

But national leaders were unable to keep the issue off the agenda for long. Third-party challengers, starting with the Greenbacks in 1874, repeatedly pressed for currency expansion. Their success in attracting support in agrarian and mining regions highlights a key difference between the nineteenth-century party system and today's. In a less nationalized polity, third parties with a substantial regional base were able to win influence at the state level and even elect federal officeholders. This success, in turn, gave Republican and Democratic state parties a strong incentive to respond to insurgencies that crosscut national party lines.[19]

Explicit pro-silver stances, which had been the exception in the mid to late 1880s, became commonplace in the plains and west in 1890–92, as more state parties came on board amid the growth and electoral success of the Populist movement.[20] By 1892, both Republican and Democratic platforms in seven of the twelve plains and western states had endorsed free coinage of silver (California, Colorado, Idaho, Montana, Nevada, Oregon, and Washington). Democrats staked out a clearer pro-silver stance than Republicans in four other states—Kansas, North Dakota, Nebraska, and Wyoming—though the GOP also claimed to support currency expansion in each state (and the Wyoming GOP endorsed free coinage in 1894).[21] This was a story of within-region party convergence toward the locally popular stance, even as that led state parties further away from their national leaders. As Summers describes the process, there was a "struggle different in each state, for control, a mixture of accommodation and intimidation, of emulation and ridicule, of cooperation, co-optation, and coalition."[22]

Meanwhile, as House Speaker Reed and other Republican congressional leaders furiously fought against silver coinage in 1889–91, western Republican newspapers overwhelmingly backed free silver, alongside their Democratic counterparts, and in contradiction to eastern newspapers of both parties. A review of news coverage reveals that ten out of twelve western Republican newspapers and three of four Democratic papers backed free coinage, as compared to just one of sixteen eastern Republican papers and none of seventeen eastern Democratic papers.[23] These state party and press positions reflected a regionally based interest group environment that did not map onto the national party alignment. Mining interests and plains state farmers traditionally leaned Republican, but they were willing to back third-party candidates (and at times even Democrats) who supported an expanded currency. Eastern financial interests opposed to silver had an important presence in both parties, exerting influence on top leaders.[24]

With this pressure bubbling up from the state level, party leaders faced steep challenges maintaining party unity in the early 1890s. In an initial effort to defuse the currency issue, Republican leaders narrowly succeeded in passing the Sherman Silver Purchase Act in July 1890. The act aimed to satisfy silver mining interests by requiring the Treasury to purchase 4.5 million ounces of silver each month. But silver and agrarian interests soon turned on the compromise and renewed the push for unlimited silver coinage.

The fate of Republicans' Federal Elections Bill demonstrates that the

strength of sectionally based economic interests was so great that it could derail a party's urgent policy priority—something that is hard to imagine today.
With Democratic gains in the North narrowing the GOP's path to a national
majority and southern white violence disenfranchising Black voters, Republican leaders understood that they had a brief window of opportunity to enact
changes that might enable the party to compete for southern electoral votes
and congressional seats. As noted above, the House passed the elections bill
in July 1890, but it faced a protracted Democratic filibuster in the Senate. In
one indicator of the importance of the measure to the party, nearly every
Republican—and a majority of all senators—signed a pledge in August 1890
committing to change the Senate rules if necessary to pass the bill.[25]

Nevertheless, a few months later, when Senate Republican Leader Nelson
Aldrich (R-RI) pushed for the rules change, a group of Republicans united
with the Democrats to sidetrack the elections bill. In effect, they killed their
own party's high-stakes initiative. Six of the eight Republican defectors were
pro-silver westerners, while a seventh—James Cameron of Pennsylvania—
had substantial personal investments in silver.[26]

Although the silver Republicans denied a quid pro quo, press coverage
leading up to and following the vote made clear that the prospect of working
with Democrats on silver coinage was an important motivation.[27] Western
newspapers praised the defectors, while northeastern supporters of the elections bill condemned their treachery. The Republican *Boston Journal* noted
that "it is becoming increasingly apparent that the silver men care a good
deal for themselves and very little for their country or the Republican Party"
and that the Republican majority in the House must "crush the life out of
free coinage, not only without compunction, but with absolute delight."[28] The
Ohio *State Journal* added that "traitors inside the lines deserve, and will be
accorded, political death" for violating Republicans' solemn "pledge" for the
elections bill.[29]

The outrage of eastern Republican editors reflected the reality that the silver Republicans had bolted on a key party priority to satisfy a local constituency demand. For all the partisan intensity evident in the battles over Reed's
Rules, this case makes plain that the early 1890s featured critical intraparty
divisions that dramatically limited the scope of polarization.

The regional divide over the currency triggered a shift in party coalitions
in 1894–96. When New York Democrat Grover Cleveland returned to the
White House in 1893, he responded to a burgeoning economic crisis by moving to repeal the Silver Purchase Act, which had strained the Treasury's fiscal
capacity. Alongside the growing agrarian movement behind the pro-inflation

People's Party, this provocation forced a showdown that culminated in the silver forces capturing the Democratic Party from below and many Gold Democrats abandoning their long-standing partisan home.

The Populists' capture of state parties across the South and West enabled the Democrats' nomination of William Jennings Bryan in 1896. As Summers puts it, "the leaven of discontent worked its way up through the party, giving the reformers the votes they needed to capture conventions and nominate candidates."[30] With Democrats firmly behind silver, those backing so-called "sound money" unified behind the Republican McKinley. Republicans' loss of support in the most committed pro-silver areas and Democrats' decline in the industrial North meant that sectional economic interests were now more closely aligned with party.[31] Party voting in Congress, which had briefly declined during the Cleveland years, rebounded after 1896. Thus, the share of party votes in the House, which had fallen to about half in 1893–96, bounced back to 70–80 percent in 1897–1903. Polarized politics had faltered, but ultimately withstood the disruption surrounding the currency.

Notably, however, this happened only after a significant reshuffling of the two parties' geographic bases. The arc of the currency issue in the 1890s demonstrates that in a decentralized constitutional order geographically concentrated policy demanders and third-party insurgencies had the capacity to force issues onto the agenda that national party leaders would have preferred to sidestep. The silver Republicans' willingness to sabotage Republicans' pursuit of the Federal Elections Bill reveals the power of regionally based factions to challenge party discipline. The Populists' subsequent success in driving the Cleveland wing out of the Democratic Party ended up contributing to a return to polarization. Yet it also suggests the potential for bottom-up forces to upend the coalitional bargains that ordinarily keep parties bound together.

CORPORATE REGULATION AND THE RISE OF THE PROGRESSIVE REPUBLICANS, 1901–10

The currency issue faded quickly in the aftermath of Bryan's defeat. New discoveries of gold in the Yukon and South Africa countered the deflationary pressures that had plagued debtors for decades, greatly reducing the pressure for government action to expand the money supply.[32]

But a new set of divisive economic issues came to the fore. A wave of corporate mergers gave rise to massive, vertically integrated firms that controlled multiple stages of the production and distribution process, often threatening smaller producers and distributors with their market power. The question of how to tackle these vast agglomerations of corporate power had barely registered on the political agenda in 1896. It became the dominant economic controversy in the first decades of the twentieth century. Should big corporations be broken up through aggressive antitrust measures? Should they be forced to register with the national government and face extensive regulation of their actions?[33]

Once again, these questions split both parties along regional and urban-rural lines, with particularly damaging effects on the Republicans. The Old Guard conservative leaders of the GOP, with their base in the Northeast and close ties to major corporations, opposed a vigorous regulatory response. These leaders were challenged by a growing progressive faction that drew its primary support in the Midwest and West, where powerful eastern companies were increasingly viewed as a threat, particularly in farm and rural communities. Faced with these challenges, the revival in polarization following the 1896 election did not prove durable. As in the early 1890s, centrifugal forces pushed back against party leaders' efforts to suppress new economic demands.

The progressive Republican movement leveraged the federal structure of the party system. The historian Paula Baker observes that while McKinley's election had "appeared to put the Republican Party in control for a generation, the party was increasingly divided on its purpose. The way was clear for new issues, ones not championed by McKinley. Insurgent governors and mayors . . . pioneered those issues."[34] Indeed, the first major progressive victories emerged at the state level, sparked by Robert La Follette's election as governor of Wisconsin (1900), followed quickly by Albert Cummins's Iowa victory (1901), along with successes in Minnesota, North Dakota, and Kansas. These state gains led directly to progressive electoral reforms and new regulatory laws targeting railroads and other corporations.[35]

Equally important, progressive Republicans put national reforms onto the agenda. Cummins, for example, pushed the so-called Iowa Idea starting in 1901, which called for denying tariff protection to trusts. This proposal quickly gained endorsements from Republican state parties in Idaho, Minnesota, Nebraska, and Wisconsin, and was sponsored on the House floor by Wisconsin Representative Joseph Babcock.[36] The proposal added to the pressure on the GOP to address concerns about high tariffs and corporate concentration, two issues that divided the conservative northeastern leadership from agrarian Republicans.

Similar dynamics occurred with respect to railroad regulation, as a state reform movement originating in the Midwest and West gave new intensity to a long-standing issue. An examination of state Republican platforms shows that calls for strong railroad regulation, rare in 1900–1902, became common by 1906–8.[37] Progressive Republicans collaborated with southern Democrats on a legislative drive on this issue, opposed by top Republican leaders in Congress, forcing a series of confrontations that divided the GOP.[38]

President Theodore Roosevelt played a complicated role in the rise of progressive republicanism. When Roosevelt was still governor of New York, he advocated for greater business regulation and taxation in the state. Conservative party members pushed for his selection as Vice President as a way to sideline him.[39] A year later, President McKinley's unexpected death placed Roosevelt in the White House. Conservative leaders worried that he would ally with progressives. As president, however, Roosevelt initially sought to tamp down the party's divisions, pushing for additional regulations but working with party leaders to limit their scope, and agreeing to sidestep tariff revisions that Old Guard leaders especially feared.[40] Toward the end of his second term, though, Roosevelt moved more decisively to the left, amid progressive gains in the states and the disruptions caused by the Panic of 1907. Roosevelt denounced the "malefactors of great wealth" who he argued had made the economic crisis worse "in order to discredit the policy of the Government . . . so that they may enjoy unmolested the fruits of their own evil-doing." The president proposed an aggressive regulatory and taxation program in his December 1907 annual message, following that up in January 1908 with another attack against his corporate opponents that left Republican leaders "silent" and Democrats "joyful."[41]

Through these actions, Roosevelt exacerbated the developing cleavage in his party. But it is wrong to attribute the divisions to Roosevelt as an individual. Instead, Roosevelt's growing progressivism gained its political potency from the alliance it promised with a burgeoning reform movement across the Midwest and West.

Changes in both the interest group structure and the press landscape also helped to undermine polarization, complementing the role of state parties and locally rooted politicians. Clemens's pioneering study demonstrates that the early twentieth century featured a proliferation of interest groups, which were seen as an alternative to party and generally drew strength from both Democrats and Republicans.[42]

For example, the Farmers' Union, which started in Texas in 1902, spread across the South, Midwest, and West in 1904–8, growing to about seven hundred thousand members.[43] It pushed for a series of progressive priorities, including railroad regulation, antitrust, public control of banking, farm credit, and lower tariffs. The Union's national leadership believed the Farmers' Alliance had been undermined by its foray into party politics and thus kept some distance from each national party.[44] More generally, farmers were a key constituency for progressive reform in both the South and Midwest, as Democrats in the South but working through both parties in the Midwest. This avoidance of party alliances characterized many of the most important policy-demanding groups of the era, including the American Federation of Labor (AFL), women's suffrage advocates, pro- and anti-immigration groups, and such temperance advocates as the Women's Christian Temperance Union and the Anti-Saloon League.[45]

The structure of interest group demands generally acted as a countervailing force to national polarization. Republicans represented industrial capitalists in the manufacturing belt and agrarian midwesterners—sectional groups with increasingly opposed policy goals. As Sanders notes, in the 1890s, eastern capitalists persuaded manufacturing workers that farmers' regional interests were antithetical to their interests, blocking the path to a national farmer-labor coalition. But within midwestern states—where farmers and workers shared similar concerns about eastern economic exploitation—a farm-labor alliance could thrive, electing progressive candidates under either the Democratic or Republican banner depending on the state context.[46] These centrifugal forces pushed against national GOP leaders' efforts to maintain a united front on corporate regulation.

The structure of the turn-of-the-century press provided further opportunities for progressive Republicans to challenge prevailing party lines, undermining polarization. Several leading midwestern Republican newspapers offered critical support to La Follette and other progressive Republicans as they battled with the conservative Old Guard.[47] Equally important, a new form of muckraking journalism emerged during this period, often showcased in mass circulation, independent magazines. Historian John M. Cooper observes that Lincoln Steffens's series of *McClure's* articles—later published as *The Shame of the Cities* in 1904—made La Follette "a national figure and his progressive Republican faction a model for other reform movements," while spurring enactment of regulatory laws in several states.[48] Other muckrakers turned their ire directly on conservative Senate leaders, as in David Graham Phillips's "The Treason of the Senate," published in monthly installments in *Cosmopolitan* in 1906. The "muckraking" press was national in scope, but its lack of ties to either party meant that it was positioned to raise the salience of issues that the GOP's national leaders preferred to avoid.

The progressive-allied press played an especially important role in fueling the insurgency that culminated in the revolt against Speaker Joe Cannon, the 1910 earthquake that marked the transition away from centralized party government in Congress. Insurgent Republicans mostly represented midwestern and western districts, where progressivism was strong. They voted alongside Democrats to remove Cannon from the Rules Committee, one of his main power bases. In her deeply researched account of the Cannon revolt, Ruth Bloch Rubin emphasizes that "reformers with strong ties to popular progressive newspapers and magazines worked with sympathetic journalists to 'spread sentiment against the present House rules.'"[49] These editors publicized Cannon's alleged abuses, helping turn him into an electoral liability for Republicans. As Cannon sought to use the tools of party discipline to punish those disloyal to him, progressive Republicans countered by "leveraging their connections with influential progressive newspaper and magazine editors . . . to reward loyal members, and rebuke—to devastating effect—those who rejoined the Speaker."[50] Insurgent leader John Nelson (R-WI) later recalled the pivotal role of local newspapers in encouraging members to stand firm against Cannon. He noted that progressive Republicans "built fires underneath [reluctant insurgents] through the newspapers in their districts, and induced certain of their constituents to bring pressure upon them, and as a result they stayed with us."[51]

The revolt against Cannon is a telling example of how mediating institutions acted as formidable countervailing forces against polarization. The election of 1896 had seemingly consolidated conservative control over the GOP. But as local economic and political demands for more aggressive regulation emerged, midwestern and western Republicans had both the incentive and the capacity to respond. A progressive movement emerged at the state level and bubbled up to Washington, targeting powerful conservative Republican leaders. Twenty-seven of the thirty-three hard-core insurgent Republicans came from agricultural areas, generally in the Midwest; just six were from the industrial heartland.[52] These progressives worked with labor and farm organizations that were not tied to either party at the national level and with both local and national news outlets that shared their policy goals. Their 1910 triumph signaled a marked shift in congressional operations, launching a long era of reduced leadership influence, decentralized power, and greater cross-party voting.[53]

Ethnocultural Politics and the Limited Reach of Polarization

Dynamics surrounding social, cultural, and racial issues further limited the scope and intensity of polarization in 1890–1910. As described in chapter 1, cleavages on these issues today tend to stack. Each party represents a set of interlocking commitments, reinforced by a nationalized system of mediating institutions, that make it far easier to view the opposing party as an implacable enemy. By contrast, cleavages on these issues in the late nine-teenth and early twentieth century tended to crosscut one another and the national party system.

One might instead have expected ethnocultural identities to reinforce partisan warfare in the late nineteenth century. After all, religion and ethnic-ity were central identities in the lives of millions of Americans, and many his-torians have argued that such ethnocultural ties were primary factors shap-ing vote choice.[54] Republicans were associated with native-born, "pietistic" Protestants, who generally believed the path to salvation depended on the individual's conduct, and therefore supported government policies to enforce a specific, Christian morality. Democrats, by contrast, gained the dispropor-tionate support of immigrants and those with an affiliation to a "liturgical" religion (e.g., Catholicism, Lutheranism, and Episcopalians), which placed responsibility for moral conduct in the hands of the church and its rituals, rather than the government. Such initiatives as temperance, immigration re-strictions, limits on the use of foreign languages in schools, and Sabbatari-anism drew support from pietistic voters. The same policies repelled many Catholics, Lutherans, and immigrants.[55]

There is no doubt that a substantial number of Republican voters were on board with policies that together seemed to set the stage for a "culture war" that might have been a forerunner for today's polarization. But the obstacles to such a program proved formidable. Once again, these obstacles grew from the fragmented institutional and cleavage structure of American politics at the turn of the century.

Pietistic Republicans enjoyed considerable success in the Midwest in the late 1880s. These voters drove state Republican parties to push temperance legislation and to enact laws that restricted the use of German (along with other foreign languages) in schools. This success proved short-lived, how-ever, as Republicans suffered a severe electoral backlash in 1889–90.

The core problem for the party was that GOP success across many mid-western states required competing for German voters. When the party em-braced nativist and dry policies, this key swing group went heavily Demo-cratic. As Richard Jensen observes, the "basic weakness of the GOP was its shelter for the pietistic reformers who harped on divisive cultural issues . . . Only if the professionals could curb the moralistic crusading of the amateurs, or if sudden new issues would appear, could the GOP recover control of the Midwest and the nation."[56]

This is precisely what happened across a series of midwestern states, in an effort led most prominently by future president William McKinley, who was elected governor of Ohio in 1891. McKinley downplayed cultural issues in favor of an inclusive appeal to a more generic nationalism, centering the tariff as a policy that protected all Americans.

McKinley took this strategy national in 1896, capturing the GOP presidential nomination despite opposition from the leading anti-immigration group, the American Protective Association (APA), which declared that it would find any candidate *other* than McKinley acceptable. Instead, as Daniel Tichenor notes, "the Republican Party's leaders sidetracked the APA, which quickly faded as a political force."[57]

The APA's plight underscores a key difference between party-group relations in the late nineteenth century and today. It has become hard to imagine either party nominating a presidential candidate who is entirely unacceptable to a major voter group widely viewed as on that party's "side."[58] But in this earlier era, with parties less firmly tied to allied groups, party leaders had considerable space to move to the center on controversial issues, even if doing so faced organized group opposition from within their preexisting coalition.

McKinley's stance helped Republicans make major gains among Catholics and German Lutherans who were repelled by William Jennings Bryan's evangelical approach. Republican success across northern cities in 1896—winning Boston, New York City, Philadelphia, Baltimore, Detroit, Cleveland, and Chicago—suggests the extent to which an appeal to protectionism combined with downplaying of cultural issues could generate Republican victories even in urban areas with substantial immigrant and Catholic populations.[59]

Far from stacking, cultural allegiances divided constituencies in multiple ways that made them an unreliable basis for building a national majority.[60] Pietistic Protestants were divided by region, with their greatest support in the overwhelmingly Democratic South and among rural Midwestern Republicans. Within northern states, each party depended on voters in both cities and rural areas. Economic interests also often crosscut religion and ethnicity, providing dueling bases for vote choice. For example, as long as Republicans did not go too far in a nativist direction, they could win over Germans and many Catholics with appeals to their interests as farmers or manufacturing workers.[61]

With the cleavage structure involving multiple, non-overlapping divisions, both national parties generally had an incentive to straddle explosive cultural issues. Strikingly, at the height of the temperance movement, national party platforms remained silent or adopted an ambiguous position. Aaron Ley and Cornell Clayton observe that Prohibition "deeply split" both parties' coalitions, with the result that "neither dominant party developed a clear position on arguably one of the most pressing issues of the day."[62]

The Prohibition Party sought to force the parties' hand, but its persistence over several decades is indicative of the refusal of either party to forge a genuine alliance with temperance advocates. State parties were more likely to take a clear stand, but in many cases this meant *both* Democrats and Republicans adopting a similar position when a state's voters clearly tilted in one direction or the other.[63] The Anti-Saloon League's ultimate success in enacting the Prohibition Amendment was partly attributable to its ability to pressure members of both parties.[64]

Similar dynamics occurred on immigration, where activist groups sought to win support in both parties. Tichenor writes that the Immigration Restriction League (IRL)—which became the most important anti-immigration group at the turn of the century—"chose to pursue new extraparty openings to directly lobby national policymakers on behalf of immigration restriction. 'Our organization is a nonpartisan one,' the IRL proudly declared, 'and we would not support or oppose a candidate for office on party grounds.'"[65]

Although national Republicans were, on balance, more supportive of restrictions than were Democrats, there was considerable diversity within both parties and overlap across them. Western Democrats joined Republicans in supporting restrictions against Chinese immigration, while eastern Republicans often joined Democrats in competing for immigrant votes with a more liberal approach.[66] When restrictionists pushed a literacy test for immigrants in 1906–7, the AFL and nativist Protestants lined up on one side, with urban ethnic groups and leading corporate interests on the other. With these group alignments crosscutting party divisions, neither party could serve as a vehicle for nativists.[67]

While ethnocultural identities were of course an important factor shaping voter allegiances, the mapping of specific religious and ethnic ties to vote choice generally varied considerably across states and localities. A particular immigrant group—such as Germans, Italians, or Jews—might vote Republican in one city and Democratic in another, depending on the orientation and efforts of the local political machine and its opponents.[68] As Paula Baker concludes, "community variations in partisan alignments suggest that it is implausible to view the parties as representatives of coherent systems of economic or social thought. Parties meant different things in different places. This political system simply lacked the coherence to support consistent, ideological parties."[69]

Indeed, the absence of clear national party stances on cultural issues and the local variation in alignments were mutually reinforcing. Party elites permitted pluralism in part because of the nature of their coalitions. This pluralism in turn allowed intraparty diversity to thrive, restricting the options available to national party leaders. In this context, state parties were able to take up a pro- or anti-temperance position where there was a local base for the position, and the national parties generally steered clear for fear of offending either constituency.

Put simply, a nationalizing cultural agenda might have appeal to southern Democrats or a handful of northern Republican state parties, but embracing it would endanger their party's ability to compete nationally. The absence of a "culture war" that might have acted as a force multiplier for polarization was no accident. Instead, it reflected a fragmented cleavage structure, partly generated and clearly reinforced by mediating institutions that allowed regional diversity to thrive.

The removal of Black rights from the national political agenda during the 1890s played an important, if complicated, role in shaping the dynamics of polarization. The initial height of polarization in 1890–91 occurred as Republicans were pushing the last major civil rights legislation of the era. There is no doubt that Democrats' all-out opposition to the Federal Elections Bill fueled the intense partisanship at the start of the Reed Rules era.[70] As discussed above, however, Republicans' defeat on the elections bill was itself rooted in the limited scope of polarization, as pro-silver Republicans defected from their party to pursue a sectional economic interest. The party system that congealed in the 1890s was polarized, at least initially, on economics, but Republicans essentially abandoned civil rights at the national level, likely reducing the intensity of partisan battles in the early 1900s.[71]

Racial issues remained an unlikely vehicle for durable partisan polarization in the 1890s–1900s due to the sharp imbalance in the political strength of egalitarian and white supremacist forces. With millions of Black voters effectively disenfranchised and many northern white voters supporting white supremacy, national Republican leaders concluded—as they had at the end of Reconstruction—that their path to control of the government did not run through appeals to equal rights for Black Americans.[72]

The remaining cleavages that were organized into politics—over economics, ethnocultural identities, and the urban-rural divide—tended to crosscut one another. This limited the scope of intense polarization to a relatively narrow set of issues, such as the tariff. And even this limited partisan polarization proved vulnerable to disruption as sectional economic divisions resurfaced in the first decade of the twentieth century.

Deck-Stacking and Turn-of-the-Century Polarization

When observers worry that today's polarization raises the specter of serious democratic backsliding, one of the main concerns is that Republicans have been using "constitutional hardball" tactics—such as laws making it harder to vote and aggressive gerrymandering—in a way that entrenches their power even as they fail to secure popular majorities (see chapter 7). These strategies find an echo in the politics of nineteenth-century statehood decisions, which featured intense focus on the partisan leanings of territories. In an important study, Charles Stewart and Barry Weingast trace Republicans' strategic use of statehood admissions to "stack" the political system in their favor in the 1860s–90s. By admitting several sparsely populated western states that leaned toward the GOP, the party gained a substantial edge in the battle to control the Senate, along with a significant Electoral College bonus.[73]

Still, within the context of a decentralized constitutional order, the differences between national and local political cleavages in the nineteenth century imposed serious limitations on the effectiveness of Republicans' deck-stacking. The politics that emerged in the newly admitted states was only loosely connected to national partisan politics. Instead, it was locally grounded, organized by local elites around local interests and political networks. Republicans were able to win more Senate seats, but at the cost of reduced intraparty unity as many of these new Republican senators became champions of free silver and corporate regulations that divided the party both in Congress and nationally. The failure of the Federal Elections Bill in 1891 reflected the tenuous loyalty of western Republicans; over the next several years, these Republicans would push an economic agenda that was anathema to Old Guard conservative leaders.

When it comes to presidential elections, David Mayhew demonstrates persuasively the uncertainty and fluidity that characterized statehood politics, greatly limiting the effectiveness of state admission deck-stacking. Ten states can be regarded as Republican partisan admissions from 1861–90.[74] Building on Mayhew, we examine how these new states voted in presidential elections during the high-polarization era that started in 1890. From 1892–1900, the GOP won thirteen of thirty presidential contests in these ten states. When one extends the time frame to 1912, the party won exactly half of the contests. Isolating the five GOP-leaning states admitted in 1889–90—presumably an easier test for deck-stacking given the condensed time period—Republicans won just eighteen of thirty (60 percent) of the presidential contests in 1892–1912, and just one of the five in 1916.

The case of statehood admissions illustrates that for much of US history, the differences between national and local political cleavages and issues tended to make many deck-stacking efforts self-correcting or at least self-limiting.[75] Republican efforts to stack the Senate fostered geographic divisions that ultimately undermined the GOP coalition.

Again, the contrast with our era is instructive. States that vote Republican (or Democratic) support broadly similar policies regardless of the region in which they are located. Changes in electoral boundaries—whether through admission of additional states, such as Washington, DC, or Puerto Rico, or through redistricting—are widely understood to have predictable political effects, as to both which party would benefit and the policy agenda that would gain strength.

In much the same way, the tightening relationship between population density and partisanship means that today's status quo—which disproportionately empowers small, rural states in the Senate—is now more robustly related to conservative Republican strength than was the case soon after many of these states were admitted to the Union. We take up the role of this geographic advantage in reinforcing asymmetric aspects of polarization in chapters 6 and 7.

Conclusion

It is by no means unusual for the two major parties in the United States to be far apart from one another in their programs or for partisans to intensely dislike the opposing party. Nonetheless, earlier cases of polarization put in sharp relief the ways in which the historical path of contemporary polarization is distinctive. Prior episodes of intense polarization—the 1790s, Civil War, and 1890–1910—proved vulnerable to disruption by crosscutting issues and coalitions. Even the longest sustained period of polarization, which featured the highest party voting of any era prior to the twenty-first century, was not consolidated until about 1896 and came to an ignominious end with the progressive Republican–Democratic revolt against Speaker Joe Cannon in 1910.[76]

The configuration of mediating institutions in these earlier eras acted as a countervailing force, repeatedly empowering interests that were not well-served by the established parties' stances. State parties—at times acting under the threat of minor party challenges—proved willing to depart from national party lines in response to locally rooted demands. Key societal groups were rarely firmly aligned with a single party, and the coalition of groups that made up a given party varied across regions. Although much of the press was partisan in the nineteenth century, it was also locally rooted, with news outlets providing coverage that reflected their local political economy rather than toeing the national party line. In this context, cleavages tended to crosscut one another, rather than stack, and emerging issues and interests could find entry into politics even if both national parties wished that they would not.

Perhaps the most noteworthy feature of party competition in these earlier periods is the extent to which state and national parties each adapted to the perceived center of voter opinion.[77] At one level, this should be no surprise; the median voter theorem tells us to expect party convergence toward the center. Yet recent work has persuasively demonstrated that contemporary parties often do not move to the median. One can view Democrats and Republicans today as coalitions of intense policy demanders that advocate for non-centrist positions on the issues their groups care about most. The parties can get away with relatively extreme positions because most voters pay only limited attention to issues, and thus voters have a "blind spot" that gives leeway to the party-group alliances.[78]

In the fragmented political system that characterized earlier eras of American history, group-party alliances were simply weaker than is the case today. This gave state and national parties more flexibility to go where they believed the votes were. Western and midwestern Republican parties could respond to the strong electoral demand for currency expansion and corporate regulation proposals that were anathema to eastern party leaders. Both parties could straddle cultural issues, such as temperance or immigration restrictions, even as many "base" voters favored a clear stand.

When one compares state party platforms across a range of issues, it is striking how often the two parties articulated a similar (often vague) position, even in periods viewed as highly polarized. This does not mean policy did not "matter" in elections; instead, it reflects a competitive party system in which party leaders had greater capacity to adapt to the electorate's perceived demands, with less constraint from party-allied groups.

In chapters 4 and 5, we trace the reasons party-group alliances have become more entrenched and national in scope. For now, it is worth noting two differences that set earlier eras apart from the contemporary party system. First, in an era of patronage, the parties were less dependent on group alliances in order to mobilize the financial resources and activist labor necessary to compete in elections. Second, in the absence of primary elections, candidates likely had greater capacity to bid for the support of centrist swing voters even if doing so alienated an existing party constituency, as McKinley did in the 1890s.

It is also important to note that there were a handful of intense policy demanders who did have the kind of firm alliance with a party that we see today. The two best examples are pro-tariff industries with the Republicans and white supremacists with the Democrats.[79] Protectionism served as a unifying policy for Republicans throughout much of the late nineteenth century, binding the party closely to industrial interests in the North and upper Midwest.[80] Yet even on the tariff, sectional economic interests at times challenged party lines. Export-oriented agrarian Republicans came to see the tariff as contrary to their constituents' interests and joined Democrats in calling for revisions in the 1870s and again in the early twentieth century.

Democrats' commitment to white supremacy was even firmer, as it benefited both from the party's dominance among southern whites and the very limited demand for civil rights among northern white voters throughout most of the period. Eventually, this alliance would also come under challenge during the 1930s–40s, as new interests elbowed their way into the Democratic coalition, capitalizing on a fragmented party system that allowed them to gain a foothold in northern states that lacked the southerners' single-minded commitment to Jim Crow.

As Black voters and pro–civil rights industrial unions became important constituencies for state Democratic parties throughout much of the North, they gradually transformed not just the party, but American politics more generally. We argue in the next chapter that the racial realignment that began in the New Deal years served as a critical trigger for a form of durable and intense party polarization that differs sharply from prior eras. Alongside the dramatic expansion in the role of the national government, the racial realignment created the conditions for Democrats and Republicans to take divergent positions on a range of important issues. Equally importantly, these triggers contributed to major changes in mediating institutions, helping turn state parties, the structure of group demands, and the media into drivers of further polarization. This would be a fateful change. The same mediating institutions that had provided openings for crosscutting divisions to enter into the party system in earlier polarized periods would now operate to reinforce partisan warfare.

PART II

The Rise of Contemporary Polarization

Triggers of a Nationalized Partisanship

From the 1930s to the 1980s, the US shifted from a decentralized and relatively pluralistic constitutional order to a much more nationalized and polarized one. In this chapter, we focus on two broad catalysts, the racial realignment of the parties and the rapid expansion of the federal government. In the next chapter, we show how these triggering events contributed to the transformation of the critical mediating institutions that had anchored that decentralized constitutional order.

The Democratic majority that took power in 1932 brought southern white supremacists and urban ethnic voters together in a broad coalition with little interest in racial justice. But the New Deal's economic policies attracted northern Black voters and encouraged the growth of an industrial labor movement that would soon embrace racial liberalism. These new constituencies gradually remade the Democratic Party from below. For decades, the national Democratic Party sought to avoid legislation on race that could fracture its coalition. But, with the civil rights battles of the 1960s, national leaders could no longer avoid the issue.

The "Long 1960s"—roughly stretching from the beginning of Lyndon Johnson's presidency to the middle of Jimmy Carter's—transformed American politics in at least two major ways. First, as the two national parties took clearer stances on race, their respective coalitions changed, paving the way for the parties to "sort" on numerous other social and cultural issues. Second, the reach of the federal government expanded significantly. This directed attention toward national policymaking and heightened the stakes of conflict.

In this chapter, we take a closer look at these developments. We also examine changes in the economy that began in the 1970s and accelerated in subsequent decades. The shift toward a more nationalized political economy reinforced the dynamics introduced by the racial realignment and expanded reach of national policymaking, propelling the transformation of mediating institutions that we take up in the next chapter.

The New Deal Era and Bottom-Up Pressures on the Democratic Party

The 1930s were in many ways a uniquely ideological period in American politics. On the left, a radicalized industrial labor movement in which communist organizers played a key role engaged in militant tactics to force employers to the bargaining table. For many hoping to push the New Deal to the left, the Soviet experiment was a source of inspiration, and communist-backed popular front organizations became a force in liberal-left circles. On the right, many looked to the rise of European fascism not as a threat to democracy, but as a model to emulate in response to the economic crisis. Fritz Kuhn's German American Bund, which openly backed Hitler, claimed one hundred thousand members at its peak. Both the Bund and the Communist parties proved fully capable of filling the twenty thousand–seat Madison Square Garden for their rallies. As Ira Katznelson argues forcefully, the continued viability of liberal democracy could not be taken for granted amid the disruptions of the Depression and the successes of radical movements in Europe: "Although American majorities were never drawn to the models crafted by the dictatorships, their seeming success did attract tens of thousands, including visible and articulate intellectuals and organizational leaders."[1]

It is tempting to dismiss today's polarization as mild compared to a time when both communists and avowed fascists could stage mass public events that garnered front-page coverage across the US. The fierce ideological divisions and heated rhetoric of the 1930s, however, did not map neatly onto the party system.

The Democratic coalition was deeply divided along regional lines, simultaneously encompassing some of the most reactionary and progressive forces in US politics. Prominent Democratic elected officials included Georgia Governor Eugene Talmadge—who expressed his admiration for *Mein Kampf*—and Martin Dies of Texas, who made a name for himself ferreting out alleged communists in New Deal agencies and labor unions.[2] Yet the party also had the backing of Labor's Non-Partisan League, which incorporated both mainstream and communist-dominated unions.[3] Few decisions angered southern conservatives more than Michigan Democratic Governor Frank Murphy's refusal to send in the National Guard to crush the 1937 sit-down strikes in the automobile industry, a major shift from the long tradition of state and federal governments using force on behalf of employers in labor disputes. Murphy's appointment to the Supreme Court just three years later—followed soon after by the appointment of South Carolina conservative James Byrnes—dramatized the ideological gulf *within* the majority Democratic Party.

Republicans were less heterogeneous but included a mix of stalwart conservatives opposed to the entire New Deal project, such as Robert Taft of Ohio, and moderate and liberal members who supported both an expanded welfare state and Roosevelt's foreign policy internationalism. Wendell Willkie, the GOP's nominee for president in 1940, had been a delegate to the 1932 Democratic National Convention and pledged to uphold most of the New Deal if elected.

These intraparty divisions gave top party leaders—especially on the Democratic side, which was in power throughout the period—an incentive to find ways to defuse ideological fights rather than to intensify them. Although Republicans sought to paint the New Deal as "communistic," the reality was that Roosevelt and other Democratic leaders were determined to balance a range of competing ideological currents.[4] Dependent on their peculiar north–south coalition to remain in power, Roosevelt and other top Democrats also sought to submerge issues—most notably, racial justice—that Black and labor movement activists attempted to push onto the national agenda. National party leaders struggled to placate both sides of their coalition by making vague gestures toward racial equality while resisting concrete policies to defeat racial discrimination. The consequences of these strategies of avoidance and delay were tragic, even as they reflected a clear strategic rationale.

Crucially, civil rights activists capitalized on the decentralized structure of mediating institutions that we have identified as a key feature of the pre-1970s political order. In particular, the political incentives for Democratic politicians in many states outside the South looked very different than they did for national party leaders. The migration of Black Americans from the South meant that Black voters became an important constituency in several northern cities and states.[5] And these new arrivals increasingly voted Democratic. Even with the racial exclusions built into many New Deal programs, it was nonetheless the case that the Works Progress Administration (WPA) and other initiatives represented a vast improvement for the more than one million Black Americans receiving government help. As the Black journalist Henry Lee Moon commented, "At no time since the curtain had dropped on the Reconstruction drama had government focused as much attention upon [Black Americans'] basic needs as did the New Deal."[6] Black newspapers, organizations, and voters recognized the severe shortcomings of the New Deal, but their response generally was to pressure Democrats to deliver on their promises of equal justice rather than to condemn the New Deal project.[7]

In pursuing this goal, civil rights advocates found important allies in the industrial labor movement, which was led by the Congress of Industrial Organizations (CIO). American unions had a notorious history of racial discrimination, but the CIO—which rocketed onto the political scene after 1935—had both strategic and ideological reasons for organizing on a biracial basis and making civil rights an important plank of its agenda. Racial exclusion was a recipe for union failure since Black workers constituted a potential group of strike-breakers in many industrial workplaces. This strategic imperative was reinforced by the genuine commitment to racial justice especially common among CIO activists who emerged from the Communist and Socialist Parties.[8]

Black workers and civil rights advocates quickly recognized the potential of an alliance with the CIO for improving the economic and political situation for Black Americans. They pushed union leaders to take clear stands on civil rights even in the face of considerable racism among rank-and-file white members.[9] With the CIO quickly becoming a crucial source of activists, votes, and energy for many northern Democrats, this union support necessarily drew the attention of ambitious politicians.

The presence of a common enemy reinforced the nascent alliance between industrial unions and Black civil rights activists. Northern Democrats increasingly saw southern Democrats as a hostile faction within the party. Southern Democrats had voted in favor of the pro-labor Wagner Act of 1935, but quickly turned against the labor movement amid the threat posed by the CIO to their region's low-wage, Jim Crow–policy regime.[10] With southern conservatives sponsoring anti-labor legislation and fighting efforts to expand the New Deal, the CIO concluded that turning the Democrats into a genuine liberal party required vanquishing the party's southern wing. Black Americans were no longer isolated in their fight against Jim Crow; their enemies now were also the main enemies of labor-oriented northern Democrats. Those same Democrats had come to see the defeat of "poll tax" southerners as the pathway to a liberal national majority.[11]

Exploiting the opportunities available in a decentralized constitutional order, civil rights advocates achieved their earliest successes at the state and local level. While national leaders had an interest in placating southern conservatives, locally rooted northern Democratic politicians had a more immediate incentive to respond to demands from their own constituents.

With Black voters and CIO unions an increasingly important constituency for many northern Democrats, state parties began to endorse civil rights legislation in their platforms. These state platforms had said little about civil rights in the 1920s and early 1930s. If anything, Republicans had been slightly more supportive than Democrats.[12] But northern Democratic state parties started to speak more forthrightly about civil rights in the late 1930s, and easily surpassed their Republican counterparts in their support for civil rights by the early to mid-1940s. Northern Democrats also pushed for enactment of state fair employment laws, with more than two dozen states enacting legislation barring racial discrimination in the years leading up to the Civil Rights Act of 1964.[13]

Although the Roosevelt administration and top party leaders in Congress sought to limit the place of civil rights on the national legislative agenda, rank-and-file northern Democrats pushed to sidestep conservative southern committee chairs' agenda control. Once again, geographic decentralization played an essential role; representatives from districts with a sizable Black population were more likely to sponsor civil rights bills, and urban population and unionization were strong predictors of members' willingness to support "discharge petitions" that would force legislation to the floor over the objections of party and committee gatekeepers.[14] These efforts responded to and reinforced civil rights movement activists' push to make racial discrimination a highly visible issue on the national agenda.

On the Republican side, ordinary voters—particularly those in rural areas and economic conservatives—showed substantial skepticism toward civil rights legislation, particularly when it came to such emergent issues as fair employment laws. A faction of hard-core midwestern and sunbelt conservatives in Congress sought to capitalize on this grassroots sentiment, arguing that taking a clear anti–civil rights position would allow the GOP to become the home for conservatives in both the North and the South. Senator Karl Mundt (R-SD)—an ally of Wisconsin's Joseph McCarthy—spearheaded an effort in 1951–52 to forge a unity ticket with southern conservative Democrats. Mundt gave a series of speeches across the US advocating for a realignment on the basis of a revised Republican platform "in the field of discrimination" that would return to the "great and noble American concepts of states' rights that the New Deal today has entirely scuttled."[15] Drawing on mass-level and activists' support, advocates of a more conservative stance on civil rights gradually captured control of several midwestern and western Republican parties in the 1940s and 1950s.

In many ways, liberal advocates of realignment on the Democratic side and conservative supporters on the GOP side shared insights that would prove prescient. Once Republicans clearly took the conservative position on civil rights and Democrats embraced the liberal one, it would lay the foundation for a nationalized party system defined by ideology. These figures were early advocates of an agenda that many others would pursue over the decades to follow, actively working to sharpen distinctions between the parties.[16]

But the time for this realignment had not yet arrived. Pressure from below notwithstanding, the northeastern wing of the GOP had the upper hand in controlling presidential nominations during the 1940s and 1950s. Its leaders favored moderate candidates who could compete in swing states such as New York, New Jersey, and Illinois, rather than the sort of archconservatives who might bring together the rural Midwest and the South.[17] For their part, Democratic leaders' reliance upon both southern and northern votes to win the White House and maintain their congressional majorities made them equally reluctant to take a clear position. The national leadership of both parties thus backed weak compromises—such as the Civil Rights Act of 1957—while avoiding action on more ambitious legislation that directly threatened the Jim Crow system.

Racial Realignment and Ideological Sorting in the 1960s

Through the 1950s and 1960s, civil rights activists led broad-based campaigns and protests that brought national attention to oppression in the South. By the mid-1960s, their activism made the compromises and evasions of earlier eras untenable for national Democratic leaders. The violent southern response to protests dramatized racial injustice for northern voters while undermining America's Cold War standing in front of a world audience.[18] With civil rights rising on the national agenda, avoiding a clear stand was no longer a viable strategy. Critically, by the time movement activists forced a national showdown, the parties had been remade underneath their national leaders. The meaning of New Deal liberalism had, for most Democrats, come to incorporate a commitment to civil rights, and this commitment was now a core element of the party's program throughout the North. These northerners controlled a clear majority of national convention delegates, meaning that Lyndon Johnson's path to renomination in 1964 required that he maintain the support of northern racial liberals.[19]

Among Republicans, the Goldwater movement, which had already begun to make noise before the 1960 election, capitalized on the racial conservatism of GOP voters and grassroots activists in defeating the northeastern moderate wing at the 1964 convention. Although Goldwater's landslide loss in the general election was a setback for the conservatives, it soon became clear that the balance of power within the GOP had shifted decisively in the conservatives' favor. Richard Nixon avoided Goldwater's explicit identification with southern segregationists in 1968, but he only beat back Ronald Reagan's convention threat by reassuring southern delegates that he would slow down school integration, oppose busing, and select a solid conservative as Vice President.[20]

The racial realignment of national party leaders had a decisive impact on the evolution of the party system. Democrats were now more clearly a liberal party and Republicans were much more closely associated with conservatism than in the Dewey and Eisenhower eras. Southern white conservatives responded by moving into the GOP orbit, first in presidential voting, then, over time, in their everyday partisanship and voting for other offices.

The shift in southern white partisanship had critical implications for how the two parties would respond to a slew of issues that rose onto the national agenda in the years following the Civil Rights Act of 1964. Neil O'Brian demonstrates that racially conservative white voters tended to be conservative on a host of other social and cultural issues, many of which were nascent and became political flashpoints only later. They were less supportive of feminism, abortion rights, gun control, gay rights, and immigration. Prior to the civil rights realignment, these social and cultural conservatives tended to be split nearly equally between the parties, with Democrats dominating them in the South and Republicans enjoying the edge in the North. But southern white voters brought their conservative views on social and cultural issues with them as they moved into the GOP in the 1960s–90s. As a result, as each of these issues became prominent on the national agenda, Republican politicians faced a party base that pushed them toward the conservative side, while Democrats increasingly drew their support from voters favoring broadly liberal positions. Instead of viewing the parties' positioning on each of these issues as cases of separate "issue evolutions," O'Brian suggests that they are connected to one another through their origins in the racial realignment.[21]

Different issues and identities motivated different voters. But Democrats' embrace of the liberal position on each new social and cultural issue, and Republicans' adoption of the conservative side, sent a clear signal to more and more voters regarding which party better fit their self-conception. Before the 1960s, Republicans were the party of professional, educated suburbanites as well as conservative rural voters. As southern white evangelicals increasingly came to define the party nationally, socially liberal and moderate suburbanites gradually moved into the Democrats' ranks, further solidifying each party's ideological identity.

Through this self-reinforcing process, a whole series of social and cultural identities came into alignment with partisanship.[22] The so-called "culture war" between Democrats and Republicans encompasses battles on a host of issues that, at least on the surface, are distinct from questions of racial equality. Yet it was the partisan realignment on race that set the stage for each party's response to these issues, with Republicans' "southern strategy" drawing on interconnected attitudes toward race, gender roles, and religious identity.[23]

In the 1940s and 1950s, critics on the left and right could plausibly accuse the parties of being so similar on many policy questions that the Democrats were, as former FDR Vice President Henry Wallace said in 1948, "only the Tweedledum version of the Republican Tweedledee."[24] Neither party could be a reliable ideological instrument as long as southern white conservatives remained ensconced in a coalition with urban northern liberals. Today, of course, it would be difficult to confuse the two parties. The racial realignment dislodged the southerners, paving the way for each party to embrace a much clearer ideology, with racial, social, and cultural issues increasingly defining their identities.

The "Long 1960s" and the Rise of Activist Federal Government

The civil rights movement that upended American politics was, of course, part of a broader period of turbulence, social unrest, and political mobilization. Out of this turbulence came a second transformative development: the expansion of an activist state that did much more, across many more issues, and in a more centralized fashion. This shift would have a lasting impact on politics. It increased the stakes of governance, bringing powerful new actors into the political arena. And it directed their energies toward Washington, DC, where more and more of the critical issues of governance were decided. These developments would in turn accelerate the emergence of polarized and nationalized parties.

Numerous scholars have identified the period of policymaking from the early 1960s to the mid to late 1970s as highly distinctive and unusually activist. Studies by David Mayhew, Matt Grossmann, Theda Skocpol, and others demonstrate that heightened policy activity occurred not only in Congress but also in the executive branch and the courts. Mayhew's famous study of major legislation identifies a dramatic "surge" or "bulge" in this period. Skocpol, highlighting both expanding policy and expanding interest group activism, calls it "the Long 1960s."[25]

Notably, at the outset, the politics around government expansion and nationalization was unusually bipartisan. Indeed, this is an important reason for Mayhew's well-known conclusion that divided government does not cause gridlock. Democrats held majorities and the White House from 1961–68, and their control of the policy agenda was no doubt critical to initiating the wave of new policy. Yet most of the biggest initiatives—from the Civil Rights Act and Voting Rights Act (VRA) to the enactment of Medicare and Medicaid, to the emergence of national environmental legislation—received broad bipartisan support (at least once it became clear that they would pass). Moreover, the rapid flow of new policy activity did not halt when Democrats lost big in the 1966 midterms, or when Richard Nixon defeated Hubert Humphrey in 1968. Nor, during the Long 1960s, was the presence of many Republican-nominated Supreme Court justices an obstacle to court activism. Indeed, Republican-nominated justices wrote many of the opinions that anchored the era's "rights revolution," including *Roe v. Wade.*

The expansion and nationalization of policy during the Long 1960s proceeded on multiple fronts—rising and more centralized social spending, a very large expansion of the federal regulatory state, and the imposition of federal control (exercised either through legislation or through decisions of the courts) over matters that had been previously left to localities, states, or the private sector.

The most traditional and straightforward aspect of this rising government activism was the growth of public spending. All told, federal nondefense spending would almost *triple* as a share of GDP between 1955 and 1975, rising from 5.7 percent of GDP to 15.7 percent of GDP. In 1965 Washington enacted two massive new health care programs, Medicare and Medicaid, which would in time grow to account for almost a quarter of federal spending. In 1972, Congress substantially increased Social Security benefits.

A striking feature of the trends in social policy was not just more spending, but the increasing role of the federal government in an American welfare state that had previously been quite decentralized.[26] Medicare, of course, was fully nationalized. Medicaid, although not fully nationalized, was far more centralized than the modest patchwork of state-level programs it replaced. In 1974 Congress enacted the Food Stamps program, creating another nationalized package of social benefits. That same year, Congress nationalized and considerably expanded Supplementary Security Income (SSI), the means-tested old age and disability program.

Even state spending became more dependent on federal decisions. Between 1955 and 1975 federal grants to the states more than quadrupled as a share of GDP. Typically, these grants came with a range of requirements that significantly expanded federal control. If groups wanted to influence how these resources were used, they would need to shift some of their attention from the states to Washington.

The expanded reach of federal regulatory policy was, if anything, more extensive. Prior to the 1960s, federal regulation focused mostly on commercial activity, and it was typically organized around particular economic sectors such as communications, finance, energy, or transportation.[27] In contrast, matters like environmental protection, occupational safety, employment discrimination and most areas of consumer protection were left to the states—which often meant that regulation was weak or absent altogether. This changed in short order with a wave of landmark laws, among them the Traffic Safety Act of 1966, the National Environmental Policy Act (1969), the Clean Air Act of 1970, the Occupational Safety and Health Act of 1970 (OSHA), the Clean Water Act of 1972, the Consumer Product Safety Act of 1972 and the Endangered Species Act of 1973.[28]

Nor was it simply a matter of these landmark bills. The Long 1960s stands out as a remarkably distinctive period in the construction of the modern regulatory state. Mayhew identifies 330 "major" laws passed between 1947 and 2002. If one focuses on the bills whose central features were regulatory or deregulatory the pattern is striking. Between 1947 and 1964, the federal government adopted only seven major regulatory laws. In the quarter century after 1977, it adopted eleven (while also passing a number of deregulatory initiatives centering on the older, sectorally focused regulations). In just the thirteen years in between, the federal government adopted *thirty-four* major regulatory laws—nearly double the number of major enactments of the other four decades combined.[29] The same period witnessed dramatic expansions in federal employment and spending related to social regulation.

Critically, the new regulation typically cut across many sectors of the economy at once. For example, all industries were subject to the Clean Air Act, the Clean Water Act, and OSHA. This breadth helped fuel the backlash within the business community.[30] Collective action on a large scale became more attractive when many firms were facing similar threats. Following a massive mobilization effort, the business community's defeat of Carter's proposed Consumer Protection Agency in 1978, along with other striking conservative victories in a Congress with large Democratic majorities, would effectively bring the Long 1960s to a close.[31]

The final dramatic shift in governance during the Long 1960s was the "rights revolution," a surge in court and legislative action to monitor and enforce equal rights guarantees for a wide range of individuals and groups. Launched by passage of the Civil Rights Act of 1964 and the Voting Rights Act of 1965 (VRA), Congress engaged in what Robert Kagan called "a truly extraordinary surge of activity" in this area.[32] Among the landmark enactments were the 1968 Fair Housing Act, Title IX of the Education Amendments of 1972, the Education for All Handicapped Children Act of 1975, and the Pregnancy Discrimination Act of 1978. Congress also passed the Immigration Act of 1965, not precisely a rights bill but one that removed extensive racial discrimination from immigration rules and would, in time, yield dramatic changes in the demographic contours of the United States. As with regulatory initiatives, Mayhew's tally of major laws shows a distinct (if somewhat less pronounced) bulge in the Long 1960s.

The rights revolution, of course, extended beyond Congress to the courts, where it had emerged earlier. As Charles Epp has noted, the share of the Supreme Court's agenda devoted to civil rights and civil liberties rose from just 9 percent in its 1933 term to 65 percent in the 1971 term.[33] While this expansion was more gradual than in most areas of the activist wave, with key cases like *Brown* being decided in the 1950s, roughly half of the increase occurred after 1960.

In one sense, much of the rights revolution constituted a *curtailment* of government activism, as the Supreme Court and other federal courts imposed new restrictions on what state and local governments could do. By 1975 states could not prohibit the sale of contraceptives or impose broad restrictions on abortions. They could not use non-physical coercion to obtain confessions, or convict and sentence to prison people who lacked an attorney, or search a person's home without a court order.

In a deeper sense, however, these decisions represented a fundamental expansion of federal authority. *Federal* judges, and ultimately the US Supreme Court, would now decide what was allowed or required on these and other fundamental matters. Importantly, almost all of these decisions were liberal, and while many of them were popular more than a few—for instance increasing protections for those accused of crimes—were not, and others may have had majority support but were highly controversial. These initiatives would play into the backlash to come.

The most dramatic illustration of the rights revolution's transformative impact on politics is the Supreme Court's seven to two *Roe v. Wade* decision in 1973. In an instant, *Roe* imposed a national policy standard on a highly controversial issue, replacing a system in which different states were free to fashion highly divergent responses. After 1973, trying to influence abortion policy in the United States became largely a matter of trying to influence the composition of the Supreme Court, which meant trying to influence who held the offices that determined court appointments. Within a decade it would become clear that the key influence on the policy views of those appointments was the party of the president who nominated them. Hence, those holding strong views on the matter had good reason to align with one party or the other.

Roe was just one component of the overall shift—in spending, regulation and the monitoring of rights—from a Washington that had ceded much authority to localities or private actors to one that was much more active and controlling. Not all issues carried such stark and swift political implications as *Roe*. The combined impact, however, justifies the assessment of the Long 1960s as a critical moment in the evolution of the American polity.

What caused this revolution in policy? Inevitably, the sources of such a broad historical shift are hard to pin down—Mayhew speaks of a "continuous tumult of causes."[34] Grossmann's careful examination of the actors who experts identify as significant for each major policy initiative leads him to stress the role of elite networks. He argues that these networks were distinctive during the Long 1960s. Rather than different actors being critical on different issues, Grossmann identifies a set of interconnected policymakers operating on multiple issues across an expanding range of policy domains. Like others, he stresses the quick succession of initiatives through a process of diffusion: "Early policy results allowed the same set of actors to build on their success."[35] Contributing to that success was a set of changes in Washington that increased the opportunities for policymaking elites to engage in rapid and extensive action: the growing administrative and technical capacities of both Congress and the executive, the opening of the courts to a wider range of litigants, and the arrival of public interest groups, who both prodded policymakers to action and helped them overcome resistance.

Beyond these proximate causes scholars generally emphasize the build-up of pressures associated with a period of unrest and social mobilization. Social movement activity was extraordinarily high during this period.[36] Though it began with the civil rights movement, it spread from there to environmentalism, consumer protection and women's issues as well as the anti-war movement. The success of the civil rights movement provided a model for effective mobilization that other groups eventually adopted in various forms. Among the emulators were conservative groups that would emerge to contest the initial wave of liberalizing mobilization.

Nor did the civil rights movement just provide a model. By weakening political resistance to federal action it helped open the floodgates to policy reform.[37] Prior to the Long 1960s resistance to national legislation often rested on assertions of "states' rights," which placed issues like environmental protection beyond Washington's purview. When such assertions became suspect in the wake of segregationist resistance to the civil rights movement that removed what James Q. Wilson called a "legitimacy barrier." In this context, the center of action could move to Washington, where it spread from issue to issue. "Once the 'legitimacy barrier' has fallen" Wilson wrote: "Political conflict takes a very different form. New programs need not await the advent of a crisis or an extraordinary majority because no program is any longer 'new'—it is seen, rather, as an extension, a modification, or an enlargement of something the government is already doing."[38]

The rise of social movements and the broadening of the agenda points to another background factor: previously unmet demand for governance and policy reform. Expansions of the role of the state occurred in every advanced industrial economy after World War II.[39] In the United States, the bulk of this expansion took place during the Long 1960s, but given the commonalities in demands arising across rich societies, some such expansion seems likely to have happened at some point. In some cases, like an expanded government role in health care, these demands were long-standing ones that had been held up by a strong conservative coalition in Congress. In other areas the expansion of the policy agenda reflected the new "post-materialist" concerns of an increasingly affluent, complex, interdependent and metropolis-centered society. Such changing conditions fostered demands for effective regulation, while producing growing attention to issues that fed the distinctive politics of the Long 1960s.[40] Many of the policy departures of the Long 1960s—such as environmental and consumer protection and relaxation of restrictions related to gender and sexuality—reflected these new circumstances.

Again, it is worth stressing the initial degree of bipartisanship. Several major laws passed *before* Johnson's landslide 1964 election. Although the large gains for Democrats that year undoubtedly helped, the wave of activism lost little momentum when Democrats yielded considerable electoral ground in 1966 and 1968. The first congressional session of Nixon's presidency saw, in Matt Grossmann's words, "landmark new liberal laws in environmental, health, labor, education, transportation, and urban policy. By the time Nixon signed general revenue sharing into law, the American state had dramatically expanded in size and scope."[41] Mayhew too sees continuity rather than change as Republican political power increased. Indeed, he notes that the Ninety-Third Congress, at the outset of Nixon's second term, stands out as arguably the most productive during the entire period.[42]

The Long 1960s was a watershed, though it would take time for the full consequences to emerge. Still, it is notable that just as the wave of policy nationalization and expansion crested in the mid to late 1970s, measures of partisan polarization in Congress began the long upward rise that has continued for almost half a century.

The changes wrought in this relatively brief but spectacular burst of policy enactments—a burst that ended by 1978 at the latest—would, in concert with racial realignment, create the conditions for a much more nationalized and polarized politics thereafter. The expanded role of Washington in public policymaking raised the stakes in politics, heightened political mobilization, increased the focus of political attention on national affairs, and contributed to the already developing process of partisan sorting.

Increased government action, and the potential for yet more action as the "legitimacy barrier" fell away, meant that control over that activity mattered more. A much wider range of issues on which many held strong opinions were now understood to be public matters, to be resolved through politics. Quite simply, winning and losing in politics became more consequential.

Awareness of these heightened consequences was greatest among groups with strong policy preferences. Understandably, they would organize, reorganize, or significantly expand their efforts to try to exercise influence over this new terrain. While much of the legislation of the Long 1960s was bipartisan, it was also overwhelmingly liberal—indeed, this strong tendency is evident whether one looks at legislation, executive action, or court decisions.[43] This liberal policy shift received critical support from the array of social movements that gained traction in the 1960s—and, in many cases, the new policies bolstered organized groups that served as key constituencies for these policies.

Equally important, these liberal policies fueled a strong organized backlash against many of the initiatives associated with the Long 1960s. Famously, Lewis Powell (who would later join the Supreme Court) penned a memo to leaders of the US Chamber of Commerce in response to these recent developments. He explained that the existential threat to American business required extensive political mobilization and laid out a blueprint for that response.[44]

The specific impact of Powell's memo is easy to exaggerate, but it is illustrative of the broader dynamic. Religious conservatives mobilized against state support for changing norms on sexuality, and, in time, abortion. Gun owners mobilized against new restrictions and fear that those restrictions would grow. As we will detail in the next chapter, the Long 1960s triggered a massive expansion of organized interests, much of it focused on the kinds of issues that became newly salient during this period.

Like racial realignment, the Long 1960s greatly advanced the nationalization of politics. It was not just that government was doing more. It was also that more of what government did was being determined in Washington. Bryan Jones, Michelle Whyman, and Sean Theriault conclude that "By the end of the broadening period, the relationship between the states and the federal government had been fundamentally transformed. The more the federal government broadened, the more it affected the leeway previously left to the states."[45]

Political actors responded. Groups shifted their resources and organizational capacities. Activists shifted their attention. They focused increasingly on helping supporters and damaging opponents in the nation's capital. As we shall see, much of this focus supplanted the more decentralized efforts and attention that had traditionally limited the intensity and duration of partisan divisions.

Again like racial realignment, the increased focus on national politics reinforced a process discussed previously: the growing incentives for both elites and voters to "sort" into parties clearly distinguished as liberal and conservative. The focus of activity in Washington facilitated the task of distinguishing the parties, especially as conservative groups mobilized in opposition to the Long 1960s.

Once begun, this process was strongly reinforcing. As we will explore in the next chapter, the more distinct the national parties became, the more liberal and conservative groups aligned with the appropriate party. Whether a group won or lost on an issue was seen to rest on the question of which party was in control. The growing connections between groups and parties put more pressure on out-of-step national politicians to change parties, retire, or adopt the party line. This activity further clarified party differences, which in turn further encouraged voters to sort, reinforcing the broader dynamic of polarization. Over time party networks that had traditionally allowed considerable internal variation, grounded in the local roots of party politics, would be brought into the process as well. This would have dramatic effects on party elites and party networks all the way down to the local level.

The Nationalization of the American Political Economy

We have emphasized the role of two critical catalysts to the transformation of American politics—racial realignment and the expanded policy activity of the federal government. These, of course, were not the only changes leading to a more nationalized and polarized system of party competition. In closing we briefly discuss a final transformation that has also contributed to the key developments in party structure, media and interest group organization that we will explore in the next chapter: the shift toward a more nationalized political economy in which local economic interests carry less independent weight.

The Constitution was expected to ensure that the nation's economic diversity found political expression. Madison, of course, put this at the heart of his understanding of political economy outlined in *Federalist*, no. 10: "A landed interest, a manufacturing interest, a mercantile interest, a moneyed interest, with many lesser interests, grow up of necessity in civilized nations. . . . The regulation of these various and interfering interests forms the principal task of modern legislation." The system's design worked especially to promote the clear articulation of *geographically based* economic interests. As explored in earlier chapters, local economic interests have indeed been a critical source of political diversity and dynamism throughout American history. To borrow a phrase from national security analysts, the American constitutional order excelled at "stove-piping" local economic interests into national politics.[46]

Today, the United States economy remains highly diverse, and much of that diversity remains rooted in geography. Since the 1970s the US has been in a transition from an industrial to a post-industrial or knowledge economy, and that economy is extremely geographically stratified.[47] A handful of mostly coastal cities house the "agglomeration economies" that now power America production. Extractive sectors—energy, mining and agriculture—have clear geographic centers, while manufacturing remains anchored in the Midwest and (increasingly) the Sunbelt. Geographic diversity remains evident in income distribution as well. Indeed, after a century of steady geographic convergence of incomes (with the South edging closer to national averages) further convergence stopped around 1980. Economic inequality among states has, if anything, increased since then.[48]

Yet in critical ways the economy, and in particular the vantage point of economic elites, has nationalized, with truly local interests playing a less prominent role. The central vehicle for this transformation was the "financialization" of the economy that began in the 1970s and accelerated over the next generation of gradual financial deregulation.[49]

Financialization had two distinct aspects. The most obvious was the growth of the financial sector itself, which roughly doubled its share of the economy and helped generate concentrations of wealth unseen in a century. The second and arguably more critical aspect, however, was the shareholder value revolution that "financialized" the entire corporate landscape. "Stakeholders," who were typically local, lost sway. Corporate behavior became increasingly responsive to signals from financial markets as firms sought to maximize share prices. Financialization in turn helped fuel a major increase in economic concentration across many sectors.[50]

Both financialization and economic consolidation muted the role of local economic elites. Economic power shifted to national or global firms. Local economic activity was increasingly absorbed in far-flung supply chains. Local banks and local manufacturing facilities were no longer sites of major decision-making. Instead, key decisions were made elsewhere, in response to the logics of financialization that transcend any particular location. Local "stakeholders" might retain geographically rooted interests, but they operated within economic structures that no longer gave those local interests as much voice.

The sociologist Josh Pacewicz, in his study of the two Iowa cities he dubs "Prairieville" and "River City" notes that in "the 1970s all but a handful of

Prairieville's and River City's largest employers were owned locally, but . . . by the . . . mid-2000s, most of [the] old family businesses were gone." A "politics disembedded from community governance" emerged as financial deregulation fueled a merger boom that "led to the acquisition of most of River City's and Prairieville's locally owned firms, and thereby thinned the ranks of business and labor leaders, robbing both cities of their traditional leadership class."[51] Within local political parties these leaders gave way to an activist political class oriented toward the forces of nationalization that were remaking American politics.

This disembedding has been reinforced by a rapidly increasing concentration of income and wealth. If we consider, say, the top 0.01 percent of the income distribution—one household in every ten thousand—their real after-tax incomes more than *quintupled* between 1979 and 2005, a period of stagnant or negative income growth for many Americans.[52] The expansion of massive fortunes has been even more extraordinary. Controlling for inflation, the total wealth in *Fortune*'s list of the 400 richest Americans increased from $225 billion in 1982 to $2.3 trillion in 2014.[53] Moreover, this remarkable wealth has translated into outsized political voice. From 1980 to 2012, the share of campaign contributions coming from the richest 0.01 percent of donors increased from 15 percent to 40 percent.[54]

This extreme expansion and concentration of wealth reinforced the nationalizing impact of financialization and consolidation because it too meant that massive economic resources were increasingly decoupled from any particular locale. There are geographic patterns in where politically active megadonors are located, with liberals concentrated in a handful of coastal blue states and conservatives much more widely spread.[55] Yet in an age of globalization, these vast fortunes are generally distinguished by their fluidity.

Economic elites are not only vastly better resourced than they were a generation ago; they are also increasingly disconnected from any particular location.[56] Neither the Koch brothers nor the Walton family have particular reason to care about the specific economic concerns of Kansas or Arkansas. These elites often share an interest in economic policy and considerable power to pursue those interests, but these interests are national, rather than linked to the distinctive location or activity from which that wealth initially sprang. This national focus is evident, for instance, in the fixation on lowering taxes on high incomes and wealth that has become the north star of Republican policymaking. What Hacker, Pierson and Zacher call "place-based economic interests" have lost political traction—a traction that historically played a critical role in limiting pressures for polarization within our two-party system.[57]

It would be a mistake to treat this nationalization of key features of the American economy as entirely separate from politics. All of the trends we describe—financialization, consolidation, and rising economic inequality—have been driven in significant part by political choices.[58] Nonetheless, the confluence of forces at work have clearly weakened the independent expression of purely local economic voices in American society. As we shall see, broad transformations in politics have served to weaken them even more.

Conclusion

A nationalizing political economy has operated alongside racial realignment and the policy revolution of the Long 1960s to reorient American politics. As these developments took hold, they would, in turn, help catalyze profound changes in the core mediating institutions of state parties, interest groups, and the media. In some cases, they gave new force and direction to dormant features of the political landscape in ways that would sharpen polarization. In others, they introduced quite new incentives and constraints for important political actors.

As the political system nationalized and began to polarize, state parties, interest groups, and media would, too. And changes in each would begin to reinforce and accelerate the nationalizing and polarizing changes taking place elsewhere. Fatefully, these crucial mediating institutions would now promote rather than impede polarization.

The Transformation of State Parties, Interest Groups, and Media

Racial realignment, ideological sorting, and the growing role of the national government contributed to the transformation of mediating institutions that in the past had acted as a brake against ever-increasing party divisions. State parties, interest groups, and the media have each become more nationalized and more closely linked to national party agendas. Rather than providing openings for interests and coalitions that crosscut the prevailing line of party division, these institutions today work in tandem to reinforce national party polarization.

The timeline of change varied. For state parties, the roots of change go all the way back to Progressive-Era reforms that weakened state parties' access to patronage and control of the nomination process. These reforms prepared the ground, but their potential impact on polarization lay dormant for decades because each party's primary electorate encompassed a broad range of ideological views. The parties' realignment on race, however, began a process of sorting that paved the way for ideological activists to impose a clearer identity on each party. At the same time, the expanded role of Washington encouraged these activists to focus on national issues rather than state or local concerns. State parties, which had long provided a foothold for locally rooted interests not well represented in national party councils, have become more similar to one another across regions. Today they often reflect national cleavages far better than they represent the local demands that one might expect to emerge from each state's political and economic landscape.

The tightening relationship between the parties and organized interest groups also followed a complicated timeline, with important alliances forming at different moments depending on the trajectory of individual issues. The common dynamic, though, is that the growing role of the national government went hand in hand with the increased activism of nationally oriented groups. Once the ideological sorting of the parties began in the 1960s, it was more common for these groups to identify one party over the other as the most hospitable home for its policy goals. As a result, groups developed strong incentives to forge broader partnerships with their favored parties, and the stakes of elections grew. Interest groups' earlier access-seeking strategy of wooing incumbents in both parties gave way to an approach focused on helping the allied party win elections.

This process of intertwining was very much a two-way street. As groups—such as specific industries, religious conservatives, environmentalists, and feminists—forged alliances with one party, they also helped shape that party's commitments and identity. Likewise, the parties used their growing influence in the policymaking process to pressure groups, telling them that they needed to be good partisan team players for their priorities to be favored. While there are still some interest groups that have not been fully drawn into this polarized dynamic, group-party alliances are now routine. The result is a mutually reinforcing cycle that has diminished the incentives for bipartisanship and moderation and dried up the supply of politicians inclined to pursue such strategies.

As with state parties and organized interests, the development of a nationalized, partisan media landscape fed off the ideological sorting of the parties and the growing centrality of national policy, but it was also influenced by distinctive dynamics. In particular, changes in technology played a critical role in nurturing media forms that were not spatially confined. This, in turn, altered business incentives. The rise of cable news, talk radio, and then social media turned attention away from local issues and toward hot-button national controversies. Meanwhile, the growth of an explicitly partisan media infrastructure, particularly on the right, fed off these new media forms. With their markets typically limited to one or two competitors, newspapers and broadcast television networks of the mid to late twentieth century had sought profits through winning as wide an audience as possible. By contrast, newer outlets operate in a landscape flooded with potential competitors, but they are able to reach national audiences. This encouraged a strategy of appealing to a narrower, but intensely loyal audience. Fox News and Rush Limbaugh, among others, demonstrated that taking on an aggressively conservative, pro-Republican approach was a pathway to both profits and political influence. These same sources undermined trust in other outlets and authoritative institutions, limiting their audience's openness to alternative channels of information and reinforcing sectarian impulses in the electorate.

Although state parties, organized groups, and the partisan media followed somewhat different timelines, the three sets of changes are best viewed as interconnected. As each nationalized and polarized, that change reinforced similar dynamics in the others. The changing media landscape helped to create the national network of ideological activists that has permeated the state parties. The new media served as a critical bridge between mass- and elite-level politics, providing consistent cues to ordinary partisans across the US, while incentivizing party leaders at all levels of government to stick with the party base. The growing nationalization and partisanship of organized groups further encouraged polarization in state parties since state party officials are often drawn from, or at least rely on, their party's allied groups. Furthermore, amid gridlock in Washington, interest groups increasingly turn to the states as a venue to pursue their goals.[1] At the same time, with state parties now much more closely aligned with their national teams, there is less space for groups to pursue the old, pluralist strategy of forging alliances with whichever party happens to hold the upper hand in a particular state or region. Together, the transformation of these three mediating institutions has fostered a political environment in which polarization has become self-reinforcing, with substantial consequences for policymaking (chapter 6) and the vulnerability of democratic institutions (chapter 7).

The Declining Autonomy of State Parties

Although it was only completed much later, the transformation of state parties has its origins in the Progressive Era—long before the transformation of other mediating institutions that we detail later in this chapter. These new rules essentially turned political parties into state-regulated public utilities, with legislatures determining how candidates would qualify for the ballot. The rules made it harder for third parties by, for example, banning "fusion" tickets in which an individual could run as the candidate of multiple parties, receiving votes on each party's line on the ballot.[2] Furthermore, ballot access rules added a new layer of administrative burdens on third parties, which prior to the 1890s could simply print their own tickets. Where nineteenth-century third parties—such as the Free-Soilers, Greenbackers, Populists, and Prohibitionists—successfully pressured state parties to adopt stances that were dissonant from those of their national leadership, these new rules helped insulate the two major parties from such challenges.

Even as these rules shielded Democrats and Republicans from third-party threats, other Progressive-Era reforms weakened state parties' capacity to exert independent influence on politicians. The enactment of direct primary laws gave ordinary voters a greater say in nominations, making it more likely that candidates could win office without developing a close relationship with their state and local party organization.[3] The gradual spread of civil service protections eliminated most patronage jobs, removing a key resource that state parties had used to create a cadre of campaign workers accountable to the party's leaders. Together, these changes instigated a gradual decline in political machines (and machine-like organizations) that had been central players in many states in the nineteenth and early twentieth centuries.

Parties could no longer put together an army of government workers and contractors to fund their campaigns and mobilize voters. Instead, party organizations came to rely more upon amateur, policy-motivated activists. Where previously state party leaders tended to focus intently on winning and often downplayed ideological appeals, their successors have found that they need a clear ideological identity to recruit campaign workers and donors.[4] As we shall see, forging such an identity became much more feasible as the national parties began to sort along liberal–conservative lines in the aftermath of the racial realignment.[5]

The Progressive Era was also a period of growing national governmental power—a process that accelerated in the New Deal years and accelerated again during the Long 1960s. This shift in governance led to a greater focus on national politics at the expense of local concerns. Ken Kollman and Pradeep Chhibber's cross-national study of party systems demonstrates that the centralization of governmental power makes winning a majority at the national level a higher priority, which in turn incentivizes voters and candidates to coordinate more closely between the congressional district and national levels. These shifts undercut regionally based third parties while making it more likely that competition in the states will track national party lines, rather than pulling in alternative directions.[6]

In the 1970s, state parties experienced further erosion of their autonomy, due to changes in the presidential nomination process and increased activity of national party committees. Racial realignment played a role in the nomination reforms; the Mississippi Freedom Democratic Party's challenge against the state's all-white delegation to the 1964 national convention led to Democrats' creation of the Special Equal Rights Committee. This committee mandated that state party delegations could only be seated in 1968 if they ensured equal opportunity to participate in party affairs regardless of race, creed, or national origin.[7] These rules set a key precedent for the more expansive McGovern–Fraser reforms to the presidential nomination process, which were enacted after Vice President Hubert Humphrey received the 1968 nomination without having entered a single primary.

The McGovern–Fraser reforms mandated that convention delegates be selected through primary or caucus elections open to all party members. This eliminated state and local party leaders' ability to control blocs of delegates, which had previously made these leaders key figures in the presidential selection process. Although McGovern–Fraser's rules only governed Democrats, many states adopted primary laws imposing the same conditions on both parties. As a result, ordinary voters and ideologically oriented activists became more important players in the presidential selection process, with state organizations losing their formal role.[8] The new process centered on a prolonged "invisible primary," in which individual candidates competed for support from a diffuse network of party actors and donors across the US. The informal vetting of candidates by this national network of donors, endorsers, and outside groups displaced the gatekeeping that party organizations had performed both in presidential races and more broadly.[9]

These new rules launched a period of greater national involvement in state party decisions. Starting in the late 1970s, the Republican National Committee (RNC) made a concerted effort to provide services, training, and funding to state and local parties. This activity, which the Democrats soon emulated, helped state parties remain viable as organizations. However, it came at the cost of reduced autonomy; state parties were now more like constituent units of a national party, with their efforts subject to greater intervention and even direction from the top.[10]

Despite this long and gradual decline in the autonomy of state parties they remained significant sources of political diversity into the 1970s and 1980s, with noteworthy regional differences persisting among both Democrats and Republicans. This geographic diversity, however, continued to erode. National party networks moved beyond their role as providers of services and training to become a critical source of fundraising in the new campaign finance environment that has emerged since the 1990s.[11]

Two related changes are most important. First, fundraising has become more national in scope; candidates increasingly rely on funds from individuals and groups outside their home areas. Federal Election Committee data shows that the share of itemized candidate contributions from out of state increased from 31 percent in 1990 to 68 percent in 2012.[12] The rise of ActBlue on the Democratic side and WinRed among Republicans has furthered candidates' ability to raise money from a national network of donors.[13] This shift, encouraged as well by the growth of social media, loosens the geographic bonds that tie members to their local constituents and to state party organizations. Indeed, Brandice Canes-Wrone and Kenneth Miller find that members of Congress who receive a greater share of their funding from outside their district are more likely to be responsive to the preferences of their national party's "donor class."[14] The greater reliance on outside contributors encourages further polarization because these donors are focused on national issues and are more extreme than ordinary voters. Indeed, a spring 2023 analysis by Open Secrets shows that out-of-state donors are increasingly likely to be "ideological" in their motivations, and less likely to be "business-oriented."[15]

Second, state party organizations themselves provide a reduced share of candidate funds as both national donors and outside groups have greatly increased their activity. Rising independent expenditures—enabled by the 2010 federal court decisions in *Citizens United* and *SpeechNow*—have swamped state parties as money flows in from nationally oriented groups. The Republican and Democratic Governors' Associations (RGA, DGA) have become major sources of funds for competitive gubernatorial races, while other national, party-affiliated organizations are now much more active in both congressional and state legislative races. These national organizations have fostered what Keith Hamm and coauthors refer to as "vertically networked parties" that "raised their money nationally and then decided opportunistically which state races to enter."[16]

Beyond explicitly partisan entities, ideologically oriented groups have also dramatically stepped up their financial role, and this spending is disproportionately on behalf of less moderate candidates. These groups, which had been minor players in state campaign finance in 2006–8, accounted in recent cycles for a majority of independent expenditures in state races. Together with national party-affiliated groups (e.g., the DGA and RGA), they made up more than 80 percent of the independent spending in state elections by 2016.[17] With national party and ideological actors driving funding, state parties are less likely to exert an independent impact as agenda-setters. Instead, Joel Paddock concludes that they operate as "small cogs in a 'party network' that includes the national party committees, congressional campaign committees, allied interest groups, state legislative campaign committees, political consultants, and candidate-centered campaign organizations."[18]

Abundant outside money and nationally oriented ideological activists have not only partly displaced state parties; they have also reshaped them in ways that reinforce polarization. These dynamics are evident when it comes to two areas which have been central to state parties' role for generations: candidate nominations and platform writing.

Just as earlier selection methods incentivized candidates to be responsive to local needs, today's nomination arrangements incentivize loyalty to the national party agenda. While ideological activists have been around for decades, the sorting of the mass public along ideological lines has made the Democratic and Republican primary electorates more clearly liberal and conservative, respectively.[19] This has further encouraged candidates to respond to demands from ideological activists. Indeed, the pool of state legislative candidates has polarized dramatically since the 1990s. The more extreme candidates' advantage over centrists has more than doubled in contested primaries, while the general election edge for moderates has virtually disappeared.[20]

The increasing entry and success of more extreme candidates has powerful effects on state parties. Successful primary challenges to incumbents remain unusual, but they can be highly consequential in signaling the boundaries of acceptable partisan behavior. Amid nationalized politics, a primary challenge in one state can send shockwaves across the US. For example, when David Brat upset House Republican Leader Eric Cantor in 2014, it persuaded House Republicans that openness to compromise on immigration posed too great a backlash risk from the party base.[21] Sarah Anderson, Daniel Butler, and Laurel Harbridge-Yong document widespread fear among members of Congress and state legislators that primary voters will penalize them for supporting compromises; their study shows that this fear contributes to a failure to reach deals even when a clear majority of voters supports them.[22] More generally, the successful challenges to Republicans deemed too moderate—or, more recently, simply insufficiently loyal to Donald Trump—have provided a vivid demonstration to other incumbents about what it takes to survive.

Open-seat primaries have become a particularly powerful channel for nationalized and polarizing forces to enter state parties. Outside groups have been especially active in funding candidates in primaries for seats that are safe for their party. Jonathan Rauch and Raymond La Raja argue that these groups tend to back more ideological and amateur candidates. Their 2017 survey of political consultants finds that 79 percent believed that outside groups were playing a more important role in recruiting and training candidates than they were five to ten years earlier, with many respondents emphasizing that these groups favor candidates with a strong ideological viewpoint.[23] Amateur candidates, drawing heavily on out-of-state and ideological political action committee (PAC) contributions, have become more successful in open-seat primaries in recent years.[24] The upshot of this outside activity is that the formal state party organization has become a "bit player in nomination struggles being fought over its head," as Rauch and La Raja put it.[25]

State and local parties themselves have been transformed. Party organizations increasingly consist of ideologically motivated, nationally focused activists, often with deep ties to outside ideological groups. As late as 1979–80, a survey of county party chairs showed that relatively few Republicans identified as "very conservative" (9.1 percent), and even fewer Democrats identified as "very liberal" (4.2 percent), with the median Republican chair identifying as "somewhat conservative" and the median Democratic chair identifying as

TABLE 5.1. Ideological Distribution of County Party Chairs, 1979–80 and 2013

	1979–80		2013	
	Democrats	Republicans	Democrats	Republicans
Very conservative	0.9%	9.1%	0.4%	28.9%
Conservative	7.2%	37.2%	2.5%	54.9%
Somewhat/slightly conservative	20.4%	34.5%	2.9%	10.5%
Moderate	29.2%	15.8%	14.4%	5.2%
Somewhat/slightly liberal*	23.1%	2.5%	14.2%	0.2%
Liberal	14.8%	0.7%	46.1%	0.2%
Very liberal	4.2%	0.1%	19.5%	0.0%
Sample Size	1,984	1,872	555	459

Sources: The 1979–80 survey data is from Cornelius P. Cotter et al., *Party Organizations in American Politics* (Pittsburgh: University of Pittsburgh Press, 1984), 42. The 2013 data is calculated from the original data by Nicholas Carnes, Melody Crowder-Meyer, Christopher Skovron, and David Broockman (see David Broockman et al., "Why Local Party Leaders Don't Support Nominating Centrists," *British Journal of Political Science* 51 (2021): 724–49). The earlier survey response options included "somewhat" conservative and liberal, while the later survey used "slightly" conservative and liberal as response options. Supplementary analysis of other county chair surveys using a range of response options indicate that it is highly unlikely that the change in options is a substantial contributor to the change in response distributions.

moderate. By 2013, fully 29 percent of Republican county chairs identified as "very conservative" and 19.5 percent of Democratic chairs identified as "very liberal," while the share of chairs who were moderates or leaned toward the opposing party's ideology had declined substantially (see table 5.1).[26] The 2013 survey found that county chairs preferred extremist candidates to centrists by a wide margin: ten to one among Republicans and two to one among Democrats. A 2019 survey, using slightly different response options, revealed that fully 84 percent of Democratic county chairs identified as liberal or extremely liberal, with an identical share of Republican chairs identifying as conservative or extremely conservative.[27]

Regional differences among party chairs have also diminished. In earlier decades, a sizable contingent of southern Democratic chairs identified as moderate or conservative, and many northeastern Republican chairs identified as moderate or, in a few cases, liberal. Today, the vast majority of Democratic chairs, regardless of region, identify as liberal or extremely liberal, while the vast majority of Republican chairs, across regions, identify as conservative or extremely conservative.[28]

All of this means that, even where state and local parties still have influence, they may not offer unique "inputs" that encourage moderation and diversity within the party. Instead, they are increasingly controlled by the same kind of ideological purists who are active throughout each level of an

increasingly integrated party system.[29] Indeed, in many respects the porous-
ness of state parties to highly motivated, well-organized, and well-funded
activists has made these mediating institutions an important vehicle for ac-
celerating polarization.

Party platforms provide further evidence of the declining heterogeneity
of state parties. In earlier chapters, we saw that party platforms often varied
regionally, with the national parties regularly opting for strategic ambiguity
on controversial issues. A further study of more than 1,700 platforms from
1918–2017 shows that Democratic and Republican state platforms emphasized
similar topics to one another prior to the 1960s–70s, with considerable attention to sectoral issues important to particular geographic areas, such as
agriculture. The parties then began to diverge, with polarization taking off
in the mid-1990s. Platform texts became more focused on hot-button social
and cultural issues and less attentive to sectoral interests.[30] This divergence
coincided with a substantial increase in polarization in Congress and in the
national platforms, suggesting that changes in state party positioning reflected broader shifts in each party's national network. Similarly, Paddock's
coding of the ideological content of platforms from 1956–2002 documents a
dramatic increase in the gap separating Democrats from Republicans across
a range of issues. In several cases, conservative Christian activists captured
GOP state parties from below, enacting hard-right planks on social issues.[31]
Gerald Gamm and coauthors trace both parties' positioning on abortion and
gay rights, also finding that state parties polarized on these social issues, with
the national parties following soon after.[32]

Gay marriage provides a recent example. Eleven state Democratic Party
chairs pushed for the inclusion of a gay marriage plank in the Democrats'
2012 national platform months before President Obama endorsed the policy.[33] Interestingly, while several of the party chairs signing the letter calling
for the plank came from liberal coastal states such as New York and California, the party chairs in Texas and Kansas also signed on, underscoring the declining regional distinctiveness within the parties. California Republicans, on
the other hand, continued to include a plank opposing gay marriage in their
2023 state platform despite moderate members' plea that this stance was far
out of step with the state's socially liberal electorate, undermining the party's
chances in swing districts.[34]

Indeed, for all of the talk of divisions between pro-Trump and "establishment" Republicans and between pro-Sanders progressives and "mainstream"
Democrats, Daniel Coffey's analysis of recent state platforms finds little
evidence of systematic factional or regional differences within each party's
platforms, concluding that "polarization, at least in this analysis, overrides

intraparty factionalism."[35] Daniel Hopkins agrees that state parties pay less attention to regional or sectoral issues that might promote factionalism, noting that polarization "is driven not simply by increasing divergence along the primary dimension of conflict but by the disappearance of other dimensions."[36]

The polarization in state platforms both reflects and reinforces the broader trend toward partisan warfare at the national level. As the national parties polarized and public attention shifted to national issues, it became harder for state parties to retain an identity distinctive from the national brand. Several studies have shown that the national parties' reputations and presidential approval, rather than the stances of state parties, increasingly shape state legislative election outcomes.[37]

State-level polarization is not simply a response to changing electoral incentives. It also reflects the commitments of the ideological activists and officials who now make up state party networks across the US. Rather than being forced to toe a line articulated at the national level, state party politics has become a key venue activists use to push a sharp ideological agenda that contributes to further polarization across each level of the federal system. We will have more to say about this in the next chapter. For now, it is enough to note that the impact of this shift is evident in state legislatures, where the parties have grown increasingly polarized across nearly every US state. It is also evident in policy choices, where Democratic- and Republican-controlled states increasingly diverge.[38]

State parties' role in exacerbating polarization is particularly evident in recent developments on the right in the wake of the Trump presidency. State Republican parties across much of the US have taken aggressive stands on behalf of the former president's lies about the 2020 election while pushing very conservative policies on abortion, classroom teaching about race and sexuality, and the rights of LGBTQ individuals.[39] Daniel Schlozman and Sam Rosenfeld note that "across the country, state organizations mimicked the performative hijinks around national culture war flashpoints," their positions reflecting "pressures from above and below [which] pointed in the same direction."[40] The 2022 primary elections, in which numerous Trump-endorsed candidates defeated more establishment-friendly alternatives, reinforced the message that extreme rhetoric can help secure GOP nominations and further solidified the shift to the right among Republican state and federal officeholders.[41]

So far, we have discussed the issues that state parties focus on, but the issues that they do *not* take up are equally important to understanding the changing role of state parties within the broader federal system. As earlier chapters make plain, throughout much of US history, state parties provided openings for interests and movements to push their favored policies onto the agenda even when those initiatives were out of step with the national party alignment. The successes of antislavery activists in the lead-up to the Civil War, agrarians pushing railroad regulation, and silver and farm interests advocating currency expansion underscore the impact that geographically rooted interests had in working through the federated party system. In each case, insurgents captured influence within their home state parties and worked with allies—including members of the other major party—to shuffle coalitional alignments and redirect policy. By contrast, it is hard to think of a single case in the past few decades in which a group of state parties pushed a position that threatened to undermine the existing polarized alignment.

Along these lines, there have been very few intraparty insurgencies that offer the potential for alliances with even a faction of the other party. Instead, the challenges that currently take place within state parties overwhelmingly consist of movements pushing a harder policy and political line versus the opposition. State parties have always offered polarizing forces a venue to push their agenda. But what is different now is that state parties are almost exclusively an instrument for polarizing movements, rarely offering a pathway for countervailing interests.

State parties now fail to play a role in supporting crosscutting cleavages because they are not the relatively autonomous actors that they were in earlier periods. Lacking both independent resources and the formal organizational levers to control nominations and channel politicians' career advancement, state parties have, in the words of Schlozman and Rosenfeld, "proven the odd men out in a system of nationalized party politics and outside groups' encroachment on party terrain."[42]

In sum, state parties remain relevant because they continue to be vehicles that ideological activists use to pursue their goals. But they do little to offer a distinctive, geographically rooted "input" into national politics. Instead, state parties are but one element of a nationalized partisan network in which ideologically oriented activists and allied organized groups pursue a common agenda across the US. Understanding contemporary polarization requires grappling with the ways in which these outside groups have expanded their role and forged tighter alliances with a single party. We turn to these groups next.

The Nationalization and Polarization of Organized Interests

Recall that organized interests were central to Madison's vision of a political order that was simultaneously fluid and self-stabilizing. He recognized that different groups of citizens would have distinctive interests, and that they would push to advance those interests. The constitutional framework could not (and should not) prevent this. It could, however, work to ensure that the fierce commitments of different groups did not coalesce into permanent and system-endangering enmities. Moreover, he suggested that the new nation's vast scale would reinforce the protections built into its structure. In *Federalist*, no. 10, Madison memorably argued that extending a republic over a large and diverse territory would thwart the emergence of concentrated and coordinated power:

> The smaller the society, the fewer probably will be the distinct parties and interests composing it; the fewer the distinct parties and interests, the more frequently will a majority be found of the same party; and the smaller the number of individuals composing a majority, and the smaller the compass within which they are placed, the more easily will they concert and execute their plans of oppression. Extend the sphere, and you take a greater variety of parties and interests; you make it less probable that a majority of the whole will have a common motive to invade the rights of other citizens or if such common motive exists, it will be more difficult for all who feel it to discover their own strength, and to act in unison with each other.

In the "extended republic," governing would require the construction of broad coalitions, resting on compromise. And even those coalitions would be impermanent ones, shifting from issue to issue and over time. No single majority would be able to act in concert.

Madison's vision was a source of inspiration for mid-twentieth-century political scientists, operating within the "pluralist" tradition, who formalized it in their models of American politics. Even more explicitly than Madison, Robert Dahl made organized interests the focal point of his understanding of American politics.[43] Like Madison, he stressed the manner in which American political institutions were likely to encourage the emergence and expression of a multiplicity of interests. And he expected the fractured structure of authority to mean that those groups would engage with different parts of the political system in different ways. The result would be a decentralized polity exhibiting constantly shifting alliances.

Writing in the midcentury, Dahl concluded that "perhaps in no other national political system is bargaining so basic a component of the political process. . . . With all its defects, [the US system] does nonetheless provide a high probability that any active and legitimate group will make itself heard effectively at some stage in the process of decision." This, in turn, made the US constitutional order "a relatively efficient system for reinforcing agreement, encouraging moderation, and maintaining social peace"[44]

Studying midcentury American politics, political scientists working within the basic pluralist framework identified a number of features that lined up well with this set of expectations.[45] Perhaps most significant for current purposes is the manner in which interest groups focused on cultivating relationships with individual politicians rather than political parties. During this period, the congressional agenda was primarily set through the committee system, and committees often featured partnerships between the Democratic chair and senior Republican member. It made sense to nurture relationships with members of both parties because successful policy action typically rested on bipartisan coalitions. The parties' own incentives reinforced this dynamic; the need to build support across diverse regions and constituencies meant there were few policy areas in which Democrats saw it in their interest to ally closely with one interest group while Republicans had an interest in allying with that group's opponents.[46]

In this period, the interest group system of the US remained relatively thin, fractured, decentralized and (with important exceptions, like labor) only weakly and intermittently connected to the two parties. Skocpol's study of mass voluntary organizations describes a universe of groups that sometimes obtained national scope but were firmly rooted in and oriented toward diverse local communities. Focusing on judicial nominations, Charles Cameron and his coauthors document that interest group competition in Washington was notably sparse and sporadic. Frank Baumgartner and Bryan Jones show that prior to the 1960s, economic interests—business, labor, trade and professional associations—had few rivals in Washington.[47] For individual members of Congress, interest group support was often critical to their success. But the relevant groups varied considerably across states and regions, depending in large part on whether the representative's local economy was focused on energy extraction, automobile manufacturing, agriculture, finance, or other industries.

But as we know, the structure of the interest group system and its fit with the rest of the American polity began to change rapidly during the "Long 1960s." In the words of Jack Walker, "Since about the time Martin Luther King, Jr. led a 'march on Washington' by thousands of citizens in the civil rights movement in 1963, there has been a march to Washington by interest groups as well."[48] The total number of national associations listed in the *Encyclopedia of Associations* grew from 5,843 in 1959 to 10,308 in 1970, 14,726 in 1980 and 22,259 in 1990, before reaching a new plateau.[49]

Critical shifts in the scale and focus of interest group activity occurred extraordinarily rapidly. Changes in membership of environmental groups are illustrative. The venerable Sierra Club, founded in 1892, had no chapters outside of California until the 1950s. In 1956 it had 10,000 members. By 1970 it had 113,000, and two decades later it had 630,000. Two important new groups emerged as Washington became the focus of environmental politics. The Environmental Defense Fund, established in 1967, had just 11,000 members in 1970—but 150,000 two decades later. Greenpeace USA was not founded until 1972; by 1990 it would have 2.3 million members. Overall, the number of nationally active environmental groups increased more than three-fold between 1961 and 1990 (from 119 to 396). A better sense of the scale of the transformation comes from changes in staff size; over the same period, the combined staff of these groups increased almost ten-fold (from 316 to 2,917).[50]

Technology undoubtedly played a role in this sweeping transformation. Revolutions in communications, information technology and transportation made it easier to address the formidable collective action problems that are especially acute for diffuse interests. But the principal catalyst for this change appears to be the expanded range of policy activity in Washington.

The nationalization of policy and of interest groups occurred over roughly the same period, and the two trends are often treated in tandem. The precise timing, however, is revealing. Considerable research has made the basic sequence clear. In Skocpol's summation: "The emergence of thousands of new nationally focused associations *followed slightly after* heightened federal legislative activism. . . . Tellingly, the same basic dynamic occurred across many specific policy areas, ranging from environmental policy to health care and expanded benefits and new services for older Americans. In each area, innovative federal measures tended to precede the bulk of voluntary group proliferation" (emphasis added).[51]

What made the expansion and nationalization of policy so critical? Political scientists have noted that new policies can provide resources or incentives that help groups mobilize. In the well-studied case of teachers' unions, for instance, new state-level legislation that spread rapidly in the 1960s and 1970s made it much easier for public-sector unions to organize. Legislation that directly subsidized collective action was also part of the interest group revolution of the 1960s and 1970s, especially in policy areas, like environmental protection and employment discrimination, where new laws enabled groups to finance their organizations through private litigation.[52]

But backlash dynamics were also pervasive in this new interest group ecology. Their prominence suggests that the primary catalyst for interest group development was heightened stakes rather than increased resources. Across a host of policy domains, what happened in politics mattered more, and more and more of what mattered happened in the nation's capital. New groups formed, and old groups retooled to focus their energies where the action was. "Government activity," in the words of Beth Leech and her coauthors, "acts as a magnet, pulling groups of all kinds to become active."[53]

One sees the same pattern in arena after arena. Several studies show that this backlash dynamic was the main force prompting a vast expansion in the business community's political activities in the mid to late 1970s.[54] The legislative onslaught of the early 1970s—especially the regulatory expansion that we discussed in the previous chapter—induced a broad, multipronged mobilization on the part of business. In the wake of significant legislative and regulatory activity on guns during the Long 1960s, the National Rifle Association (NRA) morphed from essentially a sporting club to a greatly expanded organization focused on zealous political advocacy, taking on many of the characteristics of a social movement. The antiabortion movement, of course, emerged in the aftermath of *Roe v. Wade*.

These shifts in the scope and focus of interest group activity affected American civic organizations and activism more broadly. In her panoramic study of American associational life, Skocpol has highlighted a key feature of the post-1960 transformation of special relevance to this analysis: "Nationalization" of groups meant a shift from *locally rooted* mass organizations based on bottom-up federated structures to top-down, professionally managed "groups without members." "In the advocacy explosions of the 1960s to the 1990s" Skocpol writes, "civic organizers and patrons established an unprecedented number of nationally active associations that lack popular and subnational roots."[55] Even many long-established groups shifted their orientation (becoming increasingly professionalized, policy-focused and Washington-centered) in adapting to the new associational ecosystem. Summarizing her findings Skocpol writes: "Contemporary organization-building techniques encourage citizen groups (just like trade and professional associations) to concentrate their efforts in efficiently managed headquarters located close to the federal government and the national media. Even a group aiming to speak for large numbers of Americans does not absolutely need 'members' in any meaningful sense of the word."[56]

In short, a new and expanded interest group universe took shape in the 1960s–80s in response to the heightened policy stakes in Washington, one that was more nationally focused and that more often set competing groups against one another in pitched battles over the policies they cared about.

NATIONALIZED INTEREST GROUPS IN THE NEW CONSTITUTIONAL ORDER

While interest groups proliferated, grew, and nationalized rapidly in the 1970s, a second transformation unfolded more slowly: the increasingly intimate collaboration between many powerful interest groups and political parties. Unlike the first set of processes, where the policy nationalization of the 1960s and 1970s was a clear and almost immediate catalyst, the incorporation of interest groups into increasingly coherent partisan coalitions was a drawn-out affair.

The dynamics operated in both directions. The gradual polarization of the parties changed the incentives for interest groups. The emergence of more powerful interest groups who increasingly saw parties as the vehicle for achieving their policy goals fueled further partisan polarization.

Organized interests, in the language of recent political science, are "intense policy demanders."[57] They want to influence public policy, and the stakes are often very, very large. Indeed, in the aftermath of the Long 1960s, the stakes grew larger still: Would taxes on the wealthy and corporations go up or down significantly? Would abortion be legal or not? Would pollution be tightly regulated or not (and more recently, would the federal government respond to the threat of climate change)? The answer to these questions, and many other hugely consequential ones, would come from Washington, and increasingly answers from Washington depended upon the balance of power between the parties.

The emergence of polarization didn't just raise the policy stakes; it meant the path to political success for groups was changing. Prior to the late 1970s, the parties mapped only loosely onto many major issue divides. There were supporters and opponents of strong environmental regulations in both parties. The same was true for issues like abortion and gun control. In this context—and in a legislative environment where bipartisan, "center-out" agreements were common—it made sense for interest groups to cultivate friends in both parties.[58]

The gradual sorting of the two major parties into more coherent ideological camps dramatically altered the political landscape for interest groups. One effect is obvious: for many groups, one party increasingly seemed like the natural partner for addressing their policy demands. Today it is generally easy to identify the preferable partisan partner for powerful interests. In most cases, however, this clarity emerged slowly, even if it might have long been possible to discern which party would be the more likely ally. The sorting of party elites (and, over time, their voters) led politicians who were out of step with their party's emerging consensus on issues to either change their positions, change their party, or (in time) give way through death, retirement, or political defeat.[59] Today, each party is far more internally homogeneous when it comes to politicians' positioning on the matters that concern intense policy demanders. In many cases, the distance between the positions of the two parties has grown as well.

For party leaders, the room to maneuver among groups diminished. With their own activists increasingly motivated by ideological commitments aligning them with a distinct set of policy-demanding groups, and with groups playing an increasingly critical role in candidate recruitment and contested primaries, it became much harder for party elites to resist alliances. Even if some Republican leaders were keen to distance themselves from too close a connection with evangelicals or Democratic leaders might have wanted to avoid taking a clear stand on gun control, for example, the activist base of the party pulled in a very clear direction, often forcing party elites' hand.

The sorting of the parties on policy contributed to (and in turn, was reinforced by) a second major change: the declining prospects for bipartisan policy legislation on many important issues. In part this is a simple corollary of the change just described; declining heterogeneity within each party meant that those interested in reaching across the aisle were likely to find fewer willing partners there. As politics—including the organization of state parties—nationalized, one could not count on local diversity to generate a continuous bipartisan supply of potential allies. But the decline in bipartisan opportunities also reflected a shift in the incentives for members of these increasingly sorted and evenly balanced parties; nothing should be done that would cloud the party's brand, or offer a lifeline to the other party.[60] Those who might have been open to a "center-out" coalition found themselves policed by members of their own party (including leadership). Once touted as "mavericks," these politicians were increasingly vilified as "sell-outs" or "RINOs" (Republicans in Name Only). In short, they faced growing incentives to stick with their party.[61]

Although not all groups responded in the same way or at the same time, the implications of these shifts for interest groups were immense. With "center-out" coalitions less viable, and with one party or the other more attractive (often *much* more attractive) as a long-term partner, pressure grew to pick sides. As we shall see, the behavior of party leaders, who increasingly signaled to groups that loyalty would be rewarded (and disloyalty punished), reinforced this tendency. Indeed, the entire process was self-reinforcing; as the parties picked sides on issues, interest groups found that their stake in closely fought electoral contests between the parties grew. Increasingly, they badly wanted to see one side win.

Interest groups faced incentives to both increase their political efforts and gear those efforts to helping their preferred party. Rather than spreading their money around to make friends, they sought to target the most consequential races in these partisan battles. And they became more inclined to desert friends in the "wrong" party—both because support for those politicians might damage the electoral prospects of their preferred party, and because gestures toward bipartisanship sent the wrong signal to party leaders who were monitoring the loyalty of groups.[62]

Recent studies provide broad evidence of the changing relationship between interest groups and parties. For the most part, these studies suggest that interest groups changed in response to party polarization, although we ourselves believe that the picture is more complicated and dynamic. Studies examining the policy stances of different interest groups demonstrate that interest groups associated with one party are more likely to adopt their party's stances across multiple, often unrelated policy areas.[63] The evidence suggests that interest group polarization increased especially in the 1990s, suggesting that, at least at a macro level, it was a response to the polarization of party elites and the disappearance of moderates. In a similar vein, Michael Barber and Mandi Eatough take a close look at how different industries have become more politicized since the late 1990s, with PACs in these industries moving from an "access-oriented" contribution strategy (in which they spread donations widely to incumbents in both parties) to an "ideologically oriented" strategy (which sends donations to a single party and puts priority on closely contested races).[64] Cameron and his coauthors look at the judicial branch. They show that interest group involvement in Supreme Court nominations increased sharply at two key turning points, both after the nomination of very conservative justices—in 1969 (with Nixon nominations that followed a string of high-profile Warren Court rulings that were part of the "rights revolution") and in 1987 with Regan's nomination of Robert Bork. Since 1987, virtually all nominations have been hotly contested.[65]

These studies offer panoramic views of the evolving interest group ecology, and they all confirm the growing alignment of groups with political parties as the parties polarized. This is of great value, but by their nature, these overviews will give equal weight to groups regardless of their prominence within that shifting ecology. The picture looks somewhat different when we focus on groups that are distinguished by their prominence and significance, suggesting that groups themselves often played an important role in generating elite polarization, rather than simply responding to it.

For further insight, we take a close look at four consequential areas: gun regulation, abortion, the environment, and the representation of business interests by encompassing associations. Rather than sampling all interest groups, the four sketches that follow explore the evolving interaction between the nation's parties and very powerful organized interests on issues of broad political salience. These groups, with their unusual capacities to mobilize voters and deliver other valuable resources to parties, warrant special attention.

In some respects these sketches reinforce the findings of quantitative analyses across the broader interest group environment. Yet they also point to a somewhat more complex and diverse set of dynamics in different areas. In some very important cases these increasingly organized and powerful interests influenced the positioning of parties, pushing them in a polarizing direction.

Political mobilization around *guns* is the clearest case of a sequence where a powerful group—the NRA—radicalized first and then brought one of the nation's major political parties to its position and cemented a durable political alliance. Again, developments in policy and regulation—in this case the Gun Control Act of 1968 and the 1972 creation of the independent Bureau of Alcohol, Tobacco, Firearms and Explosives—were important catalysts. Matthew Lacombe argues that another policy shift—the decline in federal (mostly military) support for NRA activities—was also significant since it removed a critical source of funding and pushed the NRA to search for a new organizational model.[66] As late as the mid-1970s, however, the NRA retained a nonpartisan stance. Indeed, the organization's leadership was contemplating a move from Washington, DC to Colorado—a move that would have represented a clear step away from politicization, reinforcing the organization's traditional identity as first and foremost a sports and recreation club. This move was thwarted in the decisive "revolt at Cincinnati" of 1978. Hard-right elements within the NRA, which had been pushing to increase the group's focus on political contestation, staged a successful coup at the organization's annual meeting. These activists were affiliated with the burgeoning New Right movement, which had taken up opposition to gun control as part of its socially conservative agenda in the late 1970s.

After 1978, the NRA's new leadership committed to an organizational strategy focused not only on the promotion of gun rights but the promotion of a broader social identity of libertarian conservatism that was then gaining strength on the political right.[67] This strategy was enormously successful, rapidly leading to a tripling of the organization's membership and a similar increase in its financial might. The NRA's leadership quickly identified the GOP as a likely partner for its ambitions. It was the GOP that gradually moved, between 1980 and 1994, to meet the policy demands of this increasingly formidable political force. By the early 1990s a full-fledged alliance had been consolidated, reinforced by the (impermanent) assault weapon ban Democrats passed in 1994 as part of a broader crime bill. The NRA played an important role in the stunning Republican electoral victories later that year.[68]

Since 1994 the NRA has been an integral part of the Republican coalition; it provides virtually no funds to Democrats. As the Democratic coalition has shifted away from rural areas and as gun control activists have become increasingly organized there are fewer Democrats for the NRA to support in any event. Yet the group's behavior suggests it has jettisoned an access-oriented strategy of giving widely to incumbents, instead channeling its campaign spending into critical Senate campaigns that determine which party controls that chamber (and the vetting of both legislation and Supreme Court nominations). The NRA's enormous success since its change in posture also suggests why the logic of partisan alliance is now so compelling. Public opinion has not shifted significantly on the issue, and the national legislature is hopelessly deadlocked. But the NRA has played a non-trivial role in boosting Republican presidential candidates and senators. And Republican Supreme Court appointments have generated a radically new reading of the Second Amendment, dramatically shifting US gun policy in the process.

The polarization of gun policy thus began with a shift at the interest group level, followed by a response from the Republican Party. For the issue to be fully absorbed into the party system, it was necessary that *both* parties, over time, identify with opposing policy demanders. Although gun control supporters have never been as well-organized as the NRA, the Democratic Party gradually became closely identified with support for gun control. As discussed in chapter 4, coalitional changes in the wake of the southern realignment meant that more and more Democratic politicians faced a party electorate inclined to support gun control measures.[69] Activist groups also gradually mobilized as mass shootings raised the salience of the gun issue. In the face of all-out GOP opposition to tightening gun laws, they found their only potential allies among the Democrats. While many Democratic Party officials worried that this position made it harder to win elections in much of the US—and thus might have hoped for an ambiguous stance—the party's own voters and activists increasingly viewed gun control as important and had the power to enforce that commitment.

Abortion—and specifically the 1973 *Roe v. Wade* decision—is often seen as the catalyst for the emergence of the Christian right as both a formidable political force and the essential electoral anchor of the modern Republican Party. The actual story, however, is more complex.

Policy initiatives did indeed trigger political mobilization on the Christian right. Abortion, however, only gradually became the major source of mobilization for evangelicals.[70] In the mid-1970s opposition to the Equal Rights Amendment fused together with concerns about gay rights, abortion, and the sexual revolution of the 1960s to generate a growing conservative backlash. Evangelical Protestants, who in the past had defined their views in opposition to Catholic doctrine, increasingly came to see liberal secularists as their primary adversaries. Backlash against changing racial dynamics were also never far from the surface in mobilizing this new constituency. Indeed, a 1978 IRS ruling that put the tax-exempt status of racially segregated Christian schools in jeopardy initially galvanized prominent evangelicals to organize a political movement. Opposition to abortion then became a key tenet of the Moral Majority organization when it formed in June 1979.[71]

The movement enjoyed a watershed success in 1980, when the GOP platform endorsed a constitutional amendment "to restore protection of the right to life for unborn children."[72] Even so, national figures and voters in both parties had mixed stances on abortion until well into the 1980s and the alliance did not consolidate until the late 1980s and early 1990s. Although abortion views were related to conservative attitudes on other issues, Republican voters were only modestly more antiabortion than were Democrats until the late 1980s. Republican elites shifted decisively on the issue before their voters did, but they did so in significant part because of the opportunities to capitalize on the organizational ferment developing among Christian conservatives.[73]

Many conservative activists saw abortion as a particularly attractive focus for simultaneously mobilizing conservative Christians and cementing an enduring alliance with the GOP. Evangelical leaders were eager partners; the share of Southern Baptist ministers identifying with the GOP increased from 27 to 85 percent in 1980–2000. As Angie Maxwell and Todd Shields note, "the transformation of evangelical fundamentalists" from a politically uninterested group into a legion of dedicated and party-aligned voters "remains one of the most radical shifts in modern American politics."[74]

On the other side, pro-choice groups mobilized with increasing intensity as the Christian right threatened abortion rights. In a sense, backlash generated backlash. State Democratic parties, responding to grassroots activists, became much more likely to take a pro-choice stance in the late 1970s and 1980s.[75] There were still many prominent antiabortion Democrats, however, until the 1990s. A key moment occurred in 1992, when pro-life Pennsylvania Governor Robert Casey Sr. was denied a speaking slot at the party's national convention following pro-choice groups' outrage over his plans to use the speech to criticize abortion rights.[76] As Democrats' alliance with pro-choice groups solidified, it became increasingly rare for a Democratic officeholder to be out of step with the party's position.

By the mid-1990s, then, the basic contours of two parties deeply at odds over abortion had coalesced, each aligned with an influential set of mobilized groups. At a minimum, however, this is not a straightforward story in which the parties polarized first, and organized interests adapted in response.

When *environmental* issues rose on the national agenda and massive environmental groups formed and grew in the Long 1960s, cleavages between the parties were weak. Most legislators in both parties had relatively moderate environmental policy positions.[77] Democratic Congresses and Republican presidents successfully negotiated major bipartisan initiatives from Nixon (the 1970 Environmental Protection Act) to George H. W. Bush (the 1990 Clean Air Act amendments). Environmental groups initially took bipartisan stances. The Sierra Club, for instance, was cautious about entering partisan politics. It remained neutral in the 1988 election, but it exclusively endorsed the Democratic candidate for president going forward.

Yet, as David Karol argues, environmentalism emerged in a political context where fossil fuel and other extractive industries like mining, along with the broader business community, were already loosely aligned with the GOP. This, combined with the Democrats' urban base, made the Democrats the more natural allies for environmentalists.[78] Indeed, the average voting records—based on their scores with the League of Conservation Voters (LCV)–of Democrats in the 1970s were closer to environmentalists, although the differences between the parties were relatively small.

Differences between Republican and Democratic legislators grew only slowly until roughly 1990, when polarization between the parties began to increase rapidly. Although extractive sectors (e.g., farming, mining, and fossil fuels) were increasingly disproportionately located in Republican districts, this does not appear to be the major driver of polarization. Karol shows that polarization increased at essentially the same rate and to the same levels in states with divided Senate delegations—that is, where senators of different parties represented exactly the same economies.[79] In short, even where local conditions might have been conducive to greater intraparty heterogeneity, legislators polarized sharply and consistently by party.

At least measured by campaign donations, environmental groups appear to have aligned with the Democrats prior to the period of rapid partisan polarization in LCV scores. We do not have data on the campaign contributions of environmental groups prior to 1990, but by that year roughly 90 percent of these groups' campaign contributions went to Democrats. The LCV did continue to give 10–20 percent of its endorsements to Republicans for another two decades.[80]

In 2010, Republicans, mobilizing partly in response to Democrats' failed cap-and-trade initiative to combat climate change, moved sharply rightward with an infusion of Tea Party candidates. The Republican share of LCV endorsements fell to near zero, and it has stayed at that level ever since. Mirror trends are evident among groups resistant to the environmental agenda. Contributions from energy and extractive industries (e.g., agribusiness, forestry, and mining) already leaned Republican in 1990 (despite Democratic majorities in Congress, which one would expect to attract "access" oriented contributions). They moved decisively toward the GOP in the years that followed.[81] In this instance, too, it is hard to make a clear case that the parties polarized before the relevant groups moved into a partisan orbit—the two processes seem to move in tandem.

Finally, consider the case of the US Chamber of Commerce, the nation's largest and most influential business association. Like so many other groups, the Chamber increased its political mobilization in response to the policy boom of the Long 1960s. The impetus was the explosion of regulatory and rights initiatives that presented serious challenges for the business community. The Chamber had always been a conservative organization, but it generally kept a low profile in partisan battles and supported and worked with members of both parties.[82]

More than the other cases, the Chamber's evolution fits the narrative, described by some political scientists, in which party polarization was the driving force behind changing interest group behavior. The decisive juncture for the Chamber occurred in 1993–94. The Chamber leadership's willingness to work with the Clinton administration on its ambitious healthcare proposals met with a furious response not only from some businesses within the Chamber but from increasingly assertive congressional Republicans. GOP leaders (including Newt Gingrich, Tom DeLay, and John Boehner) made it clear that they expected more consistent loyalty.

The combination of internal and external backlash led to a change in Chamber leadership. The revamped Chamber dramatically expanded its organizational resources and ambitions, while quickly displaying a much greater willingness to work in tandem with the GOP. The Chamber shifted its (greatly increased) campaign spending from an access-oriented strategy aimed at incumbents of both parties to one geared to helping Republicans win contested seats. Moreover, its political personnel became increasingly intertwined with the party, with many prominent Chamber officials coming from, or moving to, positions affiliated with the GOP.[83]

In each of these four cases, the "Long 1960s" represented a watershed. In each case, major groups either organized for the first time or dramatically expanded the scale of their political operations in the wake of the major expansion of Washington's policy activity. In each case, they redirected their efforts to contend with the rising stakes of politics and policymaking in Washington. In each case, they eventually developed much closer and more durable relationships with one of the major political parties—working not only to strengthen that party's commitment to their issue priorities, but also focusing their growing resources more consistently on helping that party to win contested elections viewed as critical to the chance of advancing those priorities. Taken together, these cases are also a reminder of how unusual the Republican Party is in cross-national terms; its uncompromising stance on guns, climate, abortion, and business regulation place it well outside the mainstream of major governing parties in advanced democracies.[84]

With the possible exception of the US Chamber of Commerce, it is difficult to depict these developments as ones where the parties clearly polarized *first* and interest groups *then* moved to adapt to this new political reality. In the other cases, groups either moved first and then cultivated ties with the more promising partner (the NRA) or the groups (environmental groups, both sides of the abortion divide) and their partner party both moved gradually away from the other party, while simultaneously becoming more closely interconnected.

Whatever the precise sequence, once these tightened interconnections developed, they became self-reinforcing. As groups played an increasing role within a party, they were better positioned to reward office seekers regarded as loyal. This changed the incentives for ambitious politicians, who were eager to gain and retain interest group support.

These developments went hand in hand with the transformation of state parties described earlier. Local activists and politicians were becoming more ideologically motivated, and more tightly linked to the mobilizing efforts of national groups of intense policy demanders—such as evangelical organizations and the NRA on the right, or civil rights and environmental groups on the left. Loyalty to these groups became increasingly important to political success, especially at the stages where candidates were recruited and primaries won or lost.

This tightening loop of more nationalized state parties and more nationalized and partisan groups was being reinforced by a third change—a radically new media landscape. As we shall see, an increasingly nationalized and partisan information environment has also encouraged greater in-party cohesion and out-party animus.

The New Partisan Media Landscape

Most Americans are not highly attentive to politics, and even those who are face a landscape of bewildering complexity. Directly or indirectly, the media shapes much of our thinking about politics. It follows that the specific structure of media can be highly consequential. And media structures change dramatically over time. In the United States, mass media has always been overwhelmingly private, and thus associated with the quest for profits. What generates profits, however, has changed as new technologies have emerged, bringing with them repeated radical disruptions of existing media practices.

Our efforts to place the contemporary structure of media in historical context focus on two critical aspects of media structure: localism and partisanship. There has been significant variation over time in both the strength of partisanship in media and the extent to which dominant media outlets are spatially constrained and thus incentivized to provide information about local politics.

In fact, the past generation has witnessed the emergence of a media structure without precedent in the United States, one that is simultaneously national and riven by partisanship. It is a structure highly conducive to the entrenchment of polarized politics. The impact of partisan media is perhaps obvious— although the specifics matter a great deal. The significance of declining localism is perhaps less obvious, but as we shall see there is extensive evidence that robust local news markets have de-polarizing consequences. Indeed, research on local news constitutes an important piece of evidence for our general claim that a more locally grounded politics is likely to be conducive to pluralism, overlapping cleavages, and limited and transient polarization.

For the first century after the Constitution's ratification, newspapers in the United States proudly broadcast their political affiliation. This was, in considerable part, a financial calculation. Printing costs were high and circulations were low. To stay afloat, newspapers turned to patronage, either directly through an owner with political ambitions and connections, or indirectly through reliance on printing contracts that local politicians directed their way. In either case, political loyalty followed. Many studies have documented clear differences in coverage associated with partisan affiliation.[85] It is important to stress, however, that loyalty to party—as measured by the amount of attention to candidates, public officials, and events—was compatible with considerable heterogeneity in content. As we have seen, fealty to one of the two national parties could co-exist with stark differences in position, depending in part on locality, on many of the policy issues of the day.

These partisan affiliations began to weaken in the late nineteenth century. Technological and social change both extended the reach of newspapers and diminished their incentives to cultivate explicit partisan attachments. Printing costs dropped dramatically (by 1910, the real cost of newsprint was just one-fifth of what it had been in 1870). The decline in the cost of printing presses was even more spectacular—the capital cost of a printer in 1890 was just one-fifteenth of what it had been in 1870. Urban centers were growing rapidly. The growth in newspaper circulation was extraordinary: from 2.6 million in 1870 to 33 million in 1920.[86]

In this new setting, advertising became the cornerstone of financial success, and expanding circulation the key to gaining ad revenue. Newspapers faced strong incentives to move away from their patronage-based models, and visible partisan slant in coverage became an economic liability. Just 11 percent of daily papers in large cities were independent in 1870 (although they accounted for 26 percent of circulation). By 1920, that share increased to 62 percent (and 73 percent of circulation). A notable change in tone accompanied this shift, as newspapers displayed less evident partisan bias and less charged language.[87]

This transformation fueled, and in turn was reinforced by, the growing professionalization of the news industry. Professionalization brought with it stronger norms of objectivity and nonpartisanship. The insulation of many papers from intense competition facilitated the consolidation of these norms. Holding local monopolies, newspapers often found that they could devote considerable resources to local political coverage—a feature of media structure with implications that would only become evident when these barriers to competition later crumbled. In short, the period from the late nineteenth century to the end of World War II, if not later, marked a long era of decentralized and relatively nonpartisan news. Recent research suggests that the decline in partisanship within newspapers was continuous from 1880 to 1980, with roughly half the measured decline occurring prior to 1920 and half in the following six decades.[88]

While newspapers may have continued to de-polarize until as late as 1980, other dramatic changes in the media environment began soon after World War II. Newspapers were a diminishing part of the landscape, and the ascendant parts first nationalized and then polarized. Technological developments were key, as newspapers faced increasing competition from platforms that were less spatially constrained. The rapid emergence of television after World War II (half of American homes would have TVs by the early 1950s) marked a clear shift. Media structure would steadily nationalize over the following half century, with network television leading the way, followed by the expansion of national talk radio shows, cable TV, and broadband internet.

All of these media (local TV stations excepted) share a common feature: They are not spatially restricted, and therefore face no incentive to provide local political news. Newspaper circulation and advertising revenues have declined steadily, as has the local newspaper share of total media consumption. Staffing levels fell 40 percent between 1994 and 2014. The negative impact on coverage of local politics was devastating—Pew reported a 35 percent fall in the number of full-time newspaper reporters covering state politics just between 2003 and 2014.[89]

The ascension of TV, of course, also gave rise to local television news—a medium that currently reaches a nightly audience of roughly 25 million (although audiences for the most popular late night news broadcasts have fallen by 31 percent in the past decade). Daniel Moskowitz reports that roughly 40 percent of Americans aged twenty-five to fifty-four watch some local news in an average week. Like local newspapers, these stations have incentives to provide information about local and state politics.[90]

Strong evidence of the significance of local political information comes from studies that compare political dynamics in congressional districts that map onto local TV markets (and thus have greater incentive to provide significant political coverage of those districts) with those that do not. Voters in districts with robust local TV markets are better informed about state and local politics and less likely to support extreme candidates.[91]

Robust local news environments are particularly effective in encouraging voters to consider voting for the other party's candidates. Political scientists have documented the close connection between newspapers' declining local coverage and voters' reduced focus on local politics. Where local newspapers are strong, election results are less correlated across levels of government. The greater prominence of local concerns and the greater uncertainty regarding voting intentions in turn creates incentives for local and state-level politicians to moderate and be more responsive to local voter preferences.[92]

Unfortunately, the persistence of local television news is the one significant exception within a broader shift toward media that is not anchored to local communities.[93] Network television, of course, was a profoundly nationalizing force, but in itself it was not a polarizing one; professional norms (protected by an effective oligopoly) and incentives to seek as broad an audience as possible discouraged clear partisanship. But network television was followed by the explosion of the talk radio market, the advent of cable and, finally, the development of broadband internet news media. These media not only curtailed the market for local news; in time, they altered the national media environment, including incumbent national networks.

It is worth emphasizing that a shift from local to national sources of information is likely to be polarizing *even if those national media outlets are not themselves politically polarized*. This is because voters who lack any local information are more likely to rely on partisanship as a simple cue when they vote. Moreover, if national politics is itself highly polarized, with national figures incentivized to stress partisan conflict and rally their team, these elements of politics will become more prominent when attention shifts from the local to the national. To the extent that media nationalizes, even outlets that are not prone to partisan bias are likely to reinforce the message of sharp distinctions between the parties. The incentives for even nonpartisan media to accentuate partisan discord in their coverage amplify this effect. Conflict generates attention and attention generates profits. It is thus not surprising that contemporary media pay disproportionate attention to political figures who are toward the extreme ends of the political spectrum.

Of course, on top of this, many of the emerging outlets *were* overtly partisan. Like previous technological changes, the proliferation of news outlets shifted the incentives for those producing content. Midcentury newspapers and national networks faced limited competition within their markets. This encouraged "broad tent" strategies and discouraged overt partisanship. The new formats, however, did the reverse. They opened up the potential for turning a profit by targeting narrower audiences spread over a large territory.

Crucially, the incentives these new opportunities generated were not symmetrical. Yochai Benkler, Robert Faris, and Hal Roberts have explored how the largest opportunities for partisan media emerged on the political right. Once started, this asymmetry was self-reinforcing. Positioning itself explicitly as a counterpoint to the "lame-stream media," conservative media developed its own set of norms. It worked energetically and with considerable success to sever its audience's attachments to traditional news outlets. A modest counterpart has emerged on the left in venues like MSNBC, but these outlets are smaller (especially when talk radio is taken into account) and do not exhibit the same kind of isolation from (and mistrust of) mainstream outlets. Thus the contemporary US has two distinct national media ecosystems, one firmly anchored on the right and one that stretches from the center to the moderate left.[94]

Political talk radio was the first wave of this transformation, taking off in the late 1980s. This "old" technology reemerged on AM stations as popular music formats shifted to FM and the FCC's repeal of the Fairness Doctrine in 1987 opened up space for politically charged programs targeting audiences underserved by existing outlets.[95] Rush Limbaugh was the most spectacular example. Limbaugh's national show launched the year after the Fairness Doctrine was revoked (Congress had passed legislation to cement the doctrine in statute, but the bill was vetoed by Ronald Reagan). Within four years, Limbaugh had built an audience of fourteen million a week (it eventually grew to twenty million), becoming a force that would lead Republicans to call him their "majority maker" and the "leader of the opposition" as they swept to victory in the "Gingrich revolution" of 1994. Limbaugh, moreover, was just one of many new national media figures anchored in radio—virtually all of them firmly located on the political right.[96]

Roughly a decade later, the emergence of cable television brought another disruption to the media landscape by radically expanding the variety of TV programming available to viewers. National television began to fragment and competition intensified. Although much attention understandably focuses on how the rise of cable galvanized partisan media outlets, it also generated polarization through a more mundane dynamic; cable gave those with little interest in politics greater opportunity to opt out of political news. As the less engaged changed the channel, the audience for political news that was left behind was both more attentive and more polarized.[97]

Fox News, launched in 1996, developed an innovative model that attracted a large audience and exerted considerable influence on political discourse. Fox has had great success in "capturing" its audience. Conservative news consumers are much more inclined than other citizens to identify just a handful of news outlets that they trust.[98] The network became increasingly openly partisan over time; its extensive ties to Republican elites included an active revolving door between Fox commentators and GOP elected and unelected officials. In 2018, Donald Trump ended the midterm campaign at a rally that featured a leading Fox commentator, Sean Hannity, along with the talk radio giant Limbaugh.

Fox's audience is considerably smaller than that of talk radio. That audience, however, consists of people who are quite attentive to and active in politics, and thus likely to influence others who are less attentive.[99] Evidence of Fox's impact is now extensive, and the effects are quite considerable. It boosts both Republican Party identification and the Republican vote share, while also moving viewers' political attitudes to the right. It also influences political elites. Research shows that the rise of Fox encouraged politicians of both parties to support Republican positions in congressional votes.[100]

Perhaps most important, Fox News has fostered extremism within the GOP. Zhao Li and Gregory Martin show that increased exposure to Fox increased political contributions to Tea Party candidates and boosted their vote share in Republican primaries. More broadly, they conclude that ". . . the backing of a pre-built media infrastructure with near-universal reach among party activists—a feature that very few other protest movements can claim— was a crucial mediator of the Tea Party protests' lasting impact."[101]

Of course, Fox is just one part of a distinctively isolating and polarizing right-wing media ecosystem. Much research focuses on Fox, not only because of its prominence but because several idiosyncrasies (the network's gradual rollout across the country and its varied location on the dial in different TV markets) facilitate the efforts of social scientists to measure its impact. Yet the impact of that broader ecosystem has clearly been profound. As Matt Grossmann and David Hopkins summarize: "Conservative media outlets have succeeded in massing considerable and arguably unprecedented influence over the internal politics of the Republican Party. Prominent media personalities have steadily gained power with the extended Republican network at the expense of elected officials and legislative leaders, forming an alternative set of party elites with their own priorities and interests. Republican politicians now view conservative media as a key conduit to their party 'base' and are visibly fearful of receiving negative coverage, even if satisfying the demands of the conservative media complicates their attempts to win general elections or pursue pragmatic policy achievements once in office."[102]

In other words, more than just reflecting the agenda of the Republican Party, Fox and other conservative outlets can shape that agenda and alter the balance of power within the party. The impact on the GOP agenda and approach is especially concerning. Fox, talk radio, and other right-wing sources traffic heavily in fearmongering, regularly depicting racial minorities as radical threats to America. In an analysis of Fox segments shortly before the 2020 election the top two subtopics were "Biden/Democrats support for 'extreme' racial ideology/protests" and "negative consequences of 'extreme' racial ideology/protests (e.g., violence)."[103]

By creating a clear-cut us versus them, where advocates of racial and gender egalitarianism are the enemy, these outlets exacerbate deep-seated cleavages in US society. Encouraging fear and anger is a way to build an audience—while also boosting the political temperature to dangerous levels in which opponents are no longer viewed as legitimate adversaries. The insulation of this information ecosystem makes these threat narratives especially resilient against discordant facts; indeed, by discrediting mainstream sources, right-wing outlets have built a post-truth universe in which rampant voter fraud explains the 2020 election and terrorists are routinely crossing the southern border.

The most recent technological development is the emergence of the internet as a source of news and information. Once again, technological change diminished the spatial constraints on media. Consumers gained access to additional sources of information that were largely disconnected from local settings. By the early twenty-first century, local news was forced to compete with national television, including the increasingly varied options available through cable, nationally syndicated talk radio and the full range of social media and news sites available on the internet. Unsurprisingly, the share of news consumption that is locally anchored has been in continuous decline.

The internet also produced a more immediate threat to local newspapers—competition for advertising. Most dramatically, Craigslist offered a free and easily accessible alternative to the classified ads that were traditionally a crucial source of newspaper revenue. According to data from the News Media Alliance (formerly Newspaper Association of America), US newspapers' advertising revenues fell from $49 billion in 2000 to $26 billion in 2010.[104] The loss of revenue was particularly consequential for local political news, which is costly to produce and thus tempting to jettison when a publication encounters tough times. The gradual rollout of Craigslist across the country helped social scientists to measure its impact.

It turns out to be considerable. Milena Djourelova, Ruben Durante, and Gregory Martin estimate that the entry of Craigslist into a specific market generated, on average, a 30 percent drop in local news reporting. And the impact of that on the political realm is what we should anticipate: more polarization. With the arrival of Craigslist in a particular market split-ticket voting declined significantly, and extreme candidates were strengthened. This is another indicator that voters were substituting national cues for local ones.[105]

In short, processes of nationalization and polarization have been particularly intense for the crucial mediating institution of news media. Locally grounded news once contributed to both the diversity of information and the diversity of recognizable interests in the American polity. Today's media fuels, rather than challenges, images of a highly polarized polity. It obscures local diversity and highlights national conflicts. In doing so it reinforces the polarizing trends at work in other dimensions of American political life.

For instance, the increased power of nationally oriented ideological activists within each party has been propelled, in part, by their ability to build networks unconstrained by geography. Social media in particular facilitates the rapid spread of narratives and appeals throughout each party's "base." Both parties have seized on internet-based appeals to raise money from activists across the country that can be targeted on crucial races—the success of the Democrats' ActBlue infrastructure has been particularly notable, facilitating a dramatic increase in out-of-state donations to candidates.[106]

This impact of the internet and social media underscores how important the interactions are between the changes in state parties, organized groups, and the media. While the increased nationalization of each of these domains is striking, the extent to which these changes have become mutually reinforcing is equally significant. One can see that confluence at work in the extraordinary success of Newt Gingrich in remaking the national GOP, even at the expense of a sitting Republican president.

Newt Gingrich and the Crystallization of a New Constitutional Order

The transformation of state parties, interest groups, and media took place over many decades and with different temporal rhythms. Yet one can see the strands weave together in Newt Gingrich's rise to congressional leadership in the 1990s. Acting as a political entrepreneur, Gingrich drew several emergent developments together, showing the way to a new mode of politics.

Gingrich should not be seen as a major *cause* of our current polarized politics. In his absence, it is very likely that other Republican politicians would have pushed in a broadly similar direction. Nonetheless, he was the first to demonstrate the political payoffs for Republicans adopting a new approach, which in turn encouraged changes inside Congress and more broadly in American politics.

The triggers that we elaborated in chapter 4—the racial realignment and the nationalization of policy—paved the way for Gingrich in both direct and indirect ways. Gingrich entered the House of Representatives in 1978, replacing retiring Democrat Jack Flynt, a conservative who had represented the area just south of Atlanta for twenty-four years. Gingrich could win in the once solidly Democratic district because of southern whites' loosening ties to the Democratic Party in the aftermath of the racial realignment, along with the migration of middle-class white voters to the South.

The gradual departure of southern conservative Democrats meant that Gingrich entered a House of Representatives in which the Democratic Party was becoming increasingly unified, allowing party leaders to use their procedural tools more aggressively to limit Republican influence. By the mid to late 1980s, life in the House of Representatives was becoming miserable for senior Republicans who in the past had enjoyed numerous opportunities to work with moderate and conservative Democrats to shape policy.[107] At the same time, the nationalization of policy set the stage for Gingrich to rally the growing set of activist conservative groups, such as the pro-life movement, the NRA, and anti-tax advocates on behalf of an onslaught against both the Democratic Congress and those Republicans seeking to work toward compromises.

From the time he entered the House, Gingrich's goals were to topple Democratic control of the institution and to position himself to lead a resurgent Republican majority. In pursuing this vision, Gingrich capitalized on the changes in media, interest groups, and state parties, while simultaneously encouraging further movement along that path.

In contrast to senior Republican leaders, such as Robert Michel of Illinois, who sought to work behind-the-scenes to influence legislation, Gingrich adopted a confrontational approach, laser-focused on tarnishing the Democratic House as corrupt and out of touch. In doing so, Gingrich relied heavily on the rapidly changing information environment, noting that "we are engaged in reshaping a whole nation through the news media."[108] His Conservative Opportunity Society, created in 1983, attacked Democrats through daily speeches on the House floor, broadcast on C-SPAN, making national headlines in the process. Gingrich courted both mainstream media and the emerging conservative talk radio world in stirring up ethics scandals that tarnished Democratic Speaker Jim Wright. Gingrich encouraged a self-reinforcing loop of negative news stories about Wright, leading to the Speaker's resignation in the summer of 1989.[109]

Gingrich's election as Republican Whip that same year signaled that more Republicans were embracing his strategy of confrontation. As Whip, Gingrich led the revolt against George H. W. Bush's 1990 budget deal with Democrats, a key moment marking the shifting balance of power in the GOP. In the face of mounting budget deficits, Bush had reluctantly agreed to a package of new taxes (along with deep spending cuts sought by Republicans). The Bush administration assumed Gingrich and other Republican leaders would back the deal, but Gingrich balked, mobilizing rank-and-file Republicans to reject the agreement. The upstart worked closely with newly formed interest groups, such as Grover Norquist's Americans for Tax Reform, to pressure Republicans to hold the line against any tax increases. As in the earlier push against Wright, Gingrich relied on what Julian Zelizer has called the "synergistic power of talk radio and the conservative grassroots" to fan the flames.[110] Although the tax increase eventually passed due to overwhelming Democratic support, Gingrich had taken a critical step in transforming the Republican Party.

Gingrich was quite frank about undercutting a sitting Republican president in order to accelerate the shift toward polarization: "The number one thing we had to prove in the fall of '90," Gingrich later explained, "was that, if you explicitly decided to govern from the center, we could make it so unbelievably expensive you couldn't sustain it."[111] Tom Delay, a leading Gingrich ally, explained why they rebelled against Bush: "The only way we could take over Congress . . . was to have a very clear distinction between the Democrats and the Republicans. The Bush administration muddied that distinction. The Bush administration wanted to work with Congress rather than beat Congress. And so it was contrary to what we were doing. We were trying to build a party and take over the Congress. The Bush administration was trying to run the country and be reelected."[112]

After Bush's 1992 defeat at the hands of Bill Clinton, Gingrich and his allies drew on changes in interest groups, the media, and state parties in seeking to nationalize the 1994 midterm election. Gingrich partnered with Norquist, who began his weekly Wednesday meetings of conservative groups in 1993, to pressure the Chamber of Commerce and other business groups to oppose Clinton's health care push.

Presaging Mitch McConnell's approach to the Obama administration, Gingrich sought to deny Clinton and the Democrats a record of successes to campaign on. Gingrich was also a regular on Rush Limbaugh and other conservative talk shows, mobilizing opposition to Clinton's programs and amplifying his message of partisan differentiation. As Dan Balz and Ronald Brownstein's closely reported study observes, "no medium had a greater effect on establishing the climate of the 1994 elections than talk radio."[113]

Gingrich was poised to capitalize on this climate due to his work, since 1987, as head of GOPAC, which had stepped into the void left by state parties' declining role in candidate selection. When Gingrich took over the group from Pete du Pont, he transformed it from a simple source of money for Republican candidates into a machine to educate and recruit likeminded challengers. Matthew Green and Jeffrey Crouch note that GOPAC trained a generation of state legislative and congressional candidates to "run on a unified and distinctive conservative message."[114] By distributing his audio and videotapes to candidates, delivering lectures by satellite, and appearing on numerous radio shows, Gingrich built a following among incoming members of Congress that helped to transform the GOP's culture.[115] For these members, Gingrich's national message—rather than the particular concerns of their state and local parties—became the touchstone of their mission.

Gingrich's ability to persuade nearly every Republican running in 1994 to sign the Contract with America depended on this ongoing party-building work. The goal of the Contract was to provide a clear, national Republican message that was poll-tested to resonate across much of the US and could be spread by the party's growing network of talk radio allies. The freshmen elected in the GOP wave were poised to back the incoming Speaker's vision, given that so many of them had been recruited and trained by Gingrich.[116]

Once in the majority, Gingrich and his team moved to consolidate the new regime by tightening their alliance with allied interest groups and media personalities. Limbaugh was named an honorary member of the incoming freshman class, and Gingrich ensured that radio talk show hosts were given plentiful access during his first week. In the months that followed, Republican leaders compiled a list of 250 radio hosts nationwide, cultivating them with regular talking points and interview offers.[117]

Meanwhile, Majority Whip DeLay launched the K Street project, which pressured Washington-based interest groups to hire only Republican lobbyists. DeLay compiled data on the campaign contributions of the 400 largest PACs, inviting their lobbyists in to see whether they were classified in the "friendly" or "unfriendly" column, while warning them that "if you want to play in our revolution, you have to play by our rules."[118] As the journalists

David Maraniss and Michael Weisskopf conclude, "economic interests have long worked closely with both parties, but not until the new majority rose to power with its antiregulatory agenda had so many corporations and trade associations banded together for as many issues under a single party banner."[119] Interest groups now faced much stronger incentives—and pressure—to ally with a single party in order to maintain influence.

In the aftermath of the 1994 election, a new political constellation came into clearer view. Intense party polarization became the new "normal" in American politics. The racial realignment and nationalization of policy had gradually helped to transform the operations of state parties, interest groups, and the media, facilitating Gingrich's rise as a fierce advocate of a national strategy of confrontation that would accentuate party differences. These same changes in mediating institutions meant that political actors would have incentives to continue to push along this same path. The forces that had, in the past, disrupted polarization no longer operated to do so. More often than not, they made things worse. The next two chapters consider the dramatic implications of these transformations for policymaking, the separation of powers, and the durability of American democracy.

PART III

The Crisis of the New American Constitutional Order

6

Policy by Other Means

The changes in interest groups, state parties, and the press that we traced in chapters 4 and 5 transformed the American constitutional order. Many aspects traditionally associated with the American political system—such as multidimensional interest representation, weak political parties, pronounced regional diversity, tendencies toward bipartisanship, and moderate policymaking—are based on the *interaction* between the nation's formal institutions and a set of decentralized mediating institutions. These intermediary institutions have played a role in strengthening certain potentialities of the formal governing structures while limiting others. The task of the next two chapters is to assess the new American constitutional order that has emerged as mediating institutions have nationalized and polarized even as the Constitution itself has remained unchanged. Familiar features of the "Madisonian" framework take on new and unexpected roles, while the various pieces of a system designed to disperse political authority now connect with each other in unfamiliar ways. In this chapter we consider the troubling implications for governance before we turn in the next chapter to the threats these new political arrangements pose for American democracy.

We begin by delineating the new constitutional order that has taken shape. We focus on the ways in which nationalization and polarization have interacted with traditional Madisonian arrangements to encourage a form of partisan teamsmanship that undermines the pluralistic bargaining that in the past underpinned policymaking in a system of separated institutions sharing power.

After drawing out these general features, we trace the workings of this emergent policymaking regime from the vantage point of each of the major sites of policymaking authority. We look at dynamics within Congress and then examine how these have created new opportunities for presidents, the courts, and state legislatures to shape policy.

Three broad themes stand out in our assessment of the new structures of policymaking. First, Congress, mired in gridlock, has weakened. This has not resulted in less policy change, but instead has shifted the venues in which important policy decisions are made, most notably to the Supreme Court. Second, the opportunities and constraints introduced by nationalized polarization are sharply asymmetric across the two parties. Republicans enjoy considerable advantages owing to the ways in which their policy goals and electoral coalition intersect with the new order. Third, the policymaking process in Washington manifests mounting acrimony and dysfunction. With the growing difficulty of achieving broad consensus over anything important beyond keeping the lights on (and sometimes not even that) the teams jostle to identify where they can act unilaterally, often resorting to tactics that test the boundaries of long-accepted practices.

The Emergent Constitutional Order

American constitutional arrangements are highly distinctive. They stand apart from most modern democracies on a number of critical dimensions.[1] The US electoral rules quickly and durably gave rise to a two-party system. This arrangement might have led to concentrations of political power were it not grounded in decentralized political authority. Americans looked to the constitutional separation of powers, checks and balances, and federalism to prevent the consolidation of power. Meanwhile, these features generated the fluidity among interest alignments needed to govern in a system where fractured authority might otherwise make effective governance impossible. In most democracies, by contrast, the main mechanism for limiting concentrations of power is electoral arrangements that encourage multiparty systems in which no single party is likely to dominate.

By ceding significant political authority to different institutions and then grounding each of these institutions in different constituencies with different selection processes, the Constitution made it more likely that the occupants of each would have distinctive interests and perspectives along with the power to protect them. Representatives, senators, judges, and presidents would respond to different audiences, depending on their institutional location. Critically, officeholders' ability to pursue their policy and political goals would depend on their institution's power, giving them a personal interest in defending their branch from incursions. This is stated most memorably in *Federalist*, no. 51, which offers the formula that "ambition must be made to counteract ambition." By connecting the interests of the individual to the power of their office, Madison argued that the constitutional system would be safeguarded against domination by a single branch or individual. Instead of joining in a single homogeneous coalition across institutions, fractiousness would be a built-in feature. As Rufus Miles put it in describing the American bureaucracy, "where you stand depends on where you sit."[2]

This institutional setup also amplified the importance of geographic differences—certain to be considerable given the nation's vast and varied territory. The Constitution incentivized members of Congress to be responsive to the diverse concerns of their local constituency. Federalism has meant that governors and state legislators, each with their own distinctive electoral bases, are important players in policymaking. The decentralized parties that formed to compete in this context accorded state and local organizations a key role as power brokers influencing nominations to valued offices at multiple levels. As a result, the career ladder to national power generally depended on first developing a strong connection to other locally rooted politicians and groups. This configuration gave spatially grounded interests—such as agrarian reformers, silver miners, and progressive insurgents (discussed in chapters 2 and 3)—a strong foothold even when their goals were in tension with those of national party leaders. The result has been that where one stands has depended not just on where one sits, but where one is from.

The veto-heavy structure of American political institutions also created obstacles to strong, unified parties. Legislation in the United States must run a gauntlet unparalleled in other democracies.[3] Initiatives can be blocked at four different sites (the House, the Senate, the presidency, and the courts). Each of these sites is organized in different ways, creating distinct constellations of interests and distinct political incentives. The Senate, with its now ubiquitous filibuster, offers a kind of double veto point, since both the Senate majority and a large minority can block a bill. Given these unusual arrangements, extensive bargaining within and across parties has typically been necessary to achieve major policy change. The presence of multiple veto points controlled by actors with distinct interests has strengthened the opportunities for factionalism within each party and generally made bipartisan coalitions the norm.

As we have discussed, these arrangements have long encouraged pluralism and posed formidable obstacles to disciplined partisan teamsmanship. The political parties that emerged provided much-needed coordination across branches, but they were broad, diverse coalitions that simultaneously afforded substantial space for policy entrepreneurs to carve together different, often bipartisan, coalitions across issues. The loose bargaining process that resulted meant that it made sense to avoid making permanent enemies and instead remain open to possible deals. Even when a single party has driven a policy program to enactment, eventual opposition party acceptance—even if only grudging and limited—has proven essential for its durability. There also has been a good deal of churn in coalitional patterns over time, with geographically rooted insurgent movements and new policy demands shuffling partisan lines. Although this vision of pluralism had critical blind spots when it came to class and race, the institutional framework tended to limit the scope and duration of intense national party conflict.

But the decentralized politics of earlier eras no longer exists. Today, elected officials, agency leaders, and judges are much more likely to identify their interests with those of their partisan team rather than their branch of government or geographic constituency. Recruitment into office now occurs through nationalized partisan networks that put great weight on loyalty and push similar demands across the nation's diverse landscape. Cooperation with the out-party is punished. All of this means that officials become responsive to similar constituencies and interests across branches of government and geographic locations. Where you sit—and where you are from—no longer has much effect on where you stand.

Nationalized polarization does not mean that the parties are now cohesive machines with all-powerful leaders. Moderates remain, and party factions have not disappeared. But they are different today than in the past. As we discuss shortly, internal factional fights no longer enhance the prospects for compromise or reshuffling of cleavages. Especially on the right, these factional efforts are now generally aimed at pulling the parties even further away from each other. Rather than weakening the team by building alliances with members of the other party, they seek to make their team more confrontational, intensifying polarization rather than diminishing it.

When shared partisanship thoroughly dominates institutional considerations, it short-circuits critical links in the Madisonian logic. Consider a Republican member of Congress deciding how to respond to President Donald Trump in 2017–20. Regardless of one's home state, the fear is the same: undermining the president carries serious political risks, particularly in a party primary. This fear might seem counterintuitive given Trump's low national approval ratings, but it reflects the changes in mediating institutions. In place of the relatively autonomous state parties of earlier decades, Republican members are embedded in a national network of party activists and donors who share a commitment to the same conservative policies, and to the established partisan alliances that support them. Given the sharp divide between the two parties, they are deeply hostile to any actions likely to benefit the Democratic opposition.

POLICY BY OTHER MEANS

Today's politicians also confront an interest group universe that is more national in scope and more clearly tied to party. Because today these groups more often identify their own success with party success, they have a stronger incentive to penalize failures to be a good team player. And with most powerful groups so aligned, there are no major alternative sources of support out there if a member alienates them by striking an independent course. Perhaps most important, straying from the party is swiftly penalized. Indeed, the nationalized and partisan media—Fox News, talk radio, and online platforms—leave a member susceptible to a coordinated, concerted attack for cooperating with the other party. The lengths to which individual Republicans went to court President Trump's support—exemplified by Kentucky Representative Tom Massie's decision, when facing a potential primary challenge, to purchase advertising time in South Florida on Fox News to reach Trump's Mar-a-Lago residence—attests to the accountability dynamics within the party.[4]

A common refrain is that nationalized polarization exacerbates gridlock. The reality is more complicated, though perhaps even more troubling. Congressional stalemates (reinforced by the filibuster as well as polarization) have enabled other institutions to take on a greater role in driving policy change, often effectively removing Congress from its traditional roles as an important source of responsiveness to public demands and a check on the other branches. In short, a gridlocked Congress is not the same as a gridlocked polity.

Presidents can draw on their unilateral power to move policy with little fear of congressional reversal. The courts have advanced an increasingly aggressive conservative agenda, again with little concern that a gridlocked Congress will fight back. Indeed, it is the courts that have seen the largest gain in effective political authority in the contemporary period. Meanwhile, state governments have enacted major policy changes on a host of hot-button issues, ranging from abortion to gun rights to voting rules. Increasingly, the policies that citizens encounter depend on whether they live in a Republican- or Democratic-controlled state. While these geographic policy differences partly reflect differences in state public opinion, they are powerfully shaped by party control.[5]

Nonetheless, there are critical differences between the two parties' capacities to take advantage of the current configuration. Although each party is now more ideologically cohesive and less divided by geography than in the past, their distinct electoral coalitions, policy ambitions, and media environments generate different incentives—and often considerable advantages—for Republicans as they pursue their policy goals.

A crucial component of this asymmetry is the fact that, as the two nationalized parties have taken their modern form, they have increasingly divided along an urban/non-urban axis, with less-populated, rural areas voting Republican.[6] Given American constitutional design, this spatial reorganization affords a substantial electoral dividend to the party that is popular in less dense areas. Most obviously, the rural bias in Senate representation has introduced a substantial pro-Republican skew as population density has become a more powerful predictor of voting and as it has become harder for individual Democratic incumbents to forge a reputation distinct from their party. This has allowed the GOP to hold a majority of seats in the Senate about half the time since 1998 even as they have never represented half the nation's citizens over that period.[7] As Jonathan Rodden and others have documented, Democrats also pay a "density tax" in House elections; here too Republicans have generally outperformed their national vote totals when congressional seats are allocated. Finally, a similar density tax operates in state legislative elections.

In a context of nationalized polarization, the bias against density in American electoral institutions creates different incentives for the two major parties. In effect, it means that Democrats have to build a broader coalition to achieve electoral success, competing in geographic areas that are more conservative than the national average. Democrats thus generally face a stronger incentive to moderate. By contrast, Republicans can seek a narrower coalition, especially as polarization and increasingly strong partisan identification (including increased hostility to the other party) make it more difficult for politicians to rely on an ability to attract "swing" voters.

As we will explore further in the next chapter, the density dividend has compounding effects, especially when a partisan team unified across institutional sites is willing to use its opportunities to gain durable advantages. The electoral tilt to the GOP at the state level has fueled Republican efforts to engage in widespread gerrymandering of state legislatures. In several states that are "purple" (North Carolina, Wisconsin, and Georgia), state electoral maps have virtually foreclosed Democratic control of the legislature, even when Democrats win a clear majority of the statewide vote.

Yet the cornerstone of this compounding power is the Supreme Court. Republicans have gained a firm and very conservative majority on the Supreme Court, in part through hardball tactics that the party's frequent control of the Senate enables and media on the right applauds. Increasingly operating as an ally of Republican presidents and state legislatures, the Supreme Court creates a major asymmetry between the parties' opportunities to shape policy amid congressional gridlock. This is especially the case since the Supreme Court can powerfully shape election law and also uphold, tear down, or reinterpret the decisions of other branches of government.

Although we discuss each branch and the states separately below, a key dynamic that emerges is that the various elements now fit together in a new way, one that both makes effective governance harder and that affords distinctive advantages to conservatives. Democrats' legislative priorities are especially vulnerable to the Senate filibuster, since the creation and expansion of programs generally requires sixty votes. The filibuster poses much less of a problem for Republicans' tax-cutting goals—which can be accomplished with a simple majority—and the party's deregulatory agenda, which can be pursued through executive appointments and sympathetic court rulings. Stymied legislatively, Democratic presidents increasingly rely upon regulatory policymaking to pursue their priorities—often at the explicit urging of their fellow partisans in Congress.[8] But conservative-controlled courts now pose a major additional obstacle to this strategy, leaving Democrats in a tenuous position. Meanwhile, congressional gridlock and conservative Supreme Court decisions have shifted much policymaking action to state legislatures, where Republicans tend to have an advantage due to biases resulting from their rural electoral base and (often) gerrymandering.

In sum, given Republicans' policy goals, a regime with a strong president and conservative court, alongside a gridlocked Congress and numerous Republican-controlled state legislatures, may be a substantial victory. By contrast, this setup constitutes a recipe for dysfunction and frustration for Democrats when they do make electoral gains.

Congressional Policymaking in a Polarized System

The effects of polarization on Congress are well known. Indeed, the academic discussion of growing polarization in the US began with a focus on Congress. The first prominent signs of renewed partisan strength were visible in the House of Representatives in the 1980s as party leaders started to exercise greater power and party-aligned voting rebounded from the low levels prevalent in the 1950s–70s. The rise of Newt Gingrich in the 1990s made it clear that something dramatic had changed, as decades of cordial relationships between the two parties' leaders gave way to all-out combat. By the early 2000s, party voting had reached levels not seen since the first decade of the twentieth century, with "partisan warfare" becoming the norm in the House and increasingly characteristic of the Senate. An array of books and articles have considered congressional polarization as both a central symptom and potential cause of our troubled politics.[9]

But there has been less attention to how the intensification of polarization has affected Congress's relationship to the other branches in the policymaking process.[10] The changes in state parties, interest groups, and the media environment have transformed the incentives of members of Congress so that they behave more as members of cohesive national teams than as representatives of distinctive geographic interests or protectors of Congress's authority. The juxtaposition of quasi-parliamentary parties with non-parliamentary institutions—bicameralism, the filibuster, and presidentialism—creates novel challenges to Congress's ability to legislate on high-visibility issues with broad impact. The resulting failure to enact far-reaching policy solutions to pressing problems erodes public confidence in Congress and the political system more generally, while shifting a greater share of policymaking to other venues.

There are several reasons to expect polarization to make it harder for Congress to enact policy. The connection is most clear when there is split party control of the House and Senate, or divided control across branches. With little or no preference overlap between the parties, few major policies will gain the support of, for example, a Democratic House and Republican Senate. Even under unified party control, polarization makes it less likely there will be sufficient bipartisan support to garner the sixty Senate votes necessary to defeat a filibuster.[11] Indeed, the use of the filibuster has exploded since the 1970s, with polarization encouraging the minority party to use obstruction as an everyday tactic.[12] Put simply, the minority has both the motivation and capacity to block much of the majority party's program.

These problems are compounded by the parties' incentive to engage in "strategic disagreement," resisting potentially acceptable compromises in order to preserve the ability to attack the other party's stance on an issue. In recent years, both parties have increasingly focused on messaging strategies that seek to make the other side appear extreme.[13] As political scientist Nolan McCarty observes, the value of tarnishing opponents as out of touch is likely greater as your own party moves further from the center, making strategic disagreement a greater problem under intense polarization.[14]

Acting on this logic, early in the Obama administration, Mitch McConnell urged his Senate colleagues to stick together to oppose the new president's signature initiatives instead of seeking grounds for agreement. George Voinovich, one of the few remaining Republican Senate moderates, summed up McConnell's message: "If Obama was for it, we had to be against it."[15] McConnell understood that Republican support for Obama's legislation would signal to the public that the proposed policies were not too liberal, an outcome that the GOP leader saw as essential to avoid. Where pluralism was premised on policy initiatives constituting a sort of à la carte menu, with different coalitions coming together to support different policies, McConnell sought to turn each issue into a simple test of whether one was for Obama or

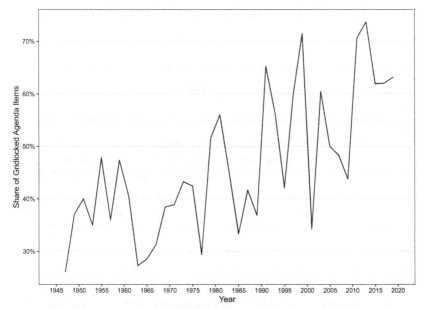

FIGURE 6.1. Share of Legislative Agenda That Is Gridlocked
Note: Figure derived from Sarah Binder dataset of gridlock and legislative enactments. We use Binder's
definition that an issue is on the national agenda when there are four or more relevant *New York Times*
editorials on it. Binder considers a range of thresholds but primarily bases her analyses on this measure.
See Sarah A. Binder, "The Struggle to Legislate in Polarized Times," in *Congress Reconsidered*, 12th ed.,
ed. Lawrence C. Dodd, Bruce I. Oppenheimer, and C. Lawrence Evans (Washington: CQ Press, 2021).

against him. This minority opposition makes it much more difficult for the
majority party to push its priorities forward, particularly given the persistence of the filibuster.[16]

Studies of congressional productivity generally bear out the expectation
that polarization makes it more difficult to legislate. In an important analysis, Sarah Binder identifies salient issues on the national policy agenda by
coding unsigned *New York Times* editorials, and then examines how often
Congress enacts a policy response to that issue. Binder finds that gridlock has
increased substantially over time. From 1947–80, the share of gridlocked issues in each Congress averaged 38 percent; this increased to 50 percent from
1981–2010 as polarization began to rise, before reaching 66 percent in 2011–20
(see figure 6.1). Binder's analysis indicates that polarization, along with di-
verging preferences of the House and Senate, drives the increased frequency
of failure. Interestingly, unified party control is no longer associated with
greater legislative success; Binder argues that this is because the need for sixty
votes in the Senate has become a more formidable obstacle amid heightened
polarization.[17]

Congress's declining capacity to carry out other legislative tasks provides further evidence of dysfunction. Most notably, Congress has become much less successful in reliably exercising its power of the purse. Congress passed a budget resolution setting a framework for tax and spending decisions in all but one year from fiscal year 1976 through 2001. It now fails to do so more than half of the time. Passing a specific budget plan opens the majority party up to messaging attacks. As a result, leaders generally only opt to do so when it paves the way to use the reconciliation process—which limits obstruction on certain tax and spending measures, enabling a simple majority to enact priority legislation. This is generally not an option when there is divided control, so Congress foregoes its authority to pass an overall budget.[18]

The process of reauthorizing programs and appropriating funds for them has also been disrupted. Regular authorization bills, which offer Congress an opportunity to set priorities for agencies and scrutinize existing programs, are now subject to delays that make them far from routine. For example, the State Department went from 2002 until 2016 without a reauthorization law. In recent years, roughly one-third of discretionary funding has taken the form of unauthorized appropriations; if one excludes defense, the one major area in which Congress has succeeded in passing annual authorization bills, more than half of discretionary spending has routinely taken the form of unauthorized appropriations.[19] Ordinary appropriations bills have also become more challenging to pass, given the need for bipartisan support to overcome a Senate filibuster. In the place of regular spending bills, Congress now more frequently governs through massive continuing resolutions that make it harder for agencies and private actors to plan.[20]

The most vivid manifestations of the broader pattern are the growing frequency and seriousness of government shutdowns and threats of debt default. The budget and appropriations process has become entangled in deeply divisive issues—some of which are not directly related to budgeting—that make it harder for Congress to carry out one of its core responsibilities.[21] High levels of gridlock have led to policy advocates strategically using omnibus spending bills and debt-ceiling deadlines to steer their non-budgetary priorities into law. This, in turn, has further complicated the challenge of reaching deals. It is often easier to find a compromise on spending totals for programs than to agree on immigration, abortion, environmental regulation, or a host of other policies that have, at times, become attached to spending legislation.

The introduction of these high-stakes showdowns reflects the growing role of extreme factions, especially on the right. The silver Republicans of the 1890s, progressive Republicans of the 1900s–20s, and Dixiecrats of the 1930s–60s were all anchored in distinctive regional interests that cleaved their

priorities from those of fellow partisans elsewhere. Tellingly, they each sought
a working alliance with the opposing party on key issues. By contrast, the most
influential intraparty factions now, such as the Tea Party and Freedom Caucus Republicans, generally seek to offer a "purer" version of the party's policy
agenda than their "establishment" colleagues. The major factions are not char-
acteristically seeking to work with the other party; instead, they draw upon
their own party's core fundraising, media, and online constituencies in a fight
for control of their party's message and identity. They harness conservative
media and fear of right-wing primary challenges to pull the party to the right.
And repeatedly, they have undercut the leadership of Republican Speakers,
leading John Boehner to resign the Speakership (2015) and Paul Ryan to retire
from Congress (2018). In 2023, they used more direct action, successfully replacing Kevin McCarthy with the more right-wing Michael Johnson.

It is important not to push the narrative of congressional dysfunction too
far. Indeed, James Curry and Frances Lee make a forceful case that less has
changed when it comes to policymaking than some accounts suggest. For
all the high-profile failures in recent years, most legislation that is ultimately
enacted has significant bipartisan support. Indeed, given frequently divided
government and supermajority rules in the Senate, legislative success—as opposed to messaging—requires building coalitions that cross party lines. Although the number of new laws has decreased, Lee and Curry note that each
law tends to be longer—as omnibus measures have become more common—
with the result that the volume of statute pages added has remained stable.[22]

These findings offer a valuable corrective to the oversimplified view that
contemporary polarization renders Congress entirely helpless. Still, the scope
of bipartisan successes outside of specific responses to immediate crises is
limited in critical ways.[23] As Binder notes, many of the laws that are widely
considered "successes" in recent years would not have been seen as accom-
plishments in earlier eras. Simply passing a continuing resolution to keep the
government running or a bill to avoid debt default may be regarded as a substantial accomplishment today. In the past, such measures were (often) routine or unnecessary.[24] Many other major laws passed by bipartisan majorities
in recent years—such as the 2018 First Step Act criminal justice reform bill
or legislation targeting the opioids epidemic—were extremely modest given
the challenges they were supposed to address. For example, to gain necessary
GOP support, the First Step Act ended up more limited than the reforms that
several Republican states had already enacted on their own.[25] A gun safety
measure enacted in the aftermath of the Uvalde, Texas school shooting in
2022 was widely praised as an example of successful bipartisanship, but it was
extremely modest.

Meanwhile, when it comes to many of the most critical issues facing the US—such as income inequality, immigration, and the declining quality of American infrastructure—the legislative response has been extremely halting, meaning that problems fester and the list of unaddressed issues grows. Action on climate change failed for decades before Democrats (with no Republican support in either chamber) finally found a path for a simple majority to act through the budget reconciliation process in 2022. As Binder concludes, "half-measures, second bests, and just-in-time legislating—or no action at all—are now the norm."[26] Even as Lee and Curry on balance offer a more positive assessment of contemporary congressional policymaking, they conclude that "today's cohesive political parties collide with the constitutional system of separation of powers and checks and balances in ways that obstruct legislative action and frequently end in stalemate."[27]

These failures are costly when it comes to the nation's capacity to address pressing problems and respond to public demands. They also damage trust in government, as the public comes to view Congress as deadlocked and dysfunctional.[28] Lee notes that even if gridlock has been a common concern throughout much of US history, "the responsibilities of the federal government today are so much broader that policy stalemate has far more wide-ranging consequences."[29] Yet situating Congress within the larger setting of nationalized polarization suggests that the result of contemporary legislative gridlock is not necessarily *less* new policy. Rather, it is a shift in *where* that policymaking takes place and, often, a shift in the substance of the resulting decisions.

The Presidency as Policymaker in a Polarized System

As Congress becomes less able to address important policy challenges, the president's power to issue executive orders and to use appointments to guide the bureaucracy loom as more potent weapons. McCarty notes that the expansion of presidential power in this context differs from earlier cases when presidents accumulated influence from the changing nature of governing tasks (e.g., the rise of the US as a superpower) or deliberate decisions of Congress to delegate in response to a crisis (e.g., New Deal legislation giving discretion to executive agencies). Instead, the president has been gaining power from Congress's inability "to provide its conventional and traditional inputs to the policy process."[30] Of course, policymaking through executive orders and appointments faces its own limitations, both in what can be accomplished and the potential for unfriendly courts to stand in the way.

Immigration policy is a telling example of both the ways in which polarization has empowered and frustrated contemporary presidents. Congress has wrestled unsuccessfully with major immigration legislation repeatedly since the George W. Bush administration. The filibuster has been the most common source of failure, though in the rare cases where legislation managed to pass the Senate, Republicans in control of the House blocked action. Amid this gridlock, the president—and the federal courts—have guided immigration policy changes.

After the DREAM Act was filibustered in 2010, President Obama issued an executive order creating the Deferred Action for Childhood Arrivals (DACA) program in 2012.[31] DACA implemented several policies that were part of the failed legislation, shielding eligible individuals from deportation and allowing them to work. Two years later, Obama expanded these protections to cover the parents of American citizens or lawful permanent residents (with the stipulation that they had lived in the US continuously since January 2010). Obama had initially claimed that he lacked the authority to institute such protections through executive action, but with the legislative pathway closed off, the president pushed the limits of his power. The Supreme Court ultimately blocked the order covering parents, while not directly ruling on the constitutionality of DACA. Obama's approach underscores the extent to which legislative gridlock has led Democratic presidents to seek to squeeze greater policymaking capacity out of their control of the executive branch, balancing this aggressiveness with the risk that conservative courts will reject these efforts.

When President Trump issued an order rescinding DACA, Congress was unable to garner the necessary support to give it a firmer legislative footing. With the courts blocking Trump's order due to procedural flaws, the policy remained clouded in uncertainty throughout his term. President Biden reinstated the program in 2021. That order, too, has been challenged in the courts, continuing the uncertainty about its future.

Beyond these battles over executive orders, Trump used his appointments at the Customs and Border Patrol, Immigration and Customs Enforcement, and US Citizenship and Immigration Services agencies to take a much more aggressive stance toward undocumented immigrants and to slow legal immigration as well.[32] This new enforcement stance was not the product of congressional legislation. Here again, gridlock in Congress paved the way for Trump's approach; there was little prospect of opponents generating the necessary supermajorities to reverse it.

Trump's declaration of a national emergency at the border took this unilateral approach to another level. After Congress rebuffed his request for border wall funding, Trump used the emergency declaration to move approximately $10 billion from military projects to fund the wall.[33] Trump's action clearly overstepped traditional understandings of the president's emergency declaration power. It also ran directly counter to Congress's explicit funding decision. In short, it challenged core congressional powers in a manner that might be expected to activate the "where you stand" features of the American constitutional order. Yet even using expedited procedures that allowed a simple majority in each chamber to pass a resolution overturning the president's order did not work, as Trump's veto power, backed by a clear majority of House and Senate Republicans, easily blocked a reversal.[34] The need to win Republican votes also undermined Democrats' efforts to use subsequent spending bills to block further reprogramming of funds.

This solidarity of Republicans across institutions stood in sharp contrast to the early 1970s, when Nixon threatened congressional control of the purse with his aggressive use of impoundments. Then, a near-unanimous Congress adopted the Congressional Budget and Impoundment Control Act of 1974, which imposed major restrictions on the president's ability to control spending.[35] That institutional reform could win bipartisan support because there was a widely shared belief that preserving Congress's power of the purse was an important priority. But in the current hyperpolarized context, Congress has shown little capacity to build the kind of broad coalition that in the past had been used to defend its prerogatives.

Although the wall case is unusual in its bold defiance of Congress in the spending arena, it is part of a much broader pattern of executive action shaping policy in a range of important policy areas—not just immigration, but also the environment, financial regulation, student loans, and public health—where Congress has been finding it difficult to legislate. As we discuss in chapter 7, the checks on unilateral presidential action have become even more frayed as legislative oversight has lost much of its bite amid partisan warfare.[36] The bottom line is that even bold presidential challenges to core congressional prerogatives are less likely to prompt an effective institutional response.

One might conclude from these developments that the presidency has emerged as a "winner" from contemporary polarization. But Congress's declining role has not necessarily translated into greater ability for presidents to achieve their own policy and political goals. This is, in part, because executive actions can often be easily reversed when the other party wins the White House.[37] But it also reflects distinctive challenges that polarization poses for governance.

On the administrative side, polarization has fostered long delays in the confirmation process, making it harder for presidents to staff agencies with allies. The resulting vacancies may undermine policy implementation; it is one thing to issue an executive order, and another to ensure it is carried out effectively. In extreme but now fairly regular cases, appointment blockades can leave important agencies—such as the National Labor Relations Board and the Consumer Finance Protection Bureau—unable to make decisions at all. Leaving aside a president's ideological interests, the uncertainties in staffing and budgeting can damage the federal government's performance, which in turn may well harm the president's standing.[38]

The core problem for contemporary presidents is that they now confront an opposition that more closely resembles a cohesive, organized parliamentary party.[39] Since it is exceedingly rare for the president's own party to control both a majority in the House and sixty Senate votes, the increased unity of the opposition makes it harder for presidents to achieve their policy goals.

In earlier eras, presidents could often negotiate directly with centrist blocs in the opposing party. But polarization, changes in the media environment, and the intense competition for majority control have led to greater pressure to toe the party line, making it much harder to pick off a handful of out-party dissidents.[40] Instead, presidents typically need to negotiate with the leaders of the opposition party. This is an altogether different proposition, since these leaders have a clear stake in the president's failure. To illustrate again with Mitch McConnell: "The single most important thing we want to achieve is for President Obama to be a one-term president."[41]

As Frances Lee shows, simply having the president make an issue a priority tends to deepen the partisan divide on that policy as the opposition party seeks to deny the president political credit for a victory.[42] This creates a catch-22: Presidents are expected to push publicly for signature initiatives that reflect their priorities but doing so incentivizes the opposition party to dig in its heels and root for failure. With the filibuster, failure is an outcome that the opposition frequently can produce. The result is a high level of legislative frustration for presidents and their supporters.

Once again, the different policy agendas of the two parties and their different relationships to the current conservative Supreme Court majority create important asymmetries. The Democratic coalition is a diverse set of policy-demanding groups, each with specific legislative goals. Thus, Democrats' core agenda involves multiple ambitious domestic policy initiatives. Many of these priorities require sixty votes to pass because they cannot be fit under the budget process's complicated rules regarding the use of reconciliation to limit obstruction.[43]

With Republicans unified in opposition to Democratic presidents' priority legislation, the result is a repeated cycle of intense disappointment. Bill Clinton, Barack Obama, and Joe Biden each entered office with control of

Congress. Each lost his House majority two years later amid not only intense Republican opposition, but also considerable internal criticism from party activists and some party elites who believed the president had failed to take advantage of the opportunities his election appeared to present.

As their legislative agenda has been increasingly frustrated, Democratic administrations have become more reliant on regulatory policymaking. Greg Elinson and Jonathan Gould observe that Obama responded to gridlock by adopting "expansive interpretations of aging statutes," issuing more major rules than his predecessors.[44] For example, with Congress unwilling to adopt climate legislation, the Obama-era Environmental Protection Act (EPA) interpreted the Clean Air Act to authorize vigorous regulation of greenhouse gas emissions—a position the Supreme Court's 2007 *Massachusetts v. EPA* supported. The administration also adopted stricter motor vehicle emission standards, expanded federal jurisdiction over water pollution, and made major changes in worker safety, consumer protection, and nutrition labeling.[45]

President Biden continued Obama's approach. In addition to approving new regulatory action on the environment, COVID prevention, guns, and consumer protection, Biden pushed against the limits on presidential power in ordering the cancellation of roughly $300 billion in student loan debt in the lead-up to the 2022 midterm election. The student loan action, which arguably rivaled Trump's boldest uses of unilateral power, won support from most congressional Democrats while being sharply attacked by Republicans. As was the case with Trump's border wall, both chambers approved a resolution overturning the order, but the vast majority of Democrats stuck with Biden in upholding his veto of that resolution. Biden's order was eventually overturned by the conservative Supreme Court majority on a party-line vote. Nonetheless, the administration succeeded in forgiving more than $127 billion in student debt through other means.[46]

As Biden's partial success in the student loan case suggests, the unilateral approach has important limitations. It is of only limited use in many policy areas, such as health care coverage (where spending is critical and statutory language more restrictive) or election reform (where the underlying statutory base is either nonexistent or has been struck down by the courts). As discussed below, with conservatives now in control of the courts, this regulatory pathway to policymaking faces increasing headwinds.

Hyperpolarization has thus generally created more problems than opportunities for Democratic presidents. President Biden's first two years in office underscore the dynamics. Despite his unusually slim margins, Biden was able to achieve remarkable unity among congressional Democrats. This unity proved sufficient to pass a broad, ambitious program through the House.

However, most of that program faltered in the Senate due to the opposition of just two senators to several key measures. Those same senators refused to support rules changes that would enable passage of other policies that they claimed to back.

Biden and the Democrats did succeed in enacting a handful of priority measures. Two major bills passed through reconciliation by holding the support of all Democratic senators—the $1.9 trillion American Rescue Plan and the Inflation Reduction Act, which included major new subsidies for a transition to clean energy, an extension of Affordable Care Act subsidies, and important regulations on drug pricing. Congress also passed two important bipartisan bills: an infrastructure measure that garnered significant GOP support by dropping many Democratic priorities and the CHIPS bill which provided substantial support to the semiconductor industry as well as new funding for research and development. However, the list of disappointments has garnered more attention; looming particularly large are the Senate failure of Biden's Build Back Better social spending plan and of voting rights and election reform legislation. Biden's first two years had seemed to offer Democrats an opportunity to rein in Republican state initiatives on gerrymandering and voting procedures that tilted the electoral playing field further in the GOP's direction; instead, the status quo prevailed in Washington, paving the way for continued state-level (and, arguably, judicial) deck-stacking (see chapter 7).

Republicans' experience with unified party control has also featured some noteworthy failures—such as the drive to privatize Social Security under George W. Bush and the bid to repeal Obamacare under Trump. But the party's top legislative priority since the 1980s—massive tax cuts—can be passed with simple majority support under the Senate's reconciliation rules.

This allows Republican presidents to deliver reliably on a signature commitment that pleases important coalition members. Furthermore, Republican presidents have used administrative and judicial appointments to shift a series of policies in a conservative direction. In many cases, simply enforcing existing regulations less strictly, issuing waivers to Republican-controlled states, and allowing numerous vacancies in disfavored agencies can contribute to achieving conservative policy goals with little prospect of a court or legislative reversal.[47]

The differences in the parties' substantive agendas, along with the conservative majority on the Supreme Court, create an asymmetry in how recent developments affect their presidents' ability to achieve their goals. Moreover, because the Democratic Party is the party that favors a strong state and activist government, perceived dysfunction in Washington contributes to a cycle of distrust that hurts Democrats' cause in the long term. By contrast, it boosts

Republican claims that government is more often a source of problems than solutions.

The Courts as Conservative Policymakers

Speaking before the conservative Federalist Society in 2018, Senator Mitch McConnell declared that his top priority was "to do everything we can, for as long as we can, to transform the federal judiciary, because everything else we do is transitory."[48] The Federalist Society itself had played a major role in incubating this long-term strategic vision, working over several decades to build a conservative legal movement that would reverse the gains that liberals had made through the courts since the 1940s.[49] Indeed, the emergence of the Federalist Society is an excellent illustration of how the new constitutional order functions. A national body closely aligned with a political party now plays a critical role in making sure that the interests of the "team" dominate, even in the judiciary, a realm that is supposed to be above partisan politics and one where individuals, once appointed, possess remarkable autonomy. This movement, funded by prominent Republican-allied groups such as Koch Industries and oil and gas companies,[50] has nurtured a national network of conservative judicial candidates and provided an effective way to vet potential nominees' ideological bona fides.

While ideology and partisanship have always played a significant role in judicial nominations, the process traditionally allowed considerable space for other factors to intrude that at times cut against the selection of die-hard loyalists. Eisenhower chose two justices who became liberal stalwarts (political rival Earl Warren and New Jersey State Judge William Brennan), Kennedy nominated personal friend Byron White, who turned out to be conservative, and Ford selected liberal John Paul Stevens. But the experiences of the Reagan and George H. W. Bush administrations were especially important in motivating Republicans to focus more intently on ideological loyalty. When two of Reagan's three selections—Sandra Day O'Connor and Anthony Kennedy—proved to be moderate voices on the court, conservative activists were disappointed. When one of Bush's two nominees—David Souter—ended up a reliable liberal vote, conservatives were infuriated.

After the Souter nomination, the ideological vetting of nominees ramped up substantially. When George W. Bush sought to nominate his friend Harriet Miers, conservatives rebelled out of fear that her ideological commitments were not firmly established. Republican Senator Sam Brownback's comment that there was a "deep concern that this would be a Souter-type candidate" underscored the conservative hostility that ultimately led Bush to withdraw the nomination.[51] In the wake of this increased attention to ideological fidelity, there have been no significant surprises in the past three decades. All nine justices today are generally reliable members of their appointing party's team.

The focus on partisan and ideological loyalty has also pervaded lower court nominations. The process for these nominations had long included decentralized elements that hindered the pursuit of an ideological agenda. For example, the system of senatorial courtesy—reflected in the use of "blue slips" allowing same-state senators to block lower court nominees—incentivized presidents to attend to local concerns and networks in making appointments for district and appeals courts. The Republican-controlled Senate dropped the use of the blue slip for appeals court nominees during the Trump administration. The Democrats have maintained that change under President Biden. Although the blue slip has continued for district courts, President Trump was particularly aggressive in appointing hard-core conservatives at all levels of the federal court system, nominating a number of individuals with very limited experience, including ten deemed unqualified by the American Bar Association.[52]

While both parties have worked to impose a clearer partisan stamp on their judicial nominations, Republicans have been more successful in remaking the courts in their party's image. The pro-Republican bias of the Senate map, combined with Republicans' ability to win the White House even while losing the popular vote (in 2000 and 2016), has given the GOP a decided advantage in nominating and confirming judges. McConnell's success in unifying his Senate Republican colleagues behind a no-holds-barred approach to the confirmation process played an important role in fully capitalizing on these advantages. In particular, Republicans' refusal to allow a vote on Obama nominee Merrick Garland in 2016 led to the seating of the conservative Neil Gorsuch in his place. Four years later, the speedy confirmation of Amy Coney Barrett in October 2020 following Justice Ruth Bader Ginsburg's death five weeks earlier ensured a conservative would be seated regardless of the November election outcome. It is a remarkable testament to the contemporary system's tilt that while Republicans were losing the popular vote for president in seven of the last eight elections, they managed to lock in a solid conservative court majority that could last for a generation.

Although legal, these tactics violated prior shared understandings regarding institutional behavior. Democrats have at times engaged in constitutional hardball of their own, but they have been less aggressive than the Republicans. For example, the party rejected calls to use its unified control of government in 2021–22 to pass legislation to roll back the GOP edge in the judiciary by expanding the size of the Supreme Court. Rural overrepresentation partly explains this party difference. Democratic majorities generally depend on winning several swing districts (and red-leaning states) in which the incumbents have substantial incentives to appear moderate. Furthermore, the media environment facing Republicans rewards sticking with the team when it pursues hardball tactics, while Democrats' greater trust in the "mainstream" media gives them a greater incentive to abide by prior governing norms. Indeed, McConnell's tactics won universal support in conservative media and among Republican voters, making it an easy decision for Republican senators to stick with their party.

McConnell also dedicated as much floor time as necessary to speed the confirmation of Trump's lower court nominees, and extended Democrats' earlier use of the nuclear option to cut down the debate time required. Where Democratic presidents and Senate leaders had allowed many lower court vacancies to sit unfilled, Trump and McConnell teamed up to take full advantage of available opportunities. Despite serving for just a single term, Donald Trump's selections comprised one-third of the Supreme Court, 30 percent of the circuit courts of appeals, and more than one-quarter of district court judges.[53] Most of Trump's selections were relatively young, ensuring that they will constitute a substantial share of judges for decades to come.

Democrats have made a concerted effort to counter Republican control of the judiciary, with President Biden outpacing Obama's relatively slow approach to judicial nominations.[54] But Democratic opportunities to reverse the conservative gains are limited given the GOP advantage in Senate apportionment, which makes it unlikely the party will enjoy unified party control for a sustained period going forward. McConnell made it clear that a future Republican majority would not hesitate to block Democratic Supreme Court nominees.[55] Republicans would also be well-positioned to stall lower court nominees, further entrenching GOP dominance throughout the judicial hierarchy. Given the pull of the Republican base, it seems likely that any plausible Republican leader would follow a similar course.

The development of a Supreme Court composed of nine ideological and partisan team players, with a solid majority coming from one side, has had major implications for governance. For all of the talk of gridlock in Washington, the reality is one of *congressional* gridlock and judicial activism. The conservative majority on the Supreme Court has driven an aggressive policy agenda that arguably outpaces, in ambition and accomplishment, that of any recent president.

The court's ambitious action has extended far beyond its high-profile decisions on issues like abortion, guns, and religion. The court has rolled back environmental regulations, such as President Obama's Clean Power Plan. In

2022 a six to three conservative majority handed down *West Virginia v. Environmental Protection Agency*—a product, as the *New York Times* noted, of "a coordinated, multiyear strategy by Republican attorneys general, conservative legal activists and their funders, several with ties to the oil and coal industries, to use the judicial system to rewrite environmental law, weakening the executive branch's ability to tackle global warming."[56] Even though no existing regulations were in dispute, the court circumscribed the EPA's authority to regulate emissions, arguing that on "major questions," unless prior law was explicit about delegation to an agency, new legislation was required—something that everyone knows will not happen given the presence of the filibuster.

The *West Virginia* decision is part of a broader effort—pursued by state attorneys general and others affiliated with the Federalist Society—to overturn the *Chevron* precedent, under which courts must defer to a government agency's interpretation of a statute that it administers unless the agency's reading of the law is unreasonable or otherwise directly contradictory to the legislative language. Overturning *Chevron* has become a priority for conservative legal activists in recent years as Democratic presidents' have increasingly come to rely on aggressive regulatory interpretations to break through legislative gridlock.[57] Indeed, in constructing its new "major questions" doctrine the court has already executed a successful end run around *Chevron*. The new doctrine gives the court the authority to tell the executive that it must go to Congress, knowing full well that Congress will likely be unable to act.

The court's actions threaten to dramatically undermine the administrative and regulatory state built over the course of the twentieth century. Beyond generally hobbling administrative capacity, this shift would leave liberal regulatory actions particularly vulnerable given the subjectivity surrounding what counts as "reasonable" or a "major question."

While these regulatory actions are especially important for Republican-allied business interests, such as the oil and gas sectors, the Supreme Court has been equally active in pursuing conservative policy goals on racial and social issues. The conservative majority has reined in the use of affirmative action in college admissions. The court has substantially curtailed efforts to curb gun violence, overturning state regulations in place for decades. Finally, the most dramatic victory for the conservative legal movement came in June 2022, with the *Dobbs* decision overturning *Roe v. Wade*.

The court has also decided a series of important cases that directly impact the political system. In nearly every case, those rulings have been widely seen as favoring the political interests of the GOP, and Republicans were strongly supportive while Democrats were strongly opposed. The court has greatly weakened the Voting Rights Act (VRA), paving the way for state efforts to make it harder to vote and allowing redistricting maps that favor Republicans at the expense of racial representation. It has imposed major new restrictions on government efforts to regulate campaign finance. It has made it harder for unions to organize. It cut off the federal courts as an avenue for addressing gerrymandering that favors one party over another.

None of these policy changes would have had the necessary support to be enacted into law through the traditional legislative route. Indeed, public opinion polls suggest that several of the decisions—especially weakening the VRA, overturning *Roe v. Wade*, imposing very sharp limitations on gun regulations, and striking down campaign finance regulations—were very unpopular. Yet there is little prospect of overturning these decisions through congressional action. Large bipartisan majorities had renewed the VRA as recently as 2006, but Senate Republicans successfully filibustered Democratic efforts to reestablish its protections, underscoring the extent to which polarization-induced gridlock shields the court from legislative responses. Similarly, Democrats are far from obtaining the necessary sixty votes to codify *Roe v. Wade* (or the committed majority needed to change the cloture rule to enable a simple majority to defeat a filibuster). Even if Democrats were able to pass legislation protecting abortion rights, the conservative bloc's recent rulings limiting the scope of Congress's commerce power would make this legislation vulnerable.[58] Indeed, on important matters, the court retains the prerogative to find new grounds for objection over time, making the challenge facing Congress a potentially Sisyphean one.

The conservative majority on the court is, of course, not unified across all issues. But following the Trump appointments, the bloc can afford to lose one vote and still emerge victorious. Chief Justice John Roberts has been the most frequent defector, angering his conservative colleagues with votes to uphold most of the Affordable Care Act and his opposition to outright reversal of *Roe v. Wade*. One possible explanation for Roberts's behavior is that the chief justice is more concerned with the court's institutional legitimacy and, accordingly, is more hesitant to issue unpopular decisions on highly visible issues. With the courts firmly in conservative hands, one could argue that this institutional interest is consistent with the long-term goals of the conservative movement. Strong, legitimate courts are good for the Republican Party as long as the conservative majority is in place. Furthermore, avoiding high-profile decisions that could spark an electoral backlash is arguably also good for the Republican Party and the conservative cause.

It is noteworthy that Roberts has been a reliable vote for conservatives on most of the key decisions on voting rights, electoral rules, campaign finance, and union power that have helped Republicans. Even if one takes the chief justice's occasional restraint at face value, there now is a solid majority of five Republican appointees who show few signs of concern that an all-out conservative agenda will undermine the court.

The presence of a conservative Supreme Court also has an important impact on the incentives and capacities of other actors in the federal system. Among its other roles, the court frequently operates as a traffic cop, indicating which actions by other actors are legally permissible and who has the right of way when different sites of authority conflict. As noted above, it limits Democratic presidents' ability to shape policy through regulatory action, even as it largely leaves in place Republican presidents' capacity to limit the effectiveness of regulations through their discretionary enforcement decisions.[59] It has also empowered state legislatures to make policy on a range of issues such as abortion, while allowing extreme partisan gerrymanders of those same legislatures that have, in several cases, locked in Republican majorities in otherwise closely divided states.

In sum, the prevalence of gridlock in Congress has created space for the federal judiciary to take on a much bolder policymaking role. With a solid conservative majority entrenched by a combination of favorable Senate geography, the vagaries of the Electoral College, aggressive hardball tactics, and good fortune, the Supreme Court has embraced a major role in driving policy changes important to the Republican Party. The scope of policy change and its implications for the political balance of power are hard to overstate. The Supreme Court has already remade or is poised to remake government policy on abortion, affirmative action, gun control, voting rights, campaign finance, labor union organization, and regulatory rulemaking.

Before the consolidation of conservative control of the courts, it was less clear whether the current configuration consistently benefited one set of policy priorities over another; after all, most successful legislative enactments have continued to be liberal initiatives and the trajectory of policy on social issues— most notably gay rights—had been moving in a progressive direction in recent decades.[60] However, the substantive policy payoff for conservatives' long institutional campaign to control the courts has now come into sharp relief.

The electoral unpopularity of many of these decisions—especially overturning *Roe v. Wade*, but also in other domains, such as environmental regulation— raises the question of whether the structural advantages described above will be sufficient to overcome the electoral liabilities associated with key tenets of the conservative agenda. For now, the critical point is that the federal judicial system's full incorporation into nationalized, polarized politics brought a dramatic expansion of its effective power and its willingness to use that power, with profound implications for the judiciary's policymaking role and long-term legitimacy.

The States as Polarized Policymakers

It is impossible to understand the impact of contemporary polarization on policymaking without close attention to the states. One might think of nationalization as shifting political contestation from states and localities to Washington. Instead, the form of nationalized polarization that has taken hold in recent decades has resulted in the two partisan teams fighting out many of the same issues across multiple levels of the federal system and institutional venues within that system.

States matter, perhaps more than they have in a long time. And in principle, the states' policy activism could be a countervailing force against nationalized polarization if it were still the case that each party's agenda and priorities varied substantially in response to local demands and interests. But today, this is more the exception than the rule amid growing partisan teamsmanship. The states have emerged as central fronts in national partisan warfare, rather than as highly diverse outposts featuring their own distinctive mixes of cleavages and policy agendas.

As described in chapter 5, state parties today are firmly entrenched in each party's national network. Rather than operating as decentralizing forces and generators of political diversity, the officials who make up state party organizations tend to emerge from a common national network of ideological activists and allied groups. They raise money from many of the same kinds of donors across states and regions, seek the support of the same powerful interest groups, and listen and respond to many of the same media voices.[61] The growing ideological polarization evident in congressional voting is equally apparent at the state legislative level, with Democrats and Republicans in a wide array of states growing further apart.[62] This is in part due to a shift in the supply of candidates, with more extreme candidates more likely to run for state legislatures than in the past. Changes in voter behavior have reinforced this shift in supply; the advantage extremist candidates enjoy in party primaries has grown dramatically since 2010, while centrists have almost entirely lost the advantage they used to enjoy in general elections.[63]

Given these changes, it should be little surprise that when a party gains power in a state, its agenda draws heavily on national party priorities. The policy-demanding groups allied with each party have played an important role in this process. Gridlock in Washington has led interest groups and movement activists to pay increased attention to the states, where the chances for legislative progress are generally better. Unified party control has become much more common in the states as party sorting has increased and gerrymandering has become more durable. As of 2023, thirty-nine states were fully controlled by a single party, the most since 1954.[64] And the filibuster is absent in virtually all state legislatures, allowing simple majorities to rule. Investing money and lobbying attention on state legislatures can have a high payoff under these conditions, particularly given that the reduced journalistic coverage of state politics tends to enhance groups' leverage and diminish the electoral costs of extremism.

As with the contemporary Supreme Court, the opportunities for bold policy departures have been especially pronounced on the political right. Alexander Hertel-Fernandez documents the role of what he calls the "conservative troika" of the American Legislative Exchange Council (ALEC), the State Policy Network, and Koch-led Americans for Prosperity in pushing a far-reaching conservative agenda across the states.[65] In Ohio, for instance, the national organizations of the troika brought with them a policy agenda centered on weakening labor unions in the state. When the state elected a Republican governor in 2010, he signed major legislation targeted public-sector unions, even though the issue had not figured in the election campaign and polling revealed no sign that it was a substantial concern in the public.[66] Nor was this episode unusual. In many areas of public policy, ALEC in particular has made aggressive use of model bills, legislator trainings, and coordinated lobbying campaigns to influence state policy.

Responding to such group efforts in the 2010s, Republican-controlled states passed major policies that restricted labor unions, limited women's access to abortion, and cut taxes on the wealthy. Conservative groups also successfully urged Republican officials in several states to resist implementation of the Affordable Care Act by refusing its Medicaid expansion and adopting rules that undermined the act's insurance marketplaces. Strikingly, this obstruction flourished even though powerful local interests, like state chambers of commerce that traditionally had considerable influence in the Republican Party, strongly favored these initiatives.[67]

While Republicans and their allied groups moved earlier and more aggressively to coordinate their efforts in the states, Democrats have sought to catch up. The States Project, founded in 2017 with funding from a handful of big donors through a dark money group, has spent heavily in targeted state races. The group also serves as a hub for liberal policy proposals, providing guidance for state legislators as they draft legislation.[68] Political scientist Jake

Grumbach notes that in recent years, Democratic state governments have created "new fuel efficiency standards and subsidies for renewable energy. They increased the state minimum wages. Many raised taxes on their wealthiest residents."[69] Most recently, Minnesota Democrats used their unified control of government to codify abortion rights, provide universal free lunch to schoolchildren, set much stricter standards for clean energy, legalize marijuana, regulate guns, protect trans individuals' rights, and allow undocumented individuals to obtain a driver's license.[70]

Stepping back from these specific examples, Grumbach draws upon a dataset covering a diverse array of 135 state policies from 1970–2014 to document the growing gap between outcomes in Democratic and Republican-controlled states. He demonstrates that the magnitude of the relationship between party control and the overall liberalism of state policy has doubled since 2000. Dramatic differences in state policy between GOP- and Democratic-controlled states have opened up in recent years when it comes to abortion, the environment, guns, health care, immigration, labor rights, gay rights, civil rights, and taxes.[71] These issues have each long been major partisan battlegrounds at the national level, but state party control was generally only very weakly related to state policy on them in the 1970s and 1980s.[72] Today, however, these issues permeate state politics, with each party's lawmakers adopting an increasingly common line regardless of their own state's unique history and composition.

Although both parties have been determined to take advantage of their opportunities at the state level in recent years, Republicans' durable edge in controlling state legislatures has given them an important advantage. From 2011–23, Republicans enjoyed a trifecta, on average, in twenty-three states; Democrats, by contrast, have on average had unified control in just 11.5 states.[73] The Supreme Court's conservative rulings have also opened a wider path for state GOP lawmaking on many issues—abortion, most famously—than in the past.

The early years of the Biden administration continued the trend toward state policy divergence. One area that had seen relatively little polarization in the past—education—has shifted considerably amid increased conservative media and elite focus on how schools address questions of equality and social justice. The attacks on discussions of race, gender, and sexuality exemplify the interplay of nationalization and federalism. A panic spread through conservative media has played out across numerous states and local communities as activists have drawn from a common playbook in challenging local educators.[74]

Conservatives' mistrust of educational institutions has also shaped higher education policy, with moves to limit tenure and academic freedom in the public university systems of several states, including Florida and Georgia. Florida Governor Ron DeSantis's rise to national prominence was boosted by a series of legislative initiatives targeting educational institutions, including the "Stop WOKE" Act (restricting discussions of race in schools and colleges) and a law undermining tenure by requiring regular five-year reviews of faculty.[75]

It is increasingly likely that young people's educational experiences will differ substantially depending on whether they live in a GOP- or Democratic-controlled state. Rather than being cordoned off to a small number of (important) policy areas, such as guns and abortion, state policy polarization permeates an ever-increasing share of the agenda.[76]

The process of state-level polarization has, of course, not been uniform. The most noteworthy exception has been the election of moderate Republican governors in such northeastern and mid-Atlantic states as Vermont, Maryland, and Massachusetts. These states each have had solid Democratic legislative majorities, dramatically limiting the potential for conservative policy change regardless of who is in the governor's office. Strikingly, however, even some of these state parties have recently been taken over by activists who echo the language and priorities of Republicans in other, more conservative parts of the US.[77] The GOP nominated pro-Trump candidates to replace their departing governors in both Massachusetts and Maryland in 2022; both lost by a wide margin.

Although Trump-aligned candidates are extremely unlikely to win general elections in blue states, their success in state party conventions and primaries across red, blue, and purple states underscores the influence of nationalized party networks throughout the US. This is not just a matter of potential further polarization on policy issues. In the wake of the January 6, 2021, insurrection and its aftermath, these state-level dynamics raise serious concerns about the future of American democracy.

In this chapter we have demonstrated how the new constitutional order has transformed policymaking, with a decline in the capacity to legislate on pressing problems, rising dysfunction and acrimony, and a pronounced shift of authority from elected politicians to appointed judges. Yet the tensions between our Constitution and the development of a nationalized system of partisan polarization are not just a threat to effective and responsive policymaking. Chapter 7 explores the emergent dangers to American democracy that result when one party in a nationalized and polarized system moves away from a commitment to free and fair elections. Drawing on the experience of earlier republics, the Framers feared a demagogic leader drawing on mass support to consolidate undue power. The presidency has turned out to be a critical focal point for threats to democratic governance, but the dangers are not simply about the executive branch. They stem from the opportunities the Constitution creates when a partisan team, operating across the American system's multiple sites of authority, comes to see democratic processes as a threat to its power and priorities.

Democracy in the Balance

Following the 2020 election Donald Trump struggled to bring the Department of Justice under firmer control. He pressured Attorney General William Barr, who had dismissed his claims that the election had been rife with fraud, to resign. According to three top Justice officials, including Jeffrey Rosen, who had taken over as acting attorney general, the president badgered them repeatedly to aggressively pursue what they considered baseless accusations. Faced with this pushback, Trump considered replacing Rosen with Jeffrey Clark, a lower-level official whose main credential was his enthusiasm for investigating the fraud claims.[1] He backed off only when he was told that mass resignations would result. The contemporaneous notes of a top Justice official suggest that during one phone conversation Trump told Rosen to "just say the election was corrupt and leave the rest to me and R[epublican] congressmen."[2] Like his request that the Georgia Secretary of State "find" eleven thousand votes and his efforts to enlist fake electors in multiple states, Trump's words to his attorney general highlight a key feature of his strategy for overturning the election. It focused on enlisting partisan allies across the nation's fractured system of political authority. It rested, in short, on the opportunities for democratic backsliding that might arise in a nationalized and polarized constitutional order.

For much of our history, American government has been held up as a model of democratic stability and ideals. This is reflected in the rhetoric regarding America's role in world politics, from the Cold War to today, as well as in the academic study of politics in our own discipline of political science, which is segmented into the study of American politics on the one hand and the rest of the world on the other. Where scholars of global politics have well-established models for understanding democratic breakdown, American politics scholarship has generally taken the stability of our institutions for granted. The biggest exceptions to this scholarly gap have been students of American political development (who study the historical contexts in which American politics has taken shape and acquired particular characteristics), as well as students of race and gender. It is impossible to think seriously about the Civil War and Reconstruction, as well as the long, uneven struggle for inclusion over the past 150 years without an acute appreciation for the limitations and vulnerabilities of American democracy. When Donald Trump was elected in 2016, these scholars were quick to pick up on the warning signs in contemporary American politics.[3]

Today, faith in American democracy is faltering. Scholars of global politics have noted that America's troubles coincide with rising concerns about democratic backsliding across a number of countries. Indeed, one might reasonably argue that there is little need for a distinctive analysis of the American case. The rise of right-wing populism, with its challenges to democratic institutions, is a global phenomenon. And the significance of global forces—deindustrialization, shifting racial and ethnic demographics, rapid cultural change, the spread of social media—is undeniable. Efforts to understand American developments should not be siloed off from these broader developments.

Yet as we stressed in chapter 1, the extent to which democratic backsliding has gained momentum in the United States remains a puzzle. The United States is a very rich country. While American democratization was long incomplete, its core electoral and governing institutions have endured for more than two centuries. Scholars of breakdown generally consider these the basic preconditions for continued democratic stability.[4] And yet the US, alone among rich and durable democracies, faces existential challenges. Why? In this chapter, we argue that our political institutions are a principal source of these dangers.

The Madisonian system *creates* distinct vulnerabilities that are absent in most democracies, and the new constitutional order has brought those vulnerabilities to the surface. The American constitutional order that developed in the wake of the Constitution's ratification rested on a set of decentralized mediating institutions that nationalized polarization has undercut. As a result, checks and balances that were supposed to support pluralism and ensure accountability no longer work the way they once did. Moreover, in the wake of these changes, important elements in today's Republican Party have both distinctive motives and distinctive opportunities to act in ways that threaten core democratic values. In short, the contemporary threat to American democracy is not general but specific.

Teamsmanship and the Rise of "Semi-Loyal" Politicians

As our discussion in chapter 6 makes clear, developments in state parties, interest groups, and the media have transformed the operation of the nation's governing institutions. In particular, they have fostered a form of partisan "teamsmanship" that crosses institutional and geographic divides.

In 1978, political sociologist Juan Linz, introduced the concept of "semi-loyal democrats."[5] Linz was interested in understanding the breakdown of democratic regimes. Semi-loyalists are political figures inside the corridors of power who do not actively engage in authoritarian behavior but provide cover for those who do. In their recent book on the threat of democratic backsliding in the United States, Steven Levitsky and Daniel Ziblatt provide a grim summary of the critical role of semi-loyalists: "Many of the politicians who preside over a democracy's collapse are just ambitious careerists trying to stay in office or perhaps win a higher one. They do not oppose democracy out of deep-seated principle but are merely indifferent to it. They tolerate or condone antidemocratic extremism because it is the path of least resistance. These politicians often tell themselves they are just doing what's necessary to get ahead. But ultimately, they become indispensable partners in democracy's demise."[6]

Displays of semi-loyalty have spread rapidly in the Republican Party. Indeed, it is fair to say that following the 2020 election semi-loyalists constituted a majority—perhaps a large majority—of Republican elected officials. At least this was evident in those settings—the national arena and closely fought states—where Republicans faced pressure to weigh in on the election. Donald Trump, of course, led the charge, but the extent to which prominent politicians backed him up is striking. The Republican Accountability Project evaluated comments from all 261 members of Congress to see if they had raised doubts about the election's legitimacy. Two hundred twenty-four had done so. A large majority of Republican House members also voted not to certify the election results. Such behavior was evident at the state level as well. Although the effort failed, *seventeen* Republican attorneys general signed off on a suit to overturn the election results in Wisconsin, Michigan, Georgia, and Pennsylvania. The overwhelming majority of state legislators in Arizona, Pennsylvania, and Wisconsin engaged in efforts to "discredit or overturn" the election results.[7]

This behavior did not fade after January 6. At both the national and state level, Republicans have engaged in widespread defense of Donald Trump, election denial, and efforts to delegitimate the ("weaponized") Department of Justice, FBI, and other legal institutions the GOP did not control. Remarkably, when far-right Republicans brought down the Speakership of Kevin McCarthy in 2023 the Republican caucus replaced him with Mike Johnson. Johnson's most notable prior action as a congressman was to orchestrate an amicus brief, signed by 126 House Republicans, asking the Supreme Court to throw out the 2020 election results from four states. In late 2023, a new biography of Mitt Romney—the GOP's 2012 presidential nominee—quoted the senator as saying that "a very large portion of my party really doesn't believe in the Constitution." Romney maintained that in Trump's post–January 6 impeachment the Senate Republican "caucus sees its job as defending the president, not determining whether he has committed impeachable offenses"[8]

"Semi-loyalist" behavior is sometimes understood as a matter of personal character. True, politicians have to decide whether to make individual sacrifices in defense of democracy, and it is appropriate to judge the choices they make. But when one observes a rapid expansion of the ranks of semi-loyalists in a single party it makes sense to ask whether the structure of incentives, rather than the mix of individual personalities, has changed.

Indeed, that is precisely what has happened. Shifts in mediating institutions have dramatically altered the key structures within which individual politicians make these fateful choices. The incentives to stick with your team have greatly intensified. Under these circumstances, when authoritarian tendencies within the party grow the pressures to act as a semi-loyalist grow as well. Loyalty to the party trumps loyalty to the Constitution.

The easiest way to see this is to recognize that it was the democratic *loyalists* within the GOP, rather than the semi-loyalists, who paid a huge professional price. Eight of the ten House Republicans who voted for the second impeachment resolution were not in office following the next election. One of the two who survived did so only because two Trump-supporting Republicans split the primary vote.

The most prominent to face a brutal backlash for her defection from her partisan team was Liz Cheney. Cheney was a nationally prominent House member, third-ranked in the party leadership. She had coasted to electoral victories in three prior Wyoming elections (in 2020, she won 74 percent of the vote in the Republican primary and 69 percent of the vote in the general election). After January 6, however, she became a prominent democratic loyalist, voting for Trump's impeachment, publicly criticizing him and his defenders for attacking the Constitution, and participating energetically in the January 6 Committee. In response, she was effectively excommunicated from the party.

Censure came from both above and below. The House Republican Conference removed her from her leadership post, replacing her with Elise Stefanik, an outspoken Trump loyalist. In February 2021, the Central Committee of the Wyoming Republican Party voted to no longer recognize her as a Republican. In February 2022 she was censured by the Republican National Committee (RNC), which defended the January 6 participants as engaged in "legitimate political discourse."[9] That August, she was crushed 68–29 percent in Wyoming's Republican primary. It was the second worst primary loss by an incumbent member of Congress in the last sixty years. (Tellingly, the worst was in 2010, when South Carolina's semi-moderate Republican Bob Inglis also fell to the wrath of the party's hard right. He was swamped by a Tea Party challenger, Trey Gowdy).

TEAMSMANSHIP AND THE BREAKDOWN OF HORIZONTAL AND VERTICAL ACCOUNTABILITY

Understanding the connection between teamsmanship and the rise of semi-loyalism provides the necessary backdrop for assessing the distinctive vulnerabilities of the American constitutional order. The argument that the American institutional framework might be unusually vulnerable to democratic backsliding may seem surprising. The view that the US constitutional system's separation of powers and federalism present potent barriers against threats emanating from authoritarian leaders and movements has a long heritage.[10] In contrast to parliamentary systems, which typically aim to protect democratic institutions primarily by encouraging multiparty coalitions, the US system has been premised on the idea that power sharing across institutions with diverse constituencies would restrain actors from behaving in ways that are dangerous to the system's stability. Ambition, as Madison said, must be made to counter ambition.

The political scientist Guillermo O'Donnell termed these institutional arrangements instances of "horizontal accountability," which he saw as one of the two main protections against authoritarianism. The other, "vertical accountability," refers to the check resulting from free and fair elections. "In institutionalized democracies," O'Donnell writes, "accountability runs not only vertically, making elected officials answerable to the ballot box, but also horizontally, across a network of relatively autonomous powers (i.e., other institutions) that can call into question, and eventually punish, improper ways of discharging the responsibilities of a given official."[11]

In the eyes of many observers, the Madisonian framework of checks and balances seems like an ideal system of horizontal accountability. Yet it is acutely vulnerable to nationalized polarization. The transformation of American mediating institutions doesn't just mean that incentives to engage in teamsmanship increase. It means that the entire Madisonian framework functions differently. In a system that fragments political authority and relies on that fragmentation as the principal safeguard for democracy, the pieces no longer fit together in the way they once did.

Most obviously, the rise of teamsmanship means that when forces operating in one part of the political system mount challenges to democratic arrangements it is much less likely than it once was that other institutional actors can and will effectively check such actions. Instead, as the case of Trump following the 2020 election makes clear, teammates may leap to the defense of their copartisan, even if this requires acting as a semi-loyalist or worse. They may block the steps needed for ambition to check ambition. Even if these copartisans do not fully control an institution, they may be able to render it incapable of providing an effective check on democratic backsliding. They may even take active steps to *facilitate* the efforts of their copartisans.

Such a breakdown of checks and balances is in itself a great risk to democracy, but it is not the only risk. A second and related risk pertains to the transformation of elite cue-giving in the constitutional order. The Madisonian system was supposed to create a diversity of information and opinion.[12] Because those situated differently would often have incentives to think and act differently, voters had a chance to receive a variety of cues from sources they considered credible. This offered an important opportunity to learn about the seriousness of antidemocratic behavior. As we will see, when congressional Republicans began to desert Richard Nixon, they didn't just put a system of checks and balances in motion. They also informed *voters* about the seriousness of the charges. With acute partisan contestation, however, the parties begin to behave more monolithically. Voters often become reliant on a narrower and more homogeneous set of cue givers.

This makes it much harder for voters to determine whether charges are serious matters or merely "partisan witch hunts." Highly partisan media strongly reinforces this effect (while also discouraging politicians from defecting from the team). In short, the breakdown of *horizontal* accountability weakens *vertical* accountability—that is, the ability of citizens to use their vote to punish abuses of power.

The increasingly partisan nature of elite cues creates the potential for a dangerously destabilizing feedback loop. Relying on highly partisan sources who stress that the election was stolen, Republican base voters have largely accepted this interpretation. In August 2023 nearly 70 percent of Republicans said that Biden was not the legitimate winner of the 2020 election.[13] Once accepted, such views may have powerful effects. They make it more and more difficult for Republican elites to challenge this belief—further reenforcing the uniformity of partisan elite cues. And they make voters more receptive to democracy challenging appeals. If Democrats are winning by cheating—and then using those victories to pursue policies Republicans fear and loathe—fighting back through every means at your disposal may feel like an act of self-defense.

A third source of vulnerability lies in the fact that the fragmentation of authority can itself be dangerous—especially where it is combined, as it often is in the United States, with partisan control over election administration. As Americans saw in 2020, there were multiple sites where Republicans could potentially have gained leverage to overturn the presidential election results. Shifting the results in just a handful of closely contested states could alter the outcome in a close election—conditions that have held in four out of the last six presidential races. The counter-majoritarian features of many key institutions exacerbate the problem. State legislatures are gerrymandered. Federal judges appointed by partisan teams wield enormous power. Like aging and rickety software, our fractured system of political authority is vulnerable to being hacked by partisan teams. Although few wanted to acknowledge it at the time, there is a good argument that this already happened in the 2000 election. Obstruction of a recount in a single state, backed up by the shakily reasoned five to four Supreme Court decision of five GOP-appointed justices in *Bush v. Gore*, determined the outcome of the election.

Finally, a fourth vulnerability warrants mention; expectations about what is possible have shifted. Social scientists have long noted that part of what makes institutions stable is the *expectation* among important actors that they will be stable. Would-be autocrats hold back in part because they anticipate that others will check their actions, increasing the likelihood that they will fail and pay a high price for having tried. Yet Americans have now seen that many Republicans are prepared to behave as semi-loyalists; that even egregious political behavior may escape punishment; and that it is loyalists, not semi-loyalists or would-be authoritarians, who will pay the price. Knowledge that such checks on attempts at backsliding are less and less likely considerably increases the prospects that such challenges will be launched. Identifying possible tipping points in such a setting is probably impossible until after the fact. But they are far easier to imagine in the United States today than they were even a decade ago.[14]

A Double Asymmetry: Motive and Opportunity

American political institutions were not designed for the political environ-ment we now face. Worse, they exhibit distinct vulnerabilities to those who might hope to seize and entrench power. Still, while "nationalized polariza-tion" describes a general feature of the contemporary environment, the risk of democratic backsliding is more specific; it resides in the contemporary Republican Party. Alarmed by the shifting demography of the nation but ad-vantaged by the nation's counter-majoritarian institutions, the GOP may now possess both the motive and opportunity to embrace the potential for demo-cratic backsliding that resides in the American constitutional order.

We have already discussed some of the factors behind the motive—a heightened sense of grievance and threat, much of it nurtured by powerful forces (especially media) in our now nationalized polity. These trends oper-ate in a nation where demographic and cultural change amplifies the sense of loss and victimization. The rise of Donald Trump was both symptom and driver of these sentiments. In the aftermath of Barack Obama's election as the first Black president, Trump appealed to those who believed that the nation's changing racial composition threatened their power and status.[15] Voters' re-action against broader cultural changes—especially a revolution in gender roles; declining religiosity; and the growing acceptance of previously mar-ginalized groups such as gay, lesbian, and trans Americans—magnified these grievances. The cultural backlash was especially resonant in less dense parts of the country, which have faced growing social dislocations as the national economy has shifted toward a "knowledge economy" anchored in metro area agglomerations and as rapid demographic change has left (older, whiter, less educated) residents of rural and small-town America feeling like "strangers in their own land."[16]

Republicans' relatively homogeneous coalition, combined with a conser-vative media environment that rewards and amplifies appeals to fear and an-ger, created a favorable context for Trump's approach of sharpening racial and cultural divides.[17] The result has been the mainstreaming of the idea within the Republican Party that many Americans are not fully legitimate members of the polity. In the words of Sarah Palin, Trump's rhetorical predecessor in the GOP, they are not part of "real America."

This is the backdrop against which we must understand the rhetorical force of baseless claims that voter fraud is widespread and that the 2020 elec-tion was stolen. Heavily reliant on voters who are receptive to and feel vali-dated by these narratives, many ordinary Republican officeholders have seen it in their interest to support challenges to established norms of restraint and tolerance, the rule of law, and the integrity and autonomy of core democratic institutions.

As Levitsky and Ziblatt argue, another peculiar feature of American institutions reinforces these tendencies. To a degree unmatched in other democracies, the American system involves an extensive set of counter-majoritarian institutions: the Senate, the Supreme Court, and the Electoral College. It also includes electoral districting rules subject to partisan control, allowing electoral minorities to govern legislatures at both the national and state level.[18] Today, *all* these arrangements systematically favor the non-metro-based party—that is, the Republican Party. In practice this further pushes the party's center of gravity toward the extreme.

The emergence of such an incentive structure represents a sharp break from the history of well-established democracies. In multiparty systems a revanchist party might gain strength, but it would have a difficult time forming the multiparty coalition needed to gain power. In such a system centrist parties are likely to remain pivotal. Likewise, in the past, a party operating in a two-party system and facing such demographic and cultural changes might be expected to respond by moderating, reaching out to ascendant groups and pulling back on hot-button racial and social issues. Instead, the transformation of the constitutional order catalyzed by nationalized polarization has changed party incentives. Republicans face increased pressure to translate that sense of victimization into dangerous challenges to democratic institutions. Rather than adapting the party's programs and appeals in response to the signals of a shifting electorate, many in the GOP seem willing to explore opportunities to diminish the ability of voters to remove them from office.

Motive, of course, must be matched with opportunity. As noted earlier, the decentralized and often antiquated structure of American institutions yields vulnerabilities that an increasingly authoritarian-leaning party can exploit. The Electoral College, powerful but potentially partisan courts, state administration of elections, the pardon system—all of these offer points of entry for those who would seek to overturn democratic outcomes and insulate themselves from accountability. The dangers are most obvious with respect to the presidency, but the presence of a would-be authoritarian president is neither necessary nor sufficient for an assault on democracy.

In the remainder of this chapter, we consider multiple pathways to democratic backsliding. Rather than exploring all possible paths, we focus on a few critical ones in some detail. All involve the severe erosion of horizontal accountability. While we begin with the presidency and weakening congressional checks on presidential power, we also explore the threats arising from the states and the courts. We emphasize that the gravest potential for backsliding may emerge from the conjunction of an authoritarian president (or presidential candidate) with state legislatures that reject core democratic values and a court majority that is willing to act as an accomplice.

We say president or presidential candidate because the danger does not lie only in the threat of a sitting president who gradually accumulates power (Viktor Orbán in Hungary). In the context of our antiquated Constitution—which contains numerous bugs that a motivated and coordinated political team holding the necessary levers of power can exploit—even a party that does not hold the presidency could conceivably succeed in breaking the foundations of representative democracy.

In short, when a partisan team increasingly sees majority rule as a threat to core interests there are multiple possible paths to democratic backsliding in the United States. This variety stems from the particular manner in which an unusually fragmented system of political authority and peculiar electoral arrangements interact with a highly polarized and nationalized party system.

Congressional Checks on Presidential Power

We begin our exploration of the various points of vulnerability by contrasting the old and new constitutional orders through a brief historical treatment of congressional oversight. Within the Madisonian system, the strongest institutional check on presidential overreach is Congress. From the earliest days of the republic, Congress has relied heavily upon its investigative power to hold presidents accountable. Investigations—potentially culminating in impeachment—are the one major instrument that Congress can exercise entirely on its own authority.[19] Although presidents have often resisted, the House and Senate have repeatedly turned to their oversight tools to challenge presidential decisions and check executive branch abuses.

One might be tempted to dismiss investigations as mere outlets for political posturing. In fact, congressional inquiries are influential precisely because they take place in front of an audience of voters. Successful investigations typically expose wrongdoing, incompetence, or questionable decisions to the public. Prior studies have shown that investigative oversight systematically reduces the incumbent president's job approval and regularly pressures presidents to adjust their policies and personnel.[20]

Beyond their importance in specific cases of legislative–executive conflict, investigations have been one of the main instruments that members of Congress have used to counter the president's advantages in contests for power. As the single most visible player in the US system, presidents are well-positioned to shape voters' judgments about policy and politics. This advantage contributes to the strong tendency for power to shift over time to the White House. Yet entrepreneurial members of Congress have repeatedly drawn upon investigations as a venue to challenge the president's preferred narrative in the public sphere, competing to shape both voters' and other elites' views.[21] Indeed, congressional oversight hearings played a critical role as Radical Republicans battled against Andrew Johnson's Reconstruction policy in the aftermath of the Civil War, as conservative southern Democrats and Republicans launched a counterattack against New Deal agencies in the late 1930s and 1940s, and, more recently, as senators challenged presidents over Vietnam, Watergate, and intelligence agency abuses in the late 1960s and 1970s. Again and again, aggressive congressional investigations have frustrated presidential efforts to gain mastery over policy and politics. In O'Donnell's terms, horizontal accountability has supported vertical accountability by giving voters important information about presidential abuses.

Today, however, growing partisan teamsmanship seriously undermines congressional oversight and enervates the power of impeachment. It has transformed the politics of both. This is most obvious under conditions where a single party controls both chambers of Congress and the presidency. Under these circumstances, majority party leaders increasingly see it as their job to protect a president of their own party from politically damaging investigations. Yet partisan warfare has also undercut oversight's effectiveness under divided party control. Impactful investigations generally rely upon persuading the public that the president or his team have done something wrong, and this informational mechanism is undercut when investigations are viewed as highly partisan. If congressional members of the president's party remain unified, they can severely damage the perceived legitimacy of oversight even when they are in the minority.

The rise of a nationalized, partisan media has both contributed to and reinforced these dynamics. The decline of "neutral arbiters" in the press means that the main signals that the public receives are likely to come from partisan elites and advocates on either side. As we discussed in chapter 5, this is particularly the case on the political right. Given the strength of Fox News and conservative media, the incentives for Republicans are especially clear. Gaining a reputation as an ardent defender of their own party's president is the path to lavish positive attention on Fox. Pursuing accusations of wrongdoing against a Republican president would generate a tidal wave of negative coverage. By contrast, gaining a reputation for going after a Democratic administration can turn a Republican member into a media celebrity, making it easy to raise campaign funds from the nationalized network of activists and groups.[22] The personal political benefits may accrue to members even when the underlying investigation has little or no substance. These incentives also operate on the Democratic side, but the weight that Democrats attach to mainstream elite news sources—such as CNN, the *New York Times*, and the *Washington Post*—generates a stronger incentive to focus on investigations that are viewed as serious and credible. The same applies to the media itself. Beyond the cost of the settlement with Dominion Voting Systems, Fox News appears to have paid little price for the astonishing revelations about its deceptive coverage of Trump's election fraud accusation—revelations that Fox's own audience probably heard little about. It seems unlikely that a mainstream news outlet could have survived a similar scandal with its reputation and audience intact.

It is thus no surprise that, while changed incentives are evident in both parties, the threat to democratic stability is much greater on the GOP side. Both Democratic and Republican presidents have sought to stretch their power through unilateral action, but the Trump case makes clear that there is a substantial Republican constituency for a president to wield power in ways that challenge basic democratic institutions. The size of that constituency also gives GOP members of Congress multiple incentives to countenance rather than resist a Republican president who uses such tactics. Among those incentives are the intense preferences of the party's interest groups, the heavily "red" electoral bases of these politicians (especially in primaries, where disloyalty is most likely to be punished), and the likelihood that influential partisan media will severely punish defection. Denying everything and attacking the other side becomes a safe strategy, particularly when partisan media is sure to amplify this message and discount alternative narratives. The net result may look like what some have described as "tribalism," but for those valuing political survival, the choice can be firmly grounded in a cold calculation of personal interest rather than emotion or identity.

Of course, partisanship has always been a factor influencing congressional oversight. Shared party ties discouraged members of Congress from policing presidents too closely. Nonetheless, serious oversight was by no means absent in earlier periods of unified government. This was especially true of the Senate, where the volume of investigative activism was far less tied to divided versus unified control throughout the twentieth century, even under conditions of high (but not nationalized) polarization.[23]

In earlier eras, the structure of mediating institutions left a lot of room for the president's copartisans to take on the White House. The relative autonomy of state parties meant that members' career paths were far less dependent on pleasing the national party and its constituencies. Through investigations, members could pursue goals beyond helping their partisan team—reelection, personal power, policy, and defending the institutional standing of Congress. This, in turn, could fuel investigations that attracted bipartisan support, making them hard to dismiss as pure partisan politics.

The New Deal and World War II offer perhaps the clearest example of the ways in which aggressive oversight checked a strong president in the earlier political context. Southern Democrats allied repeatedly with Republicans to launch investigations that targeted the Roosevelt administration and its interest group allies, most notably organized labor. For southern Democrats, the benefits of challenging a copartisan president were substantial, while the costs were low. Their own reelection was not contingent on either the national party's standing or on national leaders' faith that they were "team players." Roosevelt's failed 1938 purge brought home the critical point: In a decentralized party system, winning reelection depended on appealing to locally rooted constituencies, regardless of whether this pleased the president or other national party constituencies.[24]

Liberal and moderate Democrats reinforced the boom in oversight during the late 1930s and 1940s, motivated in part by the concern that too much power had shifted to the White House amid the Depression and war. These members led investigations that boosted their own careers while checking the executive. For example, the Truman Committee investigation of the war effort elevated Harry Truman's national profile while bolstering congressional influence over war production.[25] Critically, even many non-southern Democrats understood that their long-term interests were tied to Congress maintaining its coequal role; these members had the political space to pursue that collective interest with little fear of punishment for "disloyalty."

Importantly, the New Deal era was no aberration. As discussed in chapter 3, the Republican majorities of the first third of the twentieth century repeatedly wrestled with a regionally based faction of progressives willing to undermine the standing of GOP administrations.[26] Progressives, who had their own autonomous bases of local support, including local media, launched a series of investigations, including the high-profile Teapot Dome inquiry into corruption in the Interior and Justice Departments. Administration officials and their allies challenged Congress's authority to compel testimony during these investigations, but the Supreme Court issued landmark decisions upholding Congress's oversight powers in the face of executive resistance.[27] Unified Republican control of Congress—and a conservative Supreme Court—did not prove a serious obstacle to major investigative oversight that damaged the standing of a Republican administration.

The dynamics look quite different in the new constitutional order. With individual members' incentives now tied much more closely to their national party, oversight under unified government has dramatically declined. Copartisans show little appetite for serious oversight even when an administration provides numerous clear targets for investigators. As a result, the majority party uses its control of the committee system to block it.

A comparison of the second Iraq War to World War II is telling. From 1941–45, the Democratic Congress conducted dozens of investigations of the Roosevelt-led war effort, often uncovering lapses in management that directly led to improvements in war production. By contrast, the Republican Congresses of 2003–6 provided very limited oversight of the Iraq War despite the numerous setbacks and shortcomings plaguing the US intervention. Investigative activity—of the war as well as a host of other topics—picked up only when Democrats gained control of Congress in 2007.[28]

One might at least expect vigorous oversight under divided control to provide an effective check on the executive. Polarization does increase the incentives for the majority party to pursue aggressive investigations of an opposing party president. But these investigations bear little resemblance to earlier successful inquiries in which the constructive engagement of members of both parties lent them broad political credibility.

The contrast between the Democratic-led investigations of Donald Trump and two earlier controversial investigations under divided government—Watergate and Iran-Contra—demonstrates the extent to which partisan warfare has undermined the political power of investigations as a congressional check. In each case, die-hard presidential supporters denounced Congress for conducting a "witch hunt."[29] But in both the Watergate and Iran-Contra cases, the presence of significant bipartisan buy-in for the investigations neutralized such claims. In turn, this enabled Congress to push back against serious presidential abuses of power.

The Senate voted unanimously to create the Select Committee on Presidential Activities (which became known as the Ervin Committee) in February 1973 to investigate the Watergate break-in and any other "illegal, improper, or unethical conduct" during the 1972 presidential campaign. Even as most Republicans stuck with President Nixon, consequential fissures emerged as evidence of misconduct mounted. For example, following a series of troubling disclosures about Nixon's actions after the break-in, Senator Charles Percy (R-IL) demanded in spring 1973 that an independent special prosecutor be appointed.[30] When Nixon fired Special Prosecutor Archibald Cox in the October 1973 Saturday Night Massacre, Senator Ed Brooke (R-MA) called on the president to resign.[31]

With Republicans sending mixed signals about the investigation and the press providing wall-to-wall coverage of the scandal, Nixon's approval rating declined precipitously across partisan groups. Nixon's approval among Republicans plummeted from the 80–90 percent range to under 60 percent by fall 1973, and then dropped to about 50 percent in spring 1974; meanwhile, the president's approval among Independents fell to below 30 percent by the end of 1973.[32] Against this backdrop, one-third of the Republicans on the House Judiciary Committee voted for articles of impeachment. Realizing that he no longer had sufficient Republican support to survive an impeachment trial, Nixon resigned.

In the Iran-Contra case, the House and Senate voted overwhelmingly in January 1987 to create special select committees to investigate the arms-for-hostages deal.[33] The ten-month inquiry featured dramatic partisan fireworks, yet the willing Republican participation signaled to the Reagan administration that it could not simply stonewall. Instead, the administration established clear protocols for handling and viewing classified materials, releasing more than three thousand documents to investigators. The joint House and Senate committee report was signed by all fifteen Democrats and three of the five Senate Republicans. It was sharply critical of the administration, arguing that a "cabal of zealots" had taken a series of actions that threatened the rule of law. The remaining two Senate Republicans and all five House Republicans signed a minority report claiming that the majority had adopted a "hysterical" tone. Strikingly, the vice-chair of the Senate committee, Warren Rudman (R-NH) criticized his Republican colleagues' minority report, remarking that "I think the minority evidently believes that Republicans don't want the truth laid out. My Republican constituents want the truth laid out."[34] With the investigation generating a string of embarrassing revelations, President Reagan's political standing took a significant hit. His approval rating fell from 63 percent before news of the scandal broke to the 45–50 percent range.

Notably, Reagan's approval among Republicans, Democrats, and Independents slipped by similar margins, indicating that the investigation resonated beyond Reagan's partisan enemies.[35] A weakened Reagan lost a number of political battles during this period, including veto showdowns over the Clean Water Act and a highway reauthorization bill. The Senate also rejected Reagan's nomination of Robert Bork for the Supreme Court (with six Republicans joining all fifty-two Democrats in voting no).

Like Watergate, Iran-Contra underscores the ways in which Congress used investigations to check the most egregious presidential abuses of power. In each instance, a degree of bipartisan collaboration—even against a backdrop of substantial partisan maneuvering—enabled the investigations to fulfill an important public opinion–shaping role and to exert pressure on the administration. But that was then.

President Trump and the Collapse of Horizontal Accountability

The Trump administration provided a formidable stress test for American political institutions. From the start, President Trump supplied ample material for would-be investigators, ranging from apparent conflicts of interest, questionable business dealings, the aggressive use of executive orders on immigration and other issues, and possible campaign collusion with Russia. His decision to fire several Inspector Generals from Cabinet departments removed a traditionally independent check on executive branch mismanagement and misconduct, putting even greater onus on Congress to take its oversight role seriously.[36] With precious few exceptions, congressional Republicans responded by resisting calls for congressional scrutiny and instead defending the administration.

A telling moment came soon after Trump took office. A week before an election that Trump was expected to lose, House Oversight and Government Reform Committee Chairman Jason Chaffetz (R-UT) characterized his committee as "the tip of the spear" and described Hillary Clinton as offering "a target-rich environment." When Clinton unexpectedly lost, Chaffetz announced his retirement. Republican strategists observed that "Chaffetz is just bored with his job . . . it probably would have been a lot more fun for this Tea Party–leaning Republican to investigate Hillary Clinton's government than President Trump's."[37] Investigating Clinton would have brought Chaffetz weeks of positive coverage on conservative media; serious oversight of Trump would only bring unwanted attention. So Chaffetz, just reelected, quit. His new employer? Fox News.

House Intelligence Committee Chair Devin Nunes (R-CA) approached the Russia scandal in a way that also makes clear how ambitious Republicans viewed the politics of investigating President Trump. From the start, Nunes assiduously sought to shift blame and attention away from the White House. Nunes collaborated with White House officials' efforts to turn the scandal into a story about the Obama administration's unmasking of surveillance targets and the Hillary Clinton campaign's role in generating the Christopher Steele dossier on candidate Trump's ties to Russia. Nunes pushed forward a Republican staff memo attacking the FBI for allegedly relying on "politically motivated or questionable sources" to obtain the surveillance warrant against Trump adviser Carter Page.[38] Democratic pleas for more serious scrutiny of the Trump campaign and the White House's ties to Russia were rebuffed, as the GOP unceremoniously ended the House Intelligence Committee investigation in March 2018. The Republican majority report—adopted with no Democratic support—not only fully exonerated the president and his team, it went so far as to question the intelligence community's conclusion that Russian interference was designed to aid the Trump campaign.

Nunes's fundraising success in the wake of his ardent defense of Trump underscored the political benefits of loyalty, with one Republican consultant noting "if you've got the attention of the grassroots—particularly if you're investigating the president or defending him—it's a smart investment to make."[39] While Nunes offers the most extreme counterpoint to Madison's formula of ambition checking ambition—eventually resigning from Congress to become the CEO of the Trump Media and Technology Group—he was far from alone among Republicans in identifying his interests closely with the president's goals.

Democrats dramatically increased congressional investigative activity after they took over the House following the 2018 election. The Democratic-led investigations generated revelations that rivaled or exceeded the most egregious offenses uncovered in Watergate or Iran-Contra. The most important concerned President Trump's threat to withhold congressionally appropriated aid from Ukraine unless its government promised to investigate Joe Biden and his son Hunter. Nonetheless, congressional Republicans were unified in standing behind the president, blunting the investigation's ultimate impact. The bipartisan collaboration and presidential cooperation evident in the Iran-Contra case was nowhere to be found. Instead, Trump and his team understood that if their party stayed on the same page in dismissing serious investigations as mere partisan witch hunts—regardless of the evidence—voters would be unlikely to update their views.

Teamsmanship empowered Trump to embrace a strategy of all-out resistance that undercut Congress's ability to fulfill its constitutional responsibilities. The president declared in April 2019 that his administration would not comply with *any* subpoenas issued by the Democratic House, bragging that "we're fighting all the subpoenas."[40] Following the president's directive, administration officials routinely defied subpoenas and committee requests for information. In past showdowns over executive resistance to congressional requests for information, at least some members of the president's party typically stood up for congressional prerogatives.[41] But with Republicans lined up behind President Trump, there was little political pressure to concede Congress's authority to seek information regarding executive branch decision-making. The result was thoroughgoing resistance, abetted by the sluggishness of the courts.

THE TWO IMPEACHMENTS OF DONALD TRUMP

Trump's refusal to abide by conventional restraints on presidential abuses culminated in the battles surrounding his impeachments in 2019–20 and in the aftermath of the January 6, 2021, insurrection. House Democrats opened an impeachment inquiry in September 2019 following emergence of allegations regarding Trump's pressure on the Ukrainian government. Although the Constitution explicitly gives the House "the sole power of impeachment," White House counsel Pat Cipollone declared that President Trump "cannot permit his administration to participate in this partisan inquiry in any way."[42] The president ordered current and former officials to defy congressional subpoenas and to refuse to appear before the House committee. Although a handful of current and former officials chose to disregard the administration's guidance, nearly all of the investigators' top targets refused to testify.[43]

The administration's recalcitrance posed a clear threat to Congress's long-established constitutional role. Yet House Republicans lined up unanimously behind the president, placing their interest in defending him above their commitment to congressional prerogatives. At one point, a group led by Minority Whip Steve Scalise (R-LA) stormed a closed-door hearing to demand greater access to the proceedings and opportunities to defend the president.[44] Not a single House Republican voted in favor of impeachment, a sharp contrast to the one-third of Judiciary Committee Republicans who voted to impeach Nixon.

When the trial moved to the Senate, one might have expected the Republicans in control of the chamber to show greater independence. After all, in the more individualistic Senate, investigations had historically been nearly as common under unified control as divided government. Instead, Majority Leader McConnell led a nearly perfectly unified Republican conference. They turned back efforts to call witnesses despite revelations from former National Security Adviser John Bolton's forthcoming book, which directly linked President Trump to the decision to withhold aid until Ukraine announced an investigation into Joe Biden. Bolton offered to testify before the Senate if he were subpoenaed, but McConnell held all but two Republicans in line behind Trump, blocking Democrats' bid to have Bolton testify.[45] In the end, Mitt Romney was the only Republican to vote to convict the president. Moreover, Senate Republicans' refusal to push back against the president's war on Congress's investigative power set a potentially significant precedent.

An equally striking feature of the 2019–20 Trump impeachment saga is that the president's approval rating did not drop—and perhaps even increased modestly—over the course of the investigation.[46] This underscores the extent to which all-out partisan warfare short-circuits the public opinion–shaping role of investigations. Again, the breakdown of horizontal accountability damaged vertical accountability. With essentially every Republican official lining up behind the president, it was easy for GOP-leaning voters to conclude that the investigation was motivated solely by Democratic partisanship. The contrast with Nixon's impeachment is again telling; in the earlier case, mounting revelations of misconduct gradually sapped support for him among both Republican elites and voters. By contrast, President Trump's first impeachment trial raised doubts as to whether *any* possible action of Trump's could lead a substantial number of Senate Republicans to vote to convict.

These imaginative limits were soon tested. In the aftermath of the 2020 election, President Trump's refusal to accept the results and his promotion of a large rally to object to Congress's counting of the Electoral College results led to a violent attack on the US Capitol on January 6, 2021, temporarily disrupting Congress's constitutional duty. The insurrection followed weeks of pressure from Trump on state election officials and on Vice President Mike Pence to overturn the decision of American voters. In taking these actions, Trump had undermined the peaceful transfer of power following an election, a democratic foundation Americans had taken for granted.

It is hard to think of a more direct assault on American democracy. Indeed, the immediate response to January 6 suggested that Trump had finally gone so far that even congressional Republicans would abandon him. Senate Leader McConnell declared that night that the Congress "will not be kept out of this chamber by thugs, mobs, or threats," decrying the "failed insurrection" as an effort to "disrupt our democracy."[47] In the days following the insurrection, McConnell's allies privately indicated that he would seriously consider voting to convict Trump if the House impeached him a second time.[48]

But within a few days, the strong pull of teamsmanship reasserted itself. It quickly became clear to Republicans that state and local activists and ordinary Republican partisans were largely sticking with the defeated president. In a highly nationalized and polarized party system, Trump could count on the intense loyalty of activists throughout the US. This in turn ensured the near-unanimous, continued loyalty of House Republicans. Ultimately, just ten House Republicans voted to impeach Trump.

McConnell quickly read the tea leaves among Republicans nationally and in his own caucus. Although remaining critical of Trump's actions, he voted against conviction, citing the fact that Trump was no longer in office. Remarkably, even figures like Vice President Pence, whose life was quite clearly in danger as a result of Trump's actions, offered only muted criticism. In the end, just seven Senate Republicans voted to convict. As a result, Trump evaded the main punishment that conviction could have brought about: a bar on his running for national office again. This stark display of semi-loyalty signaled that for the GOP even the most extreme actions undermining constitutional government would no longer overcome partisan solidarity. Instead, as previously described, the Republicans facing negative consequences were the handful of members who broke with their party, insisting on accountability for the former president. The intense pressure coming from all levels of the party—local, state, and national—brings home the extent to which contemporary polarization subjects officeholders to a powerful common set of incentives regardless of regional or local differences.

The irony of the Trump impeachment trials, coming on the heels of the Clinton impeachment in 1998–99, is that the impeachment power may now become a routine tool of politics while at the same time losing its political teeth.[49] With such high partisan loyalty, impeachment may not only have lost its capacity to remove a president for misconduct, but even its ability to influence the public. When the congressional politics of investigations appears to be—and at times has become—nothing more than another manifestation of teamsmanship, there is little basis for voters to revise their beliefs. In that context, it is much less likely that investigations will fulfill their crucial role in maintaining separation of powers and checking presidential abuses.

Stepping back, the Trump case underscores one of the most troubling consequences of the transformations of the constitutional order. Congress's ability to restrain a corrupt, demagogic president has always depended on informal tools—such as the use of investigations that shape public and elite opinion—with the impeachment power looming as a final source of redress if all else fails. Partisan teamsmanship has long been a resource that presidents could draw upon in resisting congressional scrutiny, but it had always been a limited resource that had to compete with other considerations. Trump ratcheted up what it means for a member of Congress to "stick with their team." Drawing on his hold over conservative media and ordinary voters, he induced congressional Republicans to defend actions that, in earlier eras, would have been beyond the pale. The Trump case demonstrates that the absence of horizontal and vertical accountability can be self-reinforcing. Congressional Republicans' refusal to hold Trump accountable was rooted in incentives created by the party base (and associated media structures), and then that same refusal deprived voters of cues that could, in principle, change minds. And a would-be authoritarian aware of these changed incentives may feel free to act in ways that a more resilient constitutional order would have deterred.

Federalism and Democratic Backsliding

Concerns about democratic backsliding have typically focused on a potentially authoritarian president. Nonetheless, it is an oversimplification to see the threat to democracy as only originating from the White House. Spurred on by national conservative advocacy groups, such as the American Legislative Exchange Council (ALEC), Republican-controlled state legislatures have engaged in aggressive deck-stacking strategies in recent years that have made it harder for Democratic-leaning constituencies to vote and, in some cases, locked in GOP majorities even when the party loses the popular vote by a wide margin. A series of court rulings—each along partisan lines with all of the Democratic-appointed justices dissenting—have enabled these tactics by eviscerating the Voting Rights Act (VRA) and removing the threat of federal court intervention to restrain partisan gerrymandering.

As concerning as these actions are, the reaction to President Trump's false claims of election fraud in the 2020 election has taken the danger to a new level. Republican officeholders openly began to strategize about disqualifying ballots and setting aside the popular vote results in their state. Several Supreme Court justices appeared willing to endorse a doctrine—one virtually unheard of prior to the Trump-induced controversies surrounding the 2020 election—that would allow legislatures to carry out such a plan. If adopted, it could have stymied the peaceful transfer of power in a future presidential election, with devastating consequences for democratic governance.

Recent events thus suggest that the risks are broad and the sites of potential destabilization diverse. Trump's attacks on the integrity of elections were not just an immediate threat. They both revealed additional weak points in the Madisonian order and inspired state-level initiatives with clear potential to derail democratic institutions, even in the absence of an incumbent Republican president.

Analyzing the different forms that democratic backsliding takes around the world, Nancy Bermeo finds that gradual erosion is more common than the sudden transformation into a non-democracy.[50] Developments at the state level in the US, along with the behavior of the court's Republican-appointed majority, suggest that such a process of degeneration may well be underway.

Ironically, the two sites of vulnerability explored in the remainder of this chapter—federalism and the courts—are ones often heralded as key democracy-protecting features of the Constitution. Like the separation of powers that operates at the national level, federalism is often seen as an additional protector of horizontal accountability. Even when one party is ascendant at the national level, differences among the nation's states ensures that the opposition party will control important sites of political power. More fundamentally, those differences have been expected to amplify the diversity of both *interests* and *information* across a continent-spanning polity.[51] Both these qualities could be expected to provide checks against concentrations of power that might threaten democratic arrangements. As explored earlier, nationalization and polarization have muted these diversity-generating features of American federalism. In this new context, the system of decentralized authority has instead become a potential source of backsliding.

The threat to democratic stability emerging at the state level is rooted in developments that precede Donald Trump's rise to power, but the danger has reached a new level in the wake of his attacks on the legitimacy of elections. Again, it is essential to note that the motivation to undermine democracy stems from many Republicans' belief that Democratic constituencies are not full members of the American community, and that these groups' expanded political power and participation threatens values they associate with America.[52] Republicans' opportunity to act on this belief depends on the party's geographic advantages, a right-wing media landscape that incentivizes hardball tactics, and the capacity of a partisan team to initiate and support aggressive actions across a range of crucial political venues.

The resulting antidemocratic policies are not simply the disconnected products of dynamics emerging in individual states. Instead, national networks of advocates, lawmakers, and activists have pushed similar policies across the states, with the twin goals of making it easier to win within each state and deploy that control to influence the national contest for power. Claims of voter fraud, for example, draw upon the scripts of national party leaders, such as Newt Gingrich and Trump, and echoed throughout the conservative media. The Supreme Court has played an essential role in granting states wide latitude to enact policies that shift the electoral playing field in Republicans' favor, often at the expense of marginalized groups.[53] Meanwhile, congressional gridlock has stood in the way of efforts to enact national standards that might limit the scope of state-level democratic backsliding.

Two sets of election-related policies have been particularly prominent fronts in partisan battles: gerrymandering and provisions that make it harder to vote.[54] When it comes to gerrymandering, both parties have long demonstrated an eagerness to stack the deck in their favor. State legislatures governed by one party have routinely used their control of the drawing of district lines to improve their chances of holding their majority. They have also sought to boost their party's chances in congressional races. However, as the battle for majority control in the US House of Representatives has heated up since the 1990s, the gerrymandering battles have become increasingly focused on the national contest for power.

A key development occurred in Texas in 2001, when House Majority Whip Tom DeLay organized a political action committee (PAC) to help the GOP gain majority control of the Texas House of Representatives, with the goal of redrawing the state's congressional districts to boost their party's slim majority in Washington. The plan succeeded after Republicans gained a majority in the legislature in the 2002 elections. It had been rare for legislatures to redistrict in between censuses. Signaling a new willingness to ignore traditional restraints, DeLay and his allies enacted a plan that resulted in a five-seat gain for the congressional GOP.[55]

A few years later, the 2010 pro-Republican election wave provided the party with control of redistricting in numerous closely divided states. Republican legislatures used this electoral swing to lock in their majorities at home while enhancing the GOP edge in US House districts. Republicans in the battleground states of Michigan, North Carolina, Ohio, Pennsylvania, and Wisconsin—along with Democrats in Maryland, where they enjoyed control—drew lines that aggressively maximized partisan advantage.[56] The resulting district lines gave Republicans a substantial advantage in the battle for House control for the rest of the decade.[57] Democrats responded in 2016 by founding the National Democratic Redistricting Committee; led by former Attorney General Eric Holder, the organization sought to coordinate the party's effort to gain more favorable redistricting outcomes following the 2020 election.[58] Again, rather than separate efforts following distinctive local political currents in fifty states, the politics of gerrymandering today is enmeshed in the national battle for advantage.

The opportunities to engage in aggressive gerrymanders are considerably greater on the Republican side. This Republican edge is partly a result of favorable geography, because the concentration of Democratic voters in big cities makes for more "wasted votes" among Democrats across a wide range of districting plans.[59] However, the GOP's control of a greater number of state legislatures in the year following the census has boosted the party's advantage in recent cycles.

This in turn has allowed those legislators to entrench their control. Wisconsin offers a telling example. Under the lines drawn following the 2010 census, Republicans faced virtually no risk of losing control of either branch of the legislature. Even amid Democrats' 2018 wave, when the party won 53 percent of all assembly votes cast statewide, it won just 36 percent of the seats.[60] With Republicans still in the majority following the 2020 election—in part due to the prior biased map—they were able to perpetuate their gerrymander for another decade. Under the Wisconsin maps adopted for 2022–30, if both parties win 50 percent of the vote, the GOP is expected to win 62 percent of the seats in the assembly and 65 percent in the state senate. Democrats barely prevented the GOP from winning a veto-proof supermajority in the legislature in the 2022 election, despite holding their own in the statewide popular vote and winning the governor's race. Republicans also hold an edge in six of the state's eight congressional districts.[61] Tellingly, it was the Democrats' victory in a Wisconsin Supreme Court election in 2023—a race decided by a simple majority—that opened the door to a successful legal challenge of the GOP gerrymander in the state, leading to new, more competitive state district lines for the 2024 contest.[62]

Equally important, Democratic states have proven more willing to impose limitations on their legislatures' redistricting power than have Republican states. The use of nonpartisan commissions to draw lines in California (fifty-two seats) and Colorado (eight seats) limits Democrats' ability to maximize their seat share through gerrymanders, while Arizona (nine seats) was the only GOP-controlled state where an independent commission drew the lines.[63] The disparity in the use of commissions, combined with Republicans' control of more state legislatures, meant that the GOP controlled the process of drawing congressional districts in twenty states (187 seats), while Democrats controlled it in eight states (seventy-five seats) for this most recent cycle.[64]

Ironically, state-level fairness, when applied unevenly across red and blue areas, results in a more serious national imbalance. Liberal courts in Democratic-leaning states have proven more willing to rein in biased gerrymanders than have GOP-controlled courts. Democratic gerrymanders in both New York and Maryland were thrown out by state courts, greatly reducing Democrats' advantage. (Following the replacement of a swing member in 2023, however, the New York court gave Democrats a second chance to draw a gerrymandered map, which could net the party additional seats).[65] By contrast, in the few cases in which state courts have stood in the way of GOP gerrymanders—as in Florida and Ohio in 2022—their decisions were either overturned by the state supreme court (Florida), or by a federal court (Ohio). With a Democratic majority, the North Carolina Supreme Court overturned a Republican gerrymander in the state in 2022. However, when Republicans reclaimed a majority on the court in January 2023, it overturned the redistricting decisions, leading to a new GOP gerrymander.[66]

In the end, the 2021–22 redistricting cycle solidified Republicans' advantage. Christopher Warshaw, Eric McGhee, and Michal Migurski conclude that "the combination of Republicans' control of the redistricting process in far more states than Democrats and the inefficient concentration of Democrats in cities has enabled Republicans to largely maintain an advantage in the translation of votes to seats in both Congress and many state legislatures."[67] Nathaniel Rakich estimates that at the end of the process, 208 congressional districts lean Republican by 5 or more percentage points, compared to 187

Democratic-leaning districts, while the number of highly competitive seats (forty) declined from its already low levels.[68] The median House district following the 2020 redistricting cycle is more Republican than the nation as a whole, as measured by presidential vote (that is, Republicans' presidential vote share in the median House district is approximately 2.4 percent points higher than their overall popular vote share).[69]

The asymmetric partisan hardball evident in redistricting is also shaping state policies regarding voting rights and election administration. State governments have played a critical role throughout US history in both the expansion and retraction of suffrage rights. The widespread disenfranchisement of Black voters across southern states after Reconstruction stands out as an enormously consequential example of democratic backsliding implemented by state governments. Then as now, these states were backstopped by the Supreme Court. In the post-Reconstruction era, Democratic-controlled legislatures and state constitutional conventions capitalized on the Supreme Court's narrow interpretations of the Fourteenth and Fifteenth Amendments to rein in the gains Black citizens won in the aftermath of the Civil War.

A key difference between state-level backsliding in the late nineteenth century and backsliding today is that the earlier southern authoritarian enclaves were, in the words of Robert Mickey, "indigenous." Although enabled by Supreme Court rulings and southerners' influence in Congress, "the *reason* they emerged, and remained so durable, was that political–economic interests [i.e., large landowners] dominated their state parties."[70] By contrast, the antidemocratic push in the states today "is a *national* movement with *national* actors who happen to act *subnationally*," with Republican state legislators "prodded and supported by nationally coordinated networks of office seekers, activists, and donors."[71] Republican-controlled states that differ greatly in their political economies, cultures, and histories—such as North Carolina and Wisconsin—have adopted similar laws in the wake of this national network's push, often with an eye to these policies' implications for the national balance of power.[72]

Indeed, interventions to stack the deck politically generally have been greatest in the states where Republican political prospects are most uncertain. There, the stakes are potentially massive. Taking political control can mean tilting both policy results (such as undercutting labor unions) and the national political balance. Victories open up new gerrymandering possibilities and could tilt outcomes in the Electoral College.

A noteworthy example is ALEC's work spearheading the movement for strict voter identification laws since the early 2000s.[73] The group enjoyed its first successes in the non-southern states of Arizona (2004), Indiana (2005),

Wisconsin (2011), and Ohio (2011). The Supreme Court's *Shelby County* ruling (2013) lifted a key obstacle to such laws in southern states, which had been subject to "preclearance" rules that stood in the way of measures making it harder to vote. In the aftermath of *Shelby County*, strict voter ID laws that disproportionately affect minority voters have gone into effect in Arkansas, Georgia, Mississippi, and Alabama.[74] Republican-controlled states have also increasingly turned to limits on early voting and absentee balloting, while in some cases reducing the number of polling places.[75] A number of such states have imposed onerous regulatory burdens on groups that seek to register voters. The impact of these policies on voter turnout has thus far proven to be more limited than many feared—arguably in part because they generate a countermobilization among those whose rights are threatened. Yet they impose costs on individual voters and force advocacy groups to devote their resources to helping citizens navigate the additional obstacles. This means that the impact of these laws could grow over time.[76] Alongside gerrymandering, these policies threaten to allow political minorities to use temporary election wins to entrench their power.

President Trump's false claims of voter fraud in the 2020 election built upon the longer-term campaign by ALEC and other groups, backed relentlessly by right-wing media, to cast doubt on the integrity of elections. These doubts have been used to justify the enactment of legal changes ostensibly targeting fraud but in reality making it harder for Democratic constituencies to vote. Indeed, claims of a stolen election have ushered in new potential threats of democratic backsliding. Trump's refusal to acknowledge his defeat pushed these longer-term developments into dangerous new territory with his calls for state legislatures to refuse to certify Joe Biden's victory.

The *New York Times* found that at least 357 sitting Republican legislators in nine battleground states—44 percent of all GOP legislators in those states— have used their power to discredit or attempt to overturn the 2020 election.[77] For many Republicans, fealty to Trump's election lies—and the willingness to use those lies as a basis to challenge Democratic election victories—has become a test of party loyalty. State parties have gone so far as to endorse platform planks denying the 2020 election results, with Texas Republicans declaring in June 2022 that "we reject the certified results of the 2020 presidential election, and we hold that acting President Joseph Robinette Biden Jr. was not legitimately elected by the people of the United States."[78]

The possibility of Republican state election officials and legislatures setting aside a clear decision of their voters is no longer outside the set of plausible outcomes in a close presidential election. The groundwork for such an assault is being laid at the state and local level by a range of candidates and

officeholders responding to messages from the former president and his allies in conservative media. A clear majority of the party's nominees for the
House, Senate, and key statewide offices (e.g., governor, attorney general, and
secretary of state) in the 2022 midterm had denied or questioned the 2020
presidential outcome.[79] For example, in the swing state of Nevada, Republicans nominated Jim Marchant, a leader of the "America First Secretary of
State Coalition" to be in charge of administering the state's election. Marchant had peddled conspiracy theories about the 2020 results and declared he
would not have certified Biden's victory in the state. In Pennsylvania, the GOP
nominated Doug Mastriano for governor, who declared "I get to appoint the
secretary of state, who's delegated from me the power to make corrections
to elections, the voting logs, and everything. . . . I could decertify every machine in the state with the stroke of a pen."[80] Marchant was defeated by a
2 percent margin, while Mastriano fell far short in Pennsylvania. The failure
of election-denying candidates in a number of swing states averted a worst-
case scenario heading into the 2024 presidential race and indicated that there
is at least some electoral cost to nominating such candidates. Nonetheless,
more than 170 election-denying nominees emerged victorious, and several
others running in swing states were defeated by slim margins, suggesting that
considerable risk remains.[81]

The interplay between national strategists and local activists is especially
important in driving the challenge to democratic elections. RNC staff un-
rolled a detailed plan in 2022 for challenging voters in Democratic precincts.
The plan relied in part on recruiting party activists as poll workers, many of
whom were believers in Donald Trump's lies about the 2020 election. These
workers could disrupt polling places, which would then serve as the basis to
reject vote counts. The RNC also has sought to create a "nationwide district
attorney network" to push legal challenges and to stack canvassing boards
with committed activists. As the leader of the election watchdog group Issue One noted, "this is completely unprecedented in the history of American
elections that a political party would be working at this granular level to put
a network together."[82]

The combination of nationalization and polarization has enabled Republicans to embrace a far-reaching strategy at the state and local level that
has clear potential to disrupt future elections. By stacking county canvassing
boards and selecting hard-core partisans for other key posts administering
elections, the GOP has made moves that pose serious risks to the democratic
process.[83]

The most important "prize" for this strategy is the presidency. Throw-
ing the vote count into doubt would position state legislatures to certify the

Republican candidate as the recipient of their state's electoral votes even if in fact the Democrat received a majority of the ballots cast. Ultimately, the validity of those electors might be judged in the House of Representatives. There, voting based on state delegations provides Republicans with a decisive advantage. Had the House been asked to adjudicate the 2020 election, as Donald Trump hoped, California's fifty-two members would have had as much say as Wyoming's single member. And while Democrats held the majority of House seats, Republicans held the majority in twenty-six delegations, compared to the Democrats' twenty-two (Pennsylvania and Michigan had evenly split delegations).

The Courts and Democratic Backsliding

The plausibility of many of these dangers depends on the acquiescence or support of the Supreme Court. There are increasing signs that the court, as currently constituted, might well accept that supportive role. Indeed, the transformation of the court, which as discussed in chapter 6 has profoundly impacted American governance, has equally significant implications for the risks of democratic instability.

The court and its defenders have long insisted that it effectively resists the politics of teamsmanship—simply "calling balls and strikes" in the words of the current chief justice. And as in other areas of politics, the court often exemplified a kind of bipartisan politics through the 1980s, giving credence to the idea that federal judges were experts standing aside from partisan politics. But the ideological vetting of judges has ramped up dramatically since the 1990s, and today's Republican appointees are reliably far to the right of Democratic appointees.

The transition to a highly polarized court, where justices have been carefully groomed and their appointments often fiercely contested, adds to the fragility of American democracy. The risks are two-fold. The first is that a court majority supporting its "team" may make a series of decisions that gradually tilt competition in favor of one party. The second is that, at a decisive moment of political instability, the court's majority may choose to support its party patrons rather than operate as an effective check. As in our discussion of Congress and the states, the risk is that which team you are on, rather than where you sit, will determine where you stand.

Indeed, going back to Bush v. Gore, a series of important court decisions has had significant effects on political competition—all of them dividing liberal justices from conservative ones, and virtually all of them widely seen as favoring the political interests of Republicans over Democrats. *Citizens United v. FEC* (2010) made it harder to regulate corporate campaign spending. The same year, *Shelby County v. Holder* eviscerated key provisions of the VRA, encouraging Republican-controlled states to introduce a wave of new restrictions on voting. *Janus v. AFSCME* (2018) hindered the organizing efforts of unions, a key part of the Democrats' coalition. *Rucho v. Common Cause* (2019) made it clear that the federal courts would play no role in policing partisan gerrymanders, paving the way for ever more aggressive maneuvering. All of these decisions have advantaged Republicans and backstopped the partisan efforts in multiple states discussed in the previous section. Indeed, legal scholar Aziz Huq concludes from these court decisions that "the prospect of a permanent governing minority for the twenty-first century runs on judicially fashioned rails."[84]

There is no reason for confidence that this gradual process will not go further. A particularly alarming case heard in 2022, *Moore v. Harper*, threatened to intensify the partisan imbalance. Four Supreme Court justices had already suggested they might support the so-called independent state legislature doctrine, which would remove state courts' ability to check the actions of state legislatures in federal elections. Conservative activists began the push to impose the doctrine as part of their efforts to challenge laws creating independent redistricting commissions or otherwise restricting gerrymandering. Election law expert Rick Hasen noted that it would also "provide a pathway . . . to subvert the election outcomes expressing the will of the people."[85] Under this doctrine, there would be no legal recourse if a state legislature unilaterally decided to award electoral votes to the "losing" candidate. In its 2023 bipartisan decision a six to three majority of the Supreme Court rejected this extreme version of the independent state legislature doctrine—but at the same time it signaled that the court reserved to itself the authority to step in if it found a state court's intervention to be unsound.

In scenarios involving a contested state election result, Congress would retain the authority to resolve disputes. But the changes described previously in congressional politics, particularly Republican members' willingness to engage in hardball tactics in support of a demagogic leader, raise doubts that Congress would exert an effective check. As we have noted, a majority of the Republican House caucus both signed an amicus brief adopting the unprecedented position that the 2020 electoral votes of four states should be thrown out and voted (hours after the January 6 insurrection) to sustain objections to the electoral count in one or more states.[86] With a more coordinated, thorough effort at the local, state, and national level looming for future elections, it is quite plausible that a Republican-controlled Congress would accept the GOP electors selected by a legislature even if the evidence makes clear the Democratic candidate won more votes. The implications of such a scenario for the future of American democracy are nothing short of dire.

Would concern for the long-term fate of American institutions deter a sufficient number of Republicans from taking this momentous step? Possibly, but the risk that they will not has clearly grown. Several Republican county and state election officials acted as democratic loyalists in the aftermath of the 2020 election, standing up against Trump's pressure. These individuals were subjected to death threats—as well as political reprisals. Georgia Secretary of State Bradley Raffensperger survived a Republican primary challenge in 2022, but many other officials decided to withdraw from politics in the wake of the onslaught. Simply staffing election administration offices is becoming a challenge, particularly in rural counties where Trump-aligned advocates insist on the validity of conspiracy theories regarding voter fraud.[87]

The extensive pressure campaign against election officials adds to the worrying signs that many party activists and officials no longer view democracy itself as a core value. Grumbach demonstrates that Republican control of state government has, in the past two decades, become associated with democracy-eroding policies.[88] These initiatives have only become bolder since the 2020 election. A handful of state platforms have endorsed the creation of state-level electoral colleges that would replace the "one person, one vote" principle for electing statewide officers with a system that privileges rural areas. In other cases, state parties have removed references to "democratic" in their platforms, preferring instead to refer to the US as a republic.[89] If democracy means that the Democrats will win power, some Republican activists and officials evidently would be willing to sacrifice democracy.

The new constitutional order greatly increases the risks of democratic backsliding. When our parties were decentralized and our politics exhibited multiple overlapping cleavages, the structure of American political institutions offered considerable (if imperfect) protections.[90] Today those circumstances no longer hold. Indeed, under current conditions our peculiar political institutions amplify the danger. The fragmented (and often antiquated) features of the Constitution create plentiful opportunities for mischief. For instance, the peculiar structure of the Electoral College potentially empowers a handful of state legislatures to determine the outcome in a close national election. The danger is compounded if national institutions like the Supreme Court or the House of Representatives cannot be counted upon to effectively check such activities.

Our Constitution was not built to withstand nationalized partisan polarization, particularly when important elements in one of the two major national parties no longer view it as legitimate when the other side wins elections. The urgent question is whether there are feasible pathways that could move US politics away from this dangerous terrain. We take up that challenge in the concluding chapter.

8

What's Next

Our inherited political institutions are a poor fit for a fully nationalized and polarized two-party system. That combination gives rise to political incentives that promote dysfunction, limit accountability, and severely weaken government's capacity to address pressing societal problems. Even more worrisome, nationalized partisan polarization exposes previously overlooked fragilities in the fabric of American democracy itself. The specifically Madisonian guardrails against democratic backsliding (separation of powers, territorially based representation, and federalism) no longer provide secure checks against abuse. Indeed, the system's unusual allocations of authority (e.g., partisan election officials in the states, the Electoral College, a Supreme Court that is both extremely powerful and vulnerable to partisan capture) provide considerable opportunities for those abuses to endanger democratic governance.

In this conclusion, we consider the prospects for improving governance, accountability, and democratic stability. As we have argued, the most serious challenges to American democracy emanate from the contemporary Republican Party. As a result, we focus heavily on what it would take to change the party's incentives and behavior.

We begin by exploring the possibility that the system, as currently constituted, retains sufficient capacities for self-repair. We are not optimistic. Thus, we turn next to the daunting subject of reforming American political institutions. This effort is, unfortunately, as much about outlining what we think *won't* work as it is about identifying what might. Nonetheless, we see potential particularly for legislative reforms that might help to safeguard democracy and change the incentives that define the GOP.

The depth of the challenges facing US governance and democracy is clear. Strategies sufficient to address these challenges remain elusive. Yet recognizing the central contribution of our peculiar institutions to our political troubles is essential. Successful prescriptions are unlikely absent a proper diagnosis—and that diagnosis must directly involve the unusual features of our constitutional framework. While political discontent grows there remains a reservoir of reverence for the American Constitution that urgently requires reexamination.

Is the Madisonian System Self-Correcting?

It is not naive to think that a constitutional framework that has endured for almost a quarter of a millennium might have considerable capacities for self-healing. Here we briefly consider two possible ways this might happen: forces that push the GOP to the center or the emergence of new issues and cleavages that alter the political landscape and diminish the intensity of partisan polarization. We are not optimistic about the prospects for either development.

A PULL TO THE CENTER?

A common model for thinking about politics suggests that the electoral logic of competition in a two-party system will in time force parties to moderate as they pursue the "median voter" or are punished for failing to do so. First articulated by the economist Anthony Downs, the idea that electoral incentives would compel parties to gravitate toward the center has, in the words of Morris Fiorina, "served as a kind of 'master theory'" for political scientists.[1]

We have emphasized that the shift to a constitutional order that is nationalized and polarized has not had identical effects on the two parties. Democrats have clearly been affected by this transformation of politics. The party overall has become somewhat more liberal, and the strength of the Left within the party has grown. At least on the issue of immigration, the party's activist base and many of its candidates have moved pretty far from the center of the electorate.[2] Yet a number of countervailing factors remain. Democrats generally need more than a simple majority of voters to win nationally, which pushes them to construct a broad tent that has room for moderates. The policy goals of Democrats also rely much more heavily on legislation, which increases the need to accept compromises between progressive and more moderate factions. And unlike the Right, the center-left media ecosystem continues to create some incentives and support for moderation. One need only point to the selection of longtime establishment figure Joe Biden as its 2020 nominee to note a stark difference between the parties.

By contrast, the contemporary Republican Party's positioning is in clear tension with Downs's "master theory."[3] The political scientist Pippa Norris drew on a survey of 1861 party and election experts taken in 2019 to estimate the ideologies and issue positions of political parties across the world.[4] Her study shows that the GOP is a striking outlier among major parties in her sample of twenty-four western democracies—with positions on both economic policy and cultural issues that are more extreme than the center-right parties that have routinely led governments elsewhere. She finds that today's Republicans' positions resemble those of far-right parties that at times have been included as part of broader coalitions, but very rarely have led them. Democrats are on the left with respect to both economics and culture but are quite similar to center-left parties in other western democracies.

Many political observers have expected that the demographic push toward an ever more multiracial electorate, along with the liberal social attitudes of young people, would make it increasingly difficult for Republicans to continue winning elections while taking very conservative stances, particularly on the "identity-inflected" issues that have been the focal point of intense polarization.[5] With many Republican politicians showing a willingness to reject core tenets of democratic governance rather than embrace a multiracial democracy can the moderating pressures identified by the median voter approach still prevail?

Concern about the electoral challenge posed by demographic change has played a prominent role in Republican elite deliberations, most famously in the post-2012 GOP "autopsy" report, which argued that the party needed to become more welcoming for non-white voters. South Carolina Republican Lindsey Graham put the basic point more colorfully: "The demographic race we're losing badly. We're not generating enough angry white guys to stay in business for the long term."[6]

Graham said this over a decade ago. Needless to say, the reorientation he called for has not taken place. Instead, with Trump setting the tone, Republicans doubled down on accentuating and exploiting racial cleavages and associated cultural resentments, along with controversies related to gender and sexuality. Able to activate significant sources of untapped white working-class (and especially rural and exurban) votes, and able to rely on electoral institutions that gave those voters disproportionate weight, this strategy has proven modestly successful.

Perhaps surprisingly, Trump's posture has also proven appealing to some minority voters, especially men. Indeed, recent research suggests that Republicans have made significant gains among Latinos, particularly among working-class Latinos and those with conservative attitudes on immigration and policing.[7] There are also signs of Republican gains among Asian Americans and, perhaps, among Black Americans, though Black voters remain overwhelmingly Democratic.

One cannot equate racial identity with either ideology or vote choice—voters have multiple identities and commitments. The lesson for Republicans, however, has been that the party can win a reasonable share of votes from people of color without abandoning appeals that play upon racial, gender, and cultural resentments. With the party's victories still heavily reliant on attracting higher turnout and more support from non-college educated (and particularly male) white voters, the incentives to moderate on identity-inflected issues are likely to remain modest, at best.

In the long term, continued demographic shifts—along with the greater social and cultural liberalism among young voters—may make the GOP approach less and less successful. But it cannot be taken for granted that the composition of the electorate will shift rapidly enough to outpace democratic erosion.

From this perspective, recent factional battles in Republican states facing major demographic changes—such as Texas and Georgia—may offer useful lessons. In Texas, MAGA enthusiasts who have embraced a maximalist vision dominate the state Republican Party organization and Senate. The State Assembly, by contrast, has resisted some of these initiatives; in spring 2023, for example, it rejected a measure to end tenure in the state university system and to provide private school tuition vouchers, and voted to impeach Republican Attorney General Ken Paxton for multiple abuses of office. Similarly, Georgia Republicans include both MAGA enthusiasts, such as Marjorie Taylor Greene, and prominent officials who resisted election denial, such as Governor Brian Kemp and Secretary of State Brad Raffensperger. Both Kemp and Raffensberger won reelection in 2022 after standing up to Trump.

Pressure to moderate amid demographic change could ultimately transform the politics of states such as Texas and Georgia. But there is also cause for concern that Republican elected officials in those states will attempt to use their control of the electoral process to insulate their power. On issues directly related to election administration it is hard to find evidence of moderating pressures—quite the opposite. In Texas, both chambers agreed on legislation targeting election administrators in highly Democratic Harris County and abandoning the Electronic Registration Information System (ERIC), which previously ensured that voter registration rolls in Texas were updated without purging valid voters. In Georgia, Kemp signed legislation imposing new restrictions on voting by mail. Most importantly, the new law empowers the state election board—controlled by the GOP-dominated legislature—to replace county election officials. This would allow the board to target heavily Democratic Fulton County, the flashpoint of election denial claims in 2020.

At the national level things look even worse. A deep challenge comes from asymmetries in our national political institutions that allow Republicans to hold onto key power levers—including the Senate; the House; the Supreme Court; a number of critical state legislatures; and, on two recent occasions, the presidency—even when they fall short of a majority of votes. The powerful Senate is perhaps the most striking case. The Senate map, combined with rural–urban polarization virtually assures that the GOP will have the Senate majority with some frequency. The current era is the first sustained period in which a party has repeatedly held a Senate majority despite winning only a minority of votes. This has resulted in a high share of roll-call votes in which senators representing a minority of the US electorate triumphed over senators representing a majority of voters.[8]

The Republican edge in the Senate has accompanied a new willingness to use it to gain partisan advantage by blocking Democratic appointments. These advantages, combined with life terms for justices and greater life expectancy, mean that the party need only win the presidency on occasion to continue to hold a solid majority on the Supreme Court. This in turn will allow the party to win on many core policy concerns and to continue to tilt the electoral playing field to its advantage.

Parties are forced to move to the center when they otherwise cannot win sufficient electoral victories to share power. In the case of the GOP, the overrepresentation of rural voters in the US system, bolstered by deck-stacking strategies that add to the obstacles facing Democratic constituencies in many settings, may well insulate the party from such pressures even when Republicans lose the national popular vote by a substantial margin.

Reasonable people may disagree with our pessimistic reading. For example, some might point out that, despite the narrowest of majorities, Democrats after the 2020 election were able to legislate fairly extensively by forming coalitions that included politicians of both parties on everything from infrastructure to significant industrial policy initiatives to protections for gay marriage and a limited but consequential electoral reform. Most of these bipartisan legislative initiatives were quite popular in initial polling.

While Democrats lost their trifecta in the 2022 midterms—as has become the norm in midterms and was certainly to be expected given Biden's shaky approval levels—the party's losses were limited. Concerns about the robustness of democracy were more prominent in American discourse than at any time in modern political history. Republicans narrowly captured the House but failed to capture the Senate. In those races that were hotly contested there is strong evidence that Republican candidates paid an electoral price for extremism.[9] It was equally notable that the failure of a red wave to emerge did not reflect unexpected Democratic turnout—instead, it was the difficulty "MAGA" candidates had in attracting the votes of Independents and moderate Republicans that made the difference.

Squint hard and one can see the system course-correcting with voters forcing politics back to the center and punishing those who don't get the message. The behavior of a critical slice of voters pulled outcomes away from the extremes. While protecting democracy was only one issue among many, it seems to have been salient, at least as part of a package of characteristics that identified a number of prominent Republican candidates as extreme. The backlash against the Supreme Court's unpopular decision to overturn *Roe* was part of that package as well, further bolstering the argument that voters will, at times, still exact retribution against politicians when they are associated with policies that are out of step with the public's strongly held views. Expanding one's gaze beyond the 2022 election, it is not hard to see repeated examples of voter-induced course corrections. From the Reagan years through George W. Bush and Barack Obama, the half-lives of touted "emergent majorities" have been all too short.

But hold the applause. Even if Republicans at times have paid an electoral price for non-centrist positions, that price has not been steep enough to deprive it of the opportunity to regularly hold power. There remains evidence that the "out" party can often succeed not by moderating but by doing its best to generate acrimony and gridlock while waiting for the inevitable voter backlash. That is, a politics mired in conflict and dysfunction offers strategic opportunities. Despite their many differences, the two most successful congressional Republicans of the era of nationalized polarization—Newt Gingrich and Mitch McConnell—shared a fervent belief that confrontation and obstruction rather than cooperation was the best path from the minority to the majority.

Republicans show little sign of feeling pressure to move to the center. That so many election deniers had swept through Republican primaries even in moderate states was itself a sign of the strong pull of the hard right. And some of these extreme candidates came close to victory (Herschel Walker lost by less than 3 percent; Kari Lake by 0.5 percent). Those facing the clearest electoral punishment were not the ones who had denied the election results but those who had openly challenged the insurrection of January 6.

The 2022 election was disappointing for Republicans, but it hardly induced moderation. The great majority of House Republicans are from deep red districts. Fully 170 members represent districts that Donald Trump carried by at least 10 percent in 2020. Their careers are enabled and constrained by the forces of nationalization and polarization described in previous chapters. The 2022 midterms did increase the number of Republicans from Biden-won districts—from nine following the 2020 election to eighteen in 2022. Though theoretically pivotal in the closely divided House, recent experience suggests that swing-seat Republicans generally remain sufficiently worried about primary challenges to avoid confrontation with the party's very conservative majority.

Indeed, far from treating the election results as a signal that moderation was imperative, the Republican caucus immediately indicated that it planned on confrontation: investigatory hearings, impeachment threats, and debt-ceiling showdowns. Factional battles within the GOP also showed that the gravitational pull within the Republican caucus was further than ever from any hypothetical center. Leader Kevin McCarthy signaled as much as he worked laboriously to buy off the Freedom Caucus through rules concessions and opening his inner circle to extremists like Jim Jordan and Marjorie Taylor Greene. The last two Republican Speakers, Paul Ryan and John Boehner, had seen their positions crumble as a result of the far right's fierce resistance to compromise and moderation; McCarthy faced their wrath before even obtaining the position. Battleground district Republicans caused no trouble for McCarthy as he made substantial concessions to far-right conservatives in his Speakership bid. Rather than make any serious threat to work with centrist Democrats on an alternative approach, they stuck with their party brethren.

The key dynamic within the party remains. Republican moderates and mainstream conservatives are still deeply reluctant to collaborate with Democrats in a way that might risk a primary challenge. Freedom Caucus members have proven willing to block even procedural motions when they believe the leadership is not sufficiently solicitous of their demands; thus far, moderates have shied away from such a confrontational approach. Indeed, McCarthy's unprecedented concessions to the hard right were not enough to save his Speakership, as he was removed after less than a year and replaced by the vocal election denier Mike Johnson. The moderates had the votes to block Johnson but went along with the choice of the most conservative party members. We will address the question of what might be done to change these incentives.

Of course, the clearest evidence of the center's weak pull was the dominance Donald Trump asserted over the GOP as the nation approached the fateful 2024 election. One might think that a defeated ex-president who conspired to overthrow an election and faced four criminal indictments would be an unlikely standard-bearer. Yet he quickly consolidated the support of the party base and so towered over his challengers that he did not bother to participate in debates. Even as he gave speeches promising to "root out . . . the radical left thugs who live like vermin within our country," his main GOP challengers, Nikki Haley and Ron DeSantis, mostly steered clear of criticizing his authoritarian rhetoric and instead focused on his failures to deliver on right-wing policy goals.[10] And there was extensive reporting that Trump's close allies were organizing to limit checks on his authority should he succeed in regaining the White House.[11]

In short, the swing back and forth in party control, along with the handful of noteworthy bipartisan successes in the Biden years, should not be interpreted as evidence that the median voter is dictating responsiveness and moderation. Instead, the 2022 outcome attests that there still is some room for normal electoral tides—rooted in economic dissatisfaction, general discontent with the state of our politics, and other factors—to allow either party to win national elections, even if that party is further from the median voter.

Given the structural advantages described above, Republicans, in particular, need not adapt to have a reasonable shot at winning a trifecta in Washington. For Democrats, the need to compete in less hospitable states has long created a greater incentive for at least some party members to moderate. But absent willing partners in the GOP, the scope of political alternatives for Democratic moderates is also likely to be limited. The chance that electoral incentives will send powerful signals to moderate thus appears remote, at least in the absence of a major, sustained shift in the electoral balance of power.

NEW ISSUE CLEAVAGES?

A second possibility for self-healing involves the emergence of new cleavages or the weakening of existing ones. As discussed in chapters 2 and 3, throughout American political history the emergence of new issue cleavages has repeatedly disrupted polarizing trends. By diminishing the extent to which divisions "stack," such changes could reshuffle party coalitions. At a minimum, the emergence of new issues might reduce tensions if more manageable divisions replace intensely polarizing ones.

New lines of cleavage are not always easy to predict in advance, but one can identify a few possibilities in the current political environment. Most prominently, economic divisions could become more salient in partisan conflict. As our system polarized, cultural cleavages increasingly displaced economic ones within the electorate.[12] Affluent, educated white voters moved to the Democrats and working-class white voters without a college education

moved to the Republicans. Both parties have become economically heterogeneous coalitions. Income is no longer the powerful predictor of partisanship that it once was. Instead, the electoral coalitions are divided from each
other most starkly on cultural issues, especially related to race, gender, and
sexuality.

Arguably, a refocusing of political conflict around economic divisions
could disrupt existing cleavages. In addition, conflicts structured around economic divisions might be less intense and more susceptible to compromise
than conflicts structured around other social identities.[13] There is evidence
that Democratic Party elites, both in their rhetoric and their policy agenda,
have sought to focus attention on economic rather than cultural issues.[14] Stir-
rings of economic populism within the GOP are also evident, although it
is perhaps telling that the main complaint most Republicans lodge against
powerful corporations is that they have become "woke."

But here the refusal of the GOP to pivot toward a strategy that is more
racially inclusive and tolerant of changing gender norms is instructive. The
system suffers from what Sides, Tausanovitch, and Vavreck call "calcification."
While they see this largely as a matter of mass-level attitudes, we have argued that what they observe in voter predispositions reflects fundamental
change in the constitutional order. Mediating institutions play a critical role
in determining whether calcification occurs and can be sustained. Decentralized arrangements once served as generators of new issues and information
and thus as the conveyor belts for new coalitions and orientations. Yet these
mediators—state parties, media, and organized interests—no longer operate as they once did. Instead, more tightly integrated with national partisan
structures, these mediating institutions tend to reinforce existing alignments.

To take just one example of how this might act against a potential realignment or weakening of polarization, even if Democrats stress economic
issues and gear policy proposals to subsidize "red" states, Republican voters are unlikely to hear about it from their preferred media sources or from
elites whom they trust. Democrats have actually made surprising efforts to
use national policy to shift funds to "left behind" areas that now vote Republican. But the role of local economic interests in our politics has become
highly mediated.[15] In the spring 2023 debt-ceiling showdown, for example,
House Republicans voted *en masse* for a measure that repealed the Inflation
Reduction Act, which, if successful, would have rolled back energy subsidies
that were disproportionately benefiting "red" states.[16] The already developed
national partisan networks can frequently keep issues that threaten to shake
up existing alignments off the national agenda. Alternatively, as happened
with the COVID pandemic, with the help of partisan media they can frame

controversies so that potentially crosscutting issues are simply absorbed into the existing "stacked" structure of issue alignments.

The sharp partisan divide displayed in the response to the COVID pandemic speaks to the viability of another potential pathway out of polarization: the prospect that a severe national threat or crisis might transform the national agenda by constructing a common enemy. Such a scenario has clear precedent. The Cold War clearly dampened party polarization from the 1940s into the 1980s. With elites in both parties believing that the US was locked in a life-and-death struggle with Soviet communism, there was extensive bipartisanship on one of the most salient issues in American politics. This collaboration spilled over into other domains. When it came to civil rights, for example, many members of both parties saw that Jim Crow institutions were undermining America's credibility abroad.[17] Cold War pressures likely also had broader effects on party strategies. They may have disincentivized constitutional hardball moves that risked undermining the legitimacy of American political institutions. Furthermore, the presence of a serious external threat made it less likely that either party would nominate a presidential candidate who was seen as a destabilizing force. With the fall of the USSR in 1991, these restraints were removed. Political attention could shift more decisively to domestic issues, where, as described in chapters 4 and 5, the parties' constituencies and elites were moving further apart from one another.

Even so, it is important to note that the onset of polarization began *prior* to the break-up of the Soviet Union. The rise of Newt Gingrich, which reflected and brought together a range of developments in mediating institutions and electoral alignments that had been taking shape since the Long 1960s, was already well under way in 1990 (see chapter 5). In that year, House Republicans' revolt against George H. W. Bush's budget deal with Democrats marked a key shift toward a more confrontational strategy of accentuating interparty differences.[18] In any event, once polarization took root it proved resilient in the face of major foreign policy events that might have, in the past, shaken up existing political coalitions. The September 11 terrorist attacks gave rise to a short period of unity, but it soon dissipated in the face of divisions over the Iraq War and domestic policies. The 2004 Bush–Kerry contest reflected only a deepening of the sharp red–blue divide evident in the 2000 election.

More recently, while Russia's invasion of Ukraine generated condemnations from members of both parties, former president Trump and other prominent Republicans have made statements condoning Vladimir Putin's aims and approach. Although aid to Ukraine has received bipartisan backing, there is little evidence that the more dangerous international situation in the world has generated a broader cooling in the political temperature in the US. The prospect that new issues or foreign policy challenges will shift political incentives in a way that dampens polarization cannot be ruled out, but recent experience gives good reason to doubt that such developments will overwhelm the institutional shifts that have made today's polarization so different from earlier incarnations in US history.

Resurrecting the "Fractured Republic"?

If contemporary mediating institutions sustain calcification perhaps the answer is to reinvigorate Madisonian pluralism by somehow "denationalizing" these institutions, restoring a "fractured" Republic.[19] The moral costs of returning to unchecked state control over policies regarding race, gender, and the electoral rules of the game would be, in our view, unacceptable. A more fully embraced model of localized authority (what Catholic theorists call "subsidiarity") seems likely to yield a muted version of the "authoritarian enclaves" that existed prior to the political successes of the civil rights movement.[20] As noted in the last chapter, congressional gridlock and Supreme Court permissiveness have created space for maneuvering, and a number of states have already utilized this space by employing strategies to restrict voting rights and entrench the power of severely gerrymandered legislatures.[21] Republican legislatures have also become increasingly aggressive in imposing restrictions on democratically enacted initiatives in "blue" urban enclaves.

In any event, we see little prospect that critical mediating institutions can be effectively "de-nationalized." The most straightforward case is news media. The trend toward nationalization has been relentless, driven primarily by technological changes that have caused distances to radically shrink and gutted the business plans of local newspapers. There are efforts to prop up local news through new business models and philanthropy. These efforts are salutary—anything that diversifies sources of information and adds dimensions to political conflict may help limit polarization at the margins. Yet these are rearguard actions at best, with little prospect of doing more than slowing the pace of media nationalization.

The same likely holds true for the organized expression of political interests. Here again the trend toward nationalization has been long-standing and consistent. As with dramatic changes in media, technology has played an important role, shrinking distances and making nationalized collective action evermore feasible. The evolution of global capitalism has mattered as well. Increases in scale, complex supply chains, and financialization have all meant that "local" economic interests are firmly linked to (and generally subordinate to) nationalized or globalized structures of private authority. The location of power is most often far removed from the location of production. Again, it is hard to envision putting the toothpaste back in the tube.

These same developments militate against the reemergence of a decentralized system of state parties. After all, media and politically active interest groups are two of the chief organizing mechanisms for state parties. Their structures strongly shape how local politicians advance their careers.

Yet of our three sets of mediating institutions, it is state parties that offer the most meaningful opportunities for restoring a significant dimension of localized politics. This is because state party behavior is likely to reflect the incentives facing ambitious local politicians. And while nationalized interest groups and media shape those incentives, so do the political rules of the game. It is easier to imagine altering those rules than reversing the broad societal changes that have transformed the constitution of media and organized interests. It is to the challenge of political reform that we turn next.

Reforming the Constitution?

If our inherited Madisonian framework is a bad fit for a nationalized and polarized system, and the sources of nationalization and polarization are not going away, can that Madisonian framework itself be altered? Many features of the American Constitution are extreme outliers within the community of contemporary democracies. First-past-the-post elections are rare. True two-party systems are rarer still. Arrangements like the Electoral College are unheard of outside the US. No other national courts have as much power as the US Supreme Court. No other democracy introduces so many veto points into the enactment of legislation. Almost no legislative chambers diverge as far from equal representation as the Senate. Very few democracies give partisan officials so much influence over election administration. And so on.

Our unusual constitutional framework is centrally implicated in the current problems facing our polity. In some ways that framework long stifled the emergence of nationalized and polarized parties. Now that they are here, however, it is ill-equipped to handle them. Many of the problems facing the United States would be considerably more manageable if our democratic institutions were more in line with international norms.

Levitsky and Ziblatt, in *Tyranny of the Minority*, make a persuasive case that the best solution to threats to American democracy would be dramatic constitutional changes that eliminate the features that empower political minorities and thus weaken the pressures on political leaders to move to the center.[22] As they document, many of the undemocratic features of US institutions were shared, at least in part, by other democracies at the start of the

twentieth century. Those countries, however, gradually changed their institutions, while the US retained its non-majoritarian rules of the game.[23] The
pressure on Republicans to move toward the median voter would increase
dramatically if the Constitution were reformed in ways that eliminated opportunities for electoral minorities to rule.

We agree that the path of constitutional reform would offer the most powerful response to current dangers. Indeed, we have strived to demonstrate the
Constitution's essential contribution to our present difficulties. The core problem, however, is that the US is also an outlier in placing extremely high hurdles
in the way of constitutional revision. No fundamental constitutional reforms
have passed in over a century—the last being women's suffrage and the direct
election of senators.[24] There is certainly no reason to think these hurdles to
constitutional revision will be any easier to overcome in our polarized polity.

Indeed, there is a central paradox of a strategy focused on constitutional
reform. The very elements of contemporary politics such reforms are intended to address are likely to stand as insuperable barriers. Overcoming
those hurdles often requires not just very broad consensus but more specifically the acquiescence of entities upon which the status quo confers very
considerable advantages: low-population states. The overwhelming support
of state legislatures is required to utilize the standard path to constitutional
amendment. And reducing the Senate representation of states without their
consent is specifically exempted from the amendment process—the only such
provision in the Constitution.[25] Moreover, in the current context one side or
the other is likely to see any politically significant constitutional amendment
as a form of deck-stacking. Recall that in prior eras the partisan implications
of reforms were often hard to identify ahead of time—and even partisan
power plays often had unintended results. In today's world of stacked cleavages there is far less ambiguity. Given the high hurdles for amendments and
the zero-sum structure of contemporary partisan politics we see little prospect for any reforms requiring a constitutional amendment.[26]

Two Paths of Institutional Adaptation:
Responsible Parties or Empowering Factions

Since constitutional change is a remote possibility at best, we must consider
alternative visions of institutional reform. Institutional initiatives also confront the reform paradox, but in a less intense form, both because the hurdles
to be cleared are lower than for constitutional amendments and because the
impact of specific reforms on partisan balance may be less clear-cut. We first
explore the strengths and weaknesses of two plausible approaches focused

on changing the internal dynamics of the parties themselves. Both seek to address the concerns about dysfunctional polarization outlined here without ignoring the daunting political constraints. Both accept as given a setting of nationalized political contestation organized around two parties but seek to diminish the dangers associated with the contemporary constitutional order.

The first vision seeks to encourage *a responsible two-party system* by strengthening parties and empowering party leaders.[27] The argument here—perhaps dissonant to many observers—is that the main problem is that our parties are *too weak*. Supporters of this vision share a belief common among political scientists—one that we also share. Democracy is inconceivable absent parties, which play a vital role in clarifying the stakes in elections and providing a basis for accountability. The problem from this perspective is that, at present, extremists within the parties have too much power. They operate through existing opportunity structures—including primaries, partisan media, and a system of campaign finance that gives ideological donors sway—to pull their parties away from the center. Reformers in this camp hope that giving party leaders greater control—over primaries, the party's agenda, and within-party factional battles, for instance—would restore the pivotal role of the median voter. This vision rests on the idea that, because party leaders care most about being in the majority, they are not particularly attached to any extreme policy demands. Thus empowering them could shift incentives; strong party leaders would deliver a "just right" mix of party distinctiveness and moderation.

We see two basic problems with this vision. The first is that while strong and moderate parties might work well in a true parliamentary system—where the majority governs and the minority seeks to become the majority—that is not the system the United States has. In the US a party, no matter how united, has difficulty governing without a certain degree of cooperation of the other party. And if that party is also strong and well ordered, the political logic of denying that cooperation remains powerful. Such a system seems inherently zero-sum, and even a rational, majority-seeking leader would face incentives to engage in obstruction (powerfully enabled by the filibuster) and constitutional hardball. Mitch McConnell, for instance, seems to personify the orientation of a strong, election-focused leader, but it would be hard to argue that he has facilitated moderate governance. Instead, he has turned exploiting Madisonian arrangements to damage the other party into a fine art. Abolishing the filibuster might diminish this challenge, but given the prevalence of divided government, there would likely still be plenty of opportunities—and ample incentives—for parties to effectively engage in obstruction and constitutional hardball.

The second problem is also fundamental. Given the structure of contemporary mediating institutions, pressures to adapt to the median voter would seem very unlikely to be sufficient to lead a strengthened party organization to stay anchored near the middle. The most consequential—and arguably powerful—House Republican leader of the past forty years, Newt Gingrich, briefly exercised the kind of control over member advancement (e.g., committee assignments) that could, in principle, be used to discipline extremists. Instead, Gingrich generally used his power to push a maximalist version of a conservative agenda.

While advocates of stronger parties might be right that their reforms would tend to strengthen moderating impulses, the likely impact of these changes alone should not be overstated. Perhaps arrangements empowering party leaders and organizations might have *prevented* some polarization if they had been in place in, say, the 1970s. Again, however, the toothpaste is out of the tube.

The forces pulling to the extreme, including partisan media and well-resourced activist groups, are not going away. Their strength is reinforced by a system of primaries and winner-take-all elections, which means in most places state parties also feel a strong pull to the extreme. Against these daunting and now well-institutionalized pressures, giving some political resources to congressional leaders, the national party apparatus, or even state party chairs seem wholly insufficient. After all, the individuals who are most active in local, state, and national party organizations are often ideological activists drawn from the same policy-demanding groups, reinforced by supportive media, that pull the parties away from the center. There is no cadre of office-motivated "regular" party organization people waiting in the wings to steer revitalized, responsible party organizations, nor is it likely that such individuals, if they did exist, would find a viable base of support.

We have somewhat more hope for a second vision of institutional reform, which seeks to *empower centrist factions* in order to increase opportunities for moderation and consensus that are compatible with existing Madisonian institutions. Reform in this mode would seek to shift the electoral incentives of a pivotal group of legislators so that it is politically viable for them to act as an organized faction that can, at times, seize control over the agenda. Instead of seeking to transform the leadership or dramatically change the median voter in either party, this approach would try to force party leaders to share power with centrist legislators.

As Ruth Bloch Rubin shows in her study of intraparty blocs, this is actually how Congress worked at important moments in its history.[28] Crucially, the factions that Bloch Rubin discusses—such as the progressive insurgents of the early twentieth century—could exercise power apart from their national party's core constituencies because their own electoral fortunes depended on a very different constellation of interests. In these earlier instances, the constituencies differed primarily due to the decentralized interest group, state party, and media structures. In the current nationalized context, the electoral conditions for such factions are less favorable.

However, certain electoral reforms could change incentives in a way that facilitated the creation of stronger moderate factions. Three reforms that might fit this bill have been discussed in recent years: nonpartisan primaries, ranked-choice voting, and rules allowing for fusion candidacies.[29] The success of Senator Lisa Murkowski (R-AK) suggests one possible model. An Alaska initiative adopted in 2020 provides for a nonpartisan top-four primary with a general election using ranked-choice voting. This combination allowed Murkowski to win reelection in 2022 as a Republican despite losing among GOP voters by a wide margin. The Alaska State Senate elected in 2022 has also been organized by a cross-party coalition, while the Republican-led House organization includes a handful of "coalition Democrats" and "coalition Independents." These reforms and political outcomes are rooted in part in the state's distinctive political culture, but the electoral rules also play an important role in shaping incentives.

Fusion voting is another potential tool to shift electoral incentives. With the exception of a small handful of states (most notably, New York), current state election laws bar candidates from appearing on the ballot line for more than one party. Allowing fusion would raise the possibility of a third-party offering its ballot line to major party candidates who commit to specific policy or procedural principles. In a general election, the third-party line might generate greater crossover support from partisans who would be loath to cast a ballot for the opposing party. This could enable the creation of a centrist faction that bargains with the two major parties' leaders over organizing the legislative chamber.

One problem with the fusion scenario is that candidates would still also need to worry about their own party's primary. It is certainly plausible, for example, that a Republican moderate who wins a fusion race, and then proceeds to cooperate with Democrats in a handful of high-profile cases, would find herself facing a stiff primary challenge. This suggests that fusion voting, on its own, is no silver bullet. Nonetheless, the experience with cross-filing in California in the early to mid-twentieth century (which allowed candidates to appear on multiple ballot lines) suggests that such rules may foster greater fluidity in coalitions.[30]

Electoral reforms, if enacted in a sufficient number of states, thus offer the potential for at least some boost to moderate factions. There is the risk, however, that reforms carried out only in some states would constitute unilateral disarmament—potentially benefiting national actors seeking to push politics in the opposite direction. As noted earlier, this has arguably already happened with independent redistricting commissions, which are more common in Democratic than Republican states. States can serve as important demonstration projects, as is now happening with ranked-choice voting, but reformers need to remain cognizant of the danger of unintended consequences. At the end of the day, successful reform will need to have a national element. As a result, even as we acknowledge the steep obstacles, we believe that ultimately a national legislative drive will be necessary to disrupt the dangerous path that American democracy is currently following.

Strengthening moderate factions would come at a cost. The American political system, with its many veto points, is already heavily biased in favor of the status quo, providing a formidable advantage for those with already entrenched privileges. The adoption of steps to strengthen moderates would be a bitter pill for those seeking ambitious changes they consider long overdue. But the nation urgently needs to shift its political path. Gridlock and dysfunction, declining legitimacy, the ascendance of powerful and popular figures eager to trash core features of democracy and the rule of law—these are not foundations on which a more just and democratic society can be built.

A Legislative Agenda to Safeguard Democracy

For a reform pathway to succeed, it needs to address the glaring mismatch between America's political institutions and its contemporary party system. The constitutional separation of powers, checks and balances, and federalism encouraged the creation of a decentralized party system in which crosscutting cleavages routinely found expression. That party system no longer exists. It is not just that Democrats and Republicans are far apart on specific policy questions. The mediating institutions that in the past had provided numerous openings for the incorporation of locally rooted demands that crosscut national party lines have been transformed so that they instead tend to reinforce polarization. It is not at all clear that politically feasible state-level reforms to strengthen moderate factions would be enough to disrupt this dynamic.

Furthermore, given that it is the strategies of Republican officials that pose the greatest danger of democratic backsliding in the US, the essential question is what it would take to change the incentives of these politicians. The nationalized structure of contemporary mediating institutions is a major driver of Republicans' approach, and it is not at all obvious how one might break the current self-reinforcing cycle in a way that would transform Republicans' political incentives.

This is the central challenge that reform advocates must address. Given the severe obstacles to constitutional revision, the key question is what can be done *legislatively* to change the configuration of interests and pressures facing Republican politicians in particular.

Since it is very unlikely that current GOP officeholders would have an incentive to make such changes, this pathway depends on Democrats capitalizing on the next opportunity presented by unified party government. Such a window of opportunity is likely to be brief. There are sure to be many compelling policy demands that compete for attention with proposed institutional reforms. But the long-term prospects for successful governance require pursuing a reform agenda that can change the incentives facing future political candidates and officeholders.

Although we agree with some analysts that a multiparty system would be more stable, such a reform is extremely unlikely given members of Congress's attachment to single-member districts.[31] Some combination of nonpartisan primaries, ranked-choice voting, and fusion laws, however, would facilitate the emergence of an electoral base for durable centrist factions within the parties. At the same time, national legislation that provides for automatic voter registration and restricts partisan gerrymandering might shift the incentives of Republican politicians at the state level by removing these deck-stacking strategies from their repertoire. Such shifts, in turn, could potentially bolster pressure on Republicans to move toward the center of voter opinion.

Together, strengthened centrist factions and restrictions on minoritarian deck-stacking may hasten the arrival of a "tipping point" when demographic and generational change mean it is no longer electorally viable for the GOP to double down on its current strategy of appealing to its base by magnifying racial and cultural resentments. That may seem like a modest achievement, but given the precarious state of American democracy and the formidable obstacles to reform, we should embrace any opportunity that might hasten the transition to a more stable and responsive political order.

A more ambitious democracy agenda would also involve additional measures that counter minoritarian aspects of US institutions. The admission of Puerto Rico and Washington, DC as states could attenuate, if only slightly, the Senate's rural bias. This in turn would potentially shift Republicans' calculus with respect to whether strategic moderation is necessary to capture the Senate. Term limits for Supreme Court justices or court expansion (which was a fairly common practice in the nineteenth century) may also be necessary, given the prospect that the entrenched conservative majority on the court will find ways to reverse reform legislation.

The track record of Democrats on political reform following the events of 2020 is less than encouraging. Democrats can point to a modest bipartisan reform of the Electoral Count Act, but they struck out on any larger initiatives. Achieving an ambitious reform agenda will surely require elimination of the Senate filibuster, which stalled efforts at voting rights and election reform during the first two years of the Biden administration. This in turn is likely to require a larger Senate majority—a daunting aspiration given the Senate's stark minoritarian bias.

Given the urgency of the current situation those tasked with recruiting and electing candidates for national office need to focus on ensuring commitment both to democracy reform and to the rules changes necessary for such a legislative drive to succeed. While organized, politically engaged groups have a strong interest in advancing their specific—and often pressing—legislative goals, Democratic leaders must work to persuade them that their longer-term policy interests, as well as their broader stake in the future of US democracy, require a concerted push to change the rules of the game in ways that will alter the incentives of future candidates and officeholders.

Mounting dysfunction and the erosion of democratic institutions are not inevitable. We readily acknowledge that this reform agenda would face formidable political obstacles. Even if enacted, it would be highly imperfect, leaving the United States with awkward governing arrangements and biased institutions that fall well short of modern conceptions of a democratic political order. Much work would remain. But breaking the self-reinforcing dynamics that have created the present crisis in American politics requires that politicians, activists, and voters focus their energy on achieving substantial yet realistic institutional reforms. As has often been the case in the American past, highly imperfect reforms may nonetheless yield dramatic progress, expanding the circle of citizenship and improving the prospect that government may address the pressing concerns of a vast and diverse society. Today, the need for a vigorous round of highly imperfect reforms is acute.

Acknowledgments

As the endnotes attest, a book covering so much territory necessarily relies on the work of many scholars. But the endnotes are the tip of the iceberg. We have been very fortunate to turn, again and again, to a generous academic community for guidance and feedback. Knowing that we have probably overlooked someone, we deeply acknowledge our gratitude to Amel Ahmed, David Bateman, Richard Bensel, Terri Bimes, Ruth Bloch-Rubin, David Broockman, Corey Brooks, Daniel Carpenter, Devin Caughey, Ruth Collier, Jamie Druckman, Lee Drutman, Robert Fishman, Alan Gerber, Jake Grumbach, Jacob Hacker, Peter Hall, Alexander Hertel-Fernandez, Daniel Hopkins, Desmond Jagmohan, Bryan Jones, David Karol, Ray La Raja, Frances Lee, Margaret Levi, Robert Lieberman, Thomas Mann, Jane Mansbridge, Lilliana Mason, David Mayhew, Nolan McCarty, Suzanne Mettler, Robert Mickey, Michael Podhorzer, Jon Rogowski, Ariel Ron, Daniel Schlozman, David Schwartz, Theda Skocpol, Stephen Skowronek, Daniel Stid, Chloe Thurston, Daniel Tichenor, Robert Van Houweling, and Daniel Ziblatt. We gained valuable comments as well from participants in the Berkeley meeting on Madisonian Institutions and Polarization; the FSI-SSRC Conference on Political Institutions and Challenges to Democracy; a meeting of the CIFAR Successful Societies Group; the Cornell Conference on Political Institutions and Challenges to Democracy; the UC Berkeley Kadish Workshop in Law, Philosophy, and Political Theory; participants at the Max Weber Lecture at the Juan March Institute in Madrid; the University of Chicago Department of Political Science American Politics Workshop; the University of Wisconsin Law School "Con Law Schmooze"; the Harvard University American Politics Workshop; and the American Political Development Reading Group. Bateman, Carpenter, Mason, McCarty, Mettler, Thurston, and Ziblatt very generously participated in a lively one-day manuscript workshop, giving us invaluable feedback at a critical stage. We're thankful to all of these colleagues for their kindness and insight.

Paul's brother Mike Pierson went far beyond sibling obligations, giving the entire manuscript a very close and incisive read. In doing so, he spared our readers from more than a few fuzzy sentences.

We thank Anna Mikkelborg, Anna Weissman, Christian Hosam, Jack Maedgen, and Adrian Elimian for their valuable research assistance. David Bateman, Sarah Binder, David Broockman, Nicholas Carnes, Devin Caughey, David Doherty, John Frendreis, Alan Gitelson, Paul Gottemoller, John S. Jackson, Shannon Jenkins, and Douglas Roscoe all generously shared their data.

The Hewlett Foundation's Madison Initiative provided very helpful financial support.

We're grateful also to the Berkeley political science community, where an outstanding group of faculty and graduate students offer us a steady stream of new understandings of American politics.

It has been a real pleasure to work with University of Chicago Press. Sara Doskow was an early and big believer in this project, and we in turn are big believers in her. We cannot thank her enough for the dedication, skill and insight she has shown in bringing this book to completion. Laura Tsitlidze, Adriana Smith, and Michaela Luckey also worked hard and ably to meet a tight production schedule. We thank Derek Gottlieb for his excellent work preparing the index.

Paul adds: Jacob Hacker deserves special acknowledgment for an enduring intellectual relationship and friendship—both of which I treasure. I'm no longer sure which ideas are Jacob's and which are mine, so his thinking is no doubt sprinkled throughout this manuscript. I thank my family for support, insight, and invaluable distractions. Along with Mike, Kit Pierson was a steadfast, enthusiastic, and perceptive participant in the long brother-treks that at times featured extended discussions of the book's subject matter. My kids Seth and Sidra mixed curiosity about the work with loving perspective on its proper place. Tracey Goldberg offered her usual mix of patient support and wise advice for this very big undertaking. Being used to those qualities doesn't diminish my gratitude or admiration.

Eric adds: I am grateful to my family and friends for their encouragement and support—and for the many conversations in which we tried to work through what is going on in American politics and what might be done about it. Many of these discussions were with fellow alums of New College of Florida. The ideologically driven takeover of the quirky and demanding liberal arts college is a small but telling example of the dangers posed by the transformations we analyze in this book.

Notes

Chapter One

1. See Gretchen Helmke, Mary Kroeber, and Jack Paine, "Democracy by Deterrence: Norms, Constitutions, and Electoral Tilting," *American Journal of Political Science* 66 (2022): 434–50; Ashley Jardina and Robert Mickey, "White Racial Solidarity and Opposition to American Democracy," *Annals of the Academy of American and Social Sciences* 69 (2022): 79–89.

2. See, e.g., Suzanne Mettler and Robert Lieberman, *Four Threats: The Recurring Crises of American Democracy* (New York: St. Martin's Press, 2020).

3. Keith T. Poole and Howard Rosenthal, *Congress: A Political–Economic History of Roll-Call Voting* (New York: Oxford University Press, 1997).

4. See, e.g., David W. Brady and Hahrie C. Han, "A Delayed Return to Historical Norms: Congressional Party Polarization after the Second World War," *British Journal of Political Science* 37 (2007): 505–31; Marc J. Hetherington, "Putting Polarization in Perspective," *British Journal of Political Science* 39 (2009): 413–48; and Doug McAdam and Karina Kloos, "Postwar America: Bipartisan Consensus, the Median Voter, and the Absence of Social Movements," chap. 2 in *Deeply Divided: Racial Politics and Social Movements in Postwar America* (New York: Oxford University Press, 2014).

5. Frances E. Lee, "Patronage, Logrolls, and 'Polarization': Congressional Parties of the Gilded Age, 1876–1896," *Studies in American Political Development* 30 (2016): 116–27.

6. The exception is analogies to the Civil War. Until recently, such analogies tended to be seen as far-fetched, though they have gained more purchase as fears of partisan violence have escalated. See Nathan P. Kalmoe and Lilliana Mason, *Radical American Partisanship: Mapping Violent Hostility, Its Causes, and the Consequences for Democracy* (University of Chicago Press, 2022).

7. On the implications of Madison's defeats at the convention for "Madisonian" theory, see David S. Schwartz and John Mikhail, "The Other Madison Problem," *Fordham Law Review* 89 (2021): 2033–83. For the clearest articulation of Madisonian theory, see Robert A. Dahl, *A Preface to Democratic Theory* (Chicago: University of Chicago Press, 1956).

8. In light of the Virginia Plan's centralizing thrust, this thread of Madison's *Federalist Papers* writing likely reflected his own views, rather than an effort to justify arrangements that he believed fell short. See Samuel Kernell, "'The True Principles of Republican Government':

Reassessing James Madison's Political Science," in *James Madison and the Theory and Practice of Republican Government*, ed. Samuel Kernel (Stanford: Stanford University Press, 2003).

9. Robert A. Dahl and Charles E. Lindblom, *Politics, Economics, and Welfare* (New York: Harper, 1953); John G. Gunnell, *Imagining the American Polity: Political Science and the Discourse of Democracy* (University Park, PA: Penn State University Press, 2004).

10. See David B. Truman, "Federalism and the Party System," in *American Party Politics*, ed. Donald Herzberg and Gerald Pomper (New York: Holt, Rinehart & Winston, 1966); Daniel Elazar, *American Federalism: A View from the States* (New York: Thomas Y. Crowell, 1966).

11. Robert A. Dahl, *How Democratic is the American Constitution?* (New Haven: Yale University Press, 2001).

12. E. E. Schattschneider, *The Semisovereign People: A Realist's View of Democracy* (New York: Holt, Rinehart, and Winston, 1960).

13. Daniel DiSalvo, *Engines of Change: Party Factions in American Politics, 1868–2010* (New York: Oxford University Press, 2012).

14. Truman, "Federalism and the Party System," 30.

15. Nelson W. Polsby, "The American Party System," in *The New Federalist Papers*, ed. Alan Brinkley, Nelson Polsby, and Kathleen Sullivan (Washington, DC: Brookings Institution, 1997).

16. Juan Linz, "The Perils of Presidentialism," *Journal of Democracy* 1 (1990): 51–69. There is now considerable doubt about Linz's assertion that presidential systems are more vulnerable to breakdown. It is his argument about the unusual structure of American political parties that interests us here.

17. Marjorie Hershey, *Party Politics in America*, 17th ed. (New York: Routledge, 2017). There has always been an important national aspect to these party organizations—particularly rooted in competition for the presidency. Yet in other respects, the presidency limited the prospects for partisan cohesion. The election of presidents by ordinary voters, rather than by the legislature, cut against the creation of highly disciplined national parties. Presidentialism puts a premium on candidates' ability to appeal to the mass public, in contrast to parliamentary parties' greater emphasis on selecting insiders with a long record of party service. As relative "outsiders," presidents are more likely to show independence from their parties, pursuing agendas that challenge their unity. See David J. Samuels and Matthew S. Shugart, *Presidents, Parties, and Prime Ministers: How the Separation of Powers Affects Party Organization and Behavior* (New York: Cambridge University Press, 2010).

18. Daron Acemoglu and James Robinson, *Economic Origins of Dictatorship and Democracy* (New York: Cambridge University Press, 2006).

19. Earl Latham, "The Group Basis of Politics: Notes for a Theory," *American Political Science Review* 46 (1952): 376–97.

20. Benedict Anderson, *Imagined Communities* (New York: Verso, 1983).

21. Robert Mickey, *Paths Out of Dixie: The Democratization of Authoritarian Enclaves in America's Deep South, 1944–1972* (Princeton: Princeton University Press, 2015).

22. See Eric Schickler, *Racial Realignment: The Transformation of American Liberalism, 1932–1965* (Princeton: Princeton University Press, 2016).

23. See Ashley Jardina, *White Identity Politics* (New York: Cambridge University Press, 2019); and Robert Mickey, Steve Levitsky, and Lucan Way, "Is America Still Safe for Democracy?" *Foreign Affairs*, May/June 2017, https://www.foreignaffairs.com/articles/united-states/2017-04-17/america-still-safe-democracy.

24. See Desmond King and Robert C. Lieberman, "'The Latter-Day General Grant': Forceful Federal Power and Civil Rights," *Journal of Race, Ethnicity, and Politics* 6 (2021): 529–64.

25. Theda Skocpol, *Diminished Democracy: From Membership to Management in American Civic Life* (Norman: University of Oklahoma Press, 2003); Paul Pierson, "The Rise and Reconfiguration of Activist Government," in *The Transformation of American Politics: Activist Government and the Rise of Conservatism*, ed. Paul Pierson and Theda Skocpol (Princeton: Princeton University Press, 2007), 19–38; R. Shep Melnick, *Between the Lines: Interpreting Welfare Rights* (Washington, DC: Brookings Institution Press, 1994).

26. Daniel J. Hopkins, *The Increasingly United States: How and Why American Political Behavior Nationalized* (Chicago: University of Chicago Press, 2018).

27. See Beth Leech, Frank Baumgartner, Tim La Pira, and Nicholas Semanko, "Drawing Lobbyists to Washington: Government Activity and the Demand for Advocacy," *Political Research Quarterly* 58 (2005): 19–30; and Skocpol, *Diminished Democracy*.

28. Amy Lakeman, *When Theology Responds: How Politics Shapes Religious Belief*, PhD Dissertation, Harvard University, 2022.

29. Neil O'Brian shows that voters' views on racial issues were positively correlated with their views on guns, abortion, and other social and cultural issues. See Neil O'Brian, *The Roots of Polarization: From Racial Realignment to the Culture Wars* (Chicago: University of Chicago Press, 2024).

30. Frances E. Lee, *Insecure Majorities: Congress and the Perpetual Campaign* (Chicago: University of Chicago Press, 2016).

31. David A. Hopkins, *Red Fighting Blue: How Geography and Electoral Rules Polarize American Politics* (New York: Cambridge University Press, 2017).

32. It is possible to periodize American constitutional development in multiple ways. Thinking in terms of a Madisonian order and an emergent new constitutional order is useful, but we recognize that the operations of the Constitution changed dramatically over the long period we characterize as Madisonian (e.g., the Reconstruction amendments, the New Deal). Even with these major transformations, however, mediating institutions remained decentralized and, as a result, countervailing forces continued to operate in ways that limited polarization. As will become clear in the later chapters, the current constitutional order is also by no means static. On the contrary, there are good reasons to believe it is vulnerable to breakdown.

33. Shanto Iyengar, Gaurav Sood, and Yphtach Lelkes, "Affect, Not Ideology: A Social Identity Perspective on Polarization," *Public Opinion Quarterly* 76 (2012): 405–31.

34. See Nathan P. Kalmoe, *With Ballots and Bullets: Partisanship and Violence in the American Civil War* (New York: Cambridge University Press, 2020), 191; and Richard L. McCormick, *The Party Period and Public Policy: American Politics from the Age of Jackson to the Progressive Era* (New York: Oxford University Press, 1986), 170.

35. See John Zaller, *The Nature and Origins of Mass Opinion* (New York: Cambridge University Press, 1992); Gabriel S. Lenz, *Follow the Leader: How Voters Respond to Politicians' Policies and Performance* (Chicago: University of Chicago Press, 2012); and Alexander Agadjanian, "When Do Partisans Stop Following the Leader?" *Political Communication* 38 (2021): 351–69.

36. Jenna Bednar, "Polarization, Diversity, and Democratic Robustness," *Proceedings of the National Academy of Sciences* 118, no. 50 (2021), https://doi.org/10.1073/pnas.2113843118.

37. See Lilliana Mason, *Uncivil Agreement: How Politics Became Our Identity* (Chicago: University of Chicago Press, 2018). These divisions, of course, do not stack perfectly. For example, the ties between religiosity and partisanship and between education and partisanship are much

stronger for white Americans than for Black Americans and Latinos. Similarly, Latinos' partisanship shows considerable variation based on national origin and state of residence.

38. John Sides, Chris Tausanovitch, and Lynn Vavreck, *The Bitter End: The 2020 Presidential Campaign and the Challenge to American Democracy* (Princeton: Princeton University Press, 2022).

39. On the role of elite strategies in encouraging polarization, see Jennifer McCoy and Murat Somer, "Toward a Theory of Pernicious Polarization and How It Harms Democracies: Comparative Evidence and Possible Remedies," *Annals of the Academy of Political and Social Sciences* 681 (2019): 234–71.

40. See Richard Jensen, *The Winning of the Midwest: Social and Political Conflict, 1888–1896* (Chicago: University of Chicago Press, 1971).

41. Jonathan A. Rodden, *Why Cities Lose: The Deep Roots of the Urban-Rural Political Divide* (New York: Basic Books, 2018).

42. See Alvin Rabushka and Kenneth A. Shepsle, *Politics in Plural Societies: A Theory of Democratic Instability* (Columbus, OH: Charles Merrill, 1972); and Donald L. Horowitz, *Ethnic Groups in Conflict* (Berkeley: University of California Press, 1985).

43. Tom Ginsburg and Aziz Z. Huq, *How to Save a Constitutional Democracy* (Chicago: University of Chicago Press, 2018).

44. See, e.g., Steven Levitsky and Daniel Ziblatt, *How Democracies Die* (New York: Crown Publishing, 2018); and Robert R. Kaufman and Stephan Haggard, "Democratic Decline in the United States: What Can We Learn from Middle-Income Backsliding?" *Perspectives on Politics* 17, no. 2 (2019): 417–32, https://doi.org/10.1017/s1537592718003377.

45. As noted above, democracy in the US was far from complete or consolidated for most of its history, and these long-standing patterns of exclusion are critical to understanding today's potential for backsliding. Nonetheless, the basic institutions of governance under the Constitution created a system of competitive elections and divided power that has been in place for over two centuries, radically distinguishing the US from other recent backsliding cases. See Robert Mickey, "Challenges to Subnational Democracy in the United States, Past and Present," *Annals of the American Academy of Political and Social Sciences* 699 (2022): 118–29.

46. Ginsburg and Huq, *How to Save a Constitutional Democracy*, 75.

Chapter Two

1. See discussion below for evidence that these three periods have frequently been cited as analogous to contemporary polarization.

2. For example, we do not analyze the 1880s and 1910s even though the parties continued to differ from one another in important ways during these years. Incorporating these years would not change our basic story. The growing divisions that we trace in the 1870s and 1900s continued to create major problems for each party in the next decade.

3. "De-polarization" does not mean that Democrats and Republicans adopted the same positions. Party differences remained on many policy questions, including voting rights for Black Americans; furthermore, the structure of partisan divisions on many issues showed substantial continuity (see Nolan McCarty, "In Defense of DW-NOMINATE," *Studies in American Political Development* 30 (2016): 172–84). Still, Republicans' shift away from their commitment to Reconstruction undermined the sharp party cleavage that had been central to the politics of the

1860s, while economic issues, on which both parties incorporated significant factional divisions, became central to political conflict.

4. See Richard Hofstadter, *The Idea of a Party System* (Berkeley: University of California Press, 1969); and Jeffrey S. Selinger, "Rethinking the Development of Legitimate Party Opposition in the United States, 1793–1828," *Journal of the Early Republic* 18 (2012): 263–87.

5. McCormick, *The Party Period and Public Policy: American Politics from the Age of Jackson to the Progressive Era* (New York: Oxford University Press, 1986), 154.

6. Eric Foner, "The New Party Bosses," *The Nation*, June 1, 2021, https://www.thenation.com /article/politics/jon-grinspan-age-of-acrimony/.

7. On the "first culture war" and the depictions of Adams and Jefferson, see Jeffrey Pasley, *The First Presidential Contest: 1796 and the Founding of American Democracy* (Lawrence: University Press of Kansas, 2013), 224–31. See also Joanne B. Freeman, "The Election of 1800: A Study in the Logic of Political Action," *Yale Law Journal* 108 (1999): 1959–94; and Rachel Hope Cleves, *The Reign of Terror in America* (New York: Cambridge University Press, 2009).

8. Freeman, "Election of 1800," 1966–67. See Pasley, *First Presidential Contest*, 125 on the Hamilton episode.

9. Although the Federalist and Republican Parties had only just become formally organized, the 1796 presidential contest between Jefferson and Adams similarly featured a heated ideological battle in which both sides depicted the future of the American experiment as at stake (see Pasley, *First Presidential Contest*).

10. As quoted in Freeman, "Election of 1800," 1972. Freeman's account provides rich evidence for the widespread perception that the fate of the republic was at stake in 1800.

11. Freeman, "Election of 1800." Hamilton determined that Burr was a far greater threat to the republic than Jefferson and worked to persuade his Federalist colleagues to back Jefferson in the House. This is an early example of the forbearance highlighted by Steven Levitsky and Daniel Ziblatt as crucial for democratic stability (see *How Democracies Die* [New York: Crown Publishing, 2018], 8–9).

12. John L. Brooke, "The Early Republic, 1789–1815," in *Oxford Handbook of American Political History*, ed. Paula Baker and Donald T. Critchlow (New York: Oxford University Press, 2020), 49. The first formal opposition party caucus took place on April 2, 1796, in response to President Washington's initial refusal to provide documents to Congress regarding the Jay Treaty negotiations (Pasley, *The First Presidential Contest*, 151).

13. On Jefferson's strategy, see Pasley, *'The Tyranny of the Printers': Newspaper Politics in the Early American Republic* (Charlottesville: University of Virginia Press, 2001), 205. The Federalist opposition did revive with the fight over Jefferson's 1807 Embargo and in the lead-up to the War of 1812. Even so, Federalists competed in the 1812 presidential contest only by supporting anti-war Republicans, who nominated Republican DeWitt Clinton to challenge Madison (Cleves, *Reign of Terror*, 183). Republican factionalism thus held the key to Federalist national influence. The extreme secessionist stance of many Federalists, however, helped to unify the Republicans. In the aftermath of the war, party conflict was "dampened nearly to death . . . [as] Federalism collapsed as a national force" (Jeffrey Pasley, *Tyranny of the Printers*, 348).

14. Padraig Riley, *Slavery and the Democratic Conscience: Political Life in Jeffersonian America* (Philadelphia: University of Pennsylvania Press, 2016), 94, 132. Madison's controversial decision in 1816 to sign a bill rechartering the Bank of the United States—which had been a centerpiece of the Federalist program—exemplifies the divisions among the governing Republicans.

15. See, e.g., Joyce Appleby, *Capitalism and a New Social Order: The Republican Vision of the 1790s* (New York: NYU Press, 1984); Charles Beard, *Economic Origins of Jeffersonian Democracy* (New York: MacMillan, 1915); and Drew R. McCoy, *The Elusive Republic: Political Economy in the Jeffersonian Era* (Chapel Hill: University of North Carolina Press, 1980).

16. See Roland M. Baumann, "Philadelphia's Manufacturers and the Excise Taxes of 1794: The Forging of the Jeffersonian Coalition," *The Pennsylvania Magazine of History and Biography* 106 (1992): 3–39; Lawrence A. Peskin, "How the Republicans Learned to Love Manufacturing: The First Parties and the 'New Economy,'" *Journal of the Early Republic* 22 (2002): 235–62; Alfred Young, "The Mechanics and the Jeffersonians: New York, 1789–1801," *Labor History* 5 (1964): 247–76.

17. Young, "Mechanics and Jeffersonians," 272.

18. Baumann, "Philadelphia's Manufacturers and the Excise Taxes of 1794," 23–26. The Revenue Act imposed excise taxes on a variety of products, including refined sugar and snuff. It also imposed licensing requirements and taxes on liquor and wine sales.

19. Peskin, "How the Republicans Learned to Love Manufacturing," 240. Commenting on the shift in Pennsylvania, Baumann notes that "in theory there was an abiding faith in the superiority of agriculture, in practice the Jeffersonians early abandoned free trade and often adopted full fledge mercantilist ideas before 1800" ("Philadelphia's Manufacturers and the Excise Taxes of 1794," 39).

20. Brooke, "Early Republic, 1789–1815," 52.

21. As quoted in Peskin, "How the Republicans Learned to Love Manufacturing," 235. Along similar lines, Douglas Irwin notes that "Treasury secretaries in the later Jefferson and Madison administrations issued reports on manufactures which were strikingly similar to Hamilton's earlier report that Jefferson and Madison had opposed" ("The Aftermath of Hamilton's 'Report on Manufactures,'" *Journal of Economic History* 64 (2004): 801).

22. Peskin, "How the Republicans Learned to Love Manufacturing," 259.

23. Riley, *Slavery and the Democratic Conscience*, 94.

24. Riley, *Slavery and the Democratic Conscience*, 108–14.

25. James J. Gigantino notes that "Jersey Democratic Republicans advanced abolitionism to showcase their political suitability as adherents to the true spirit of 1776" (*The Ragged Road to Abolition: Slavery and Freedom in New Jersey, 1775–1865* [Philadelphia: University of Pennsylvania Press, 2015], 65). Similarly, David Gellman observes that "Black voicings did not line up neatly along partisan lines" in New York. Republicans in the state had sought to "make political hay out of the antislavery leanings of their Federalist opponents" early in the 1790s, but "the century's end witnessed bipartisan support for the gradual abolition of slavery in New York" (*Emancipating New York: The Politics of Slavery and Freedom, 1777–1827* [Baton Rouge: Louisiana State University Press, 2006], 131). The Republican press in the state sought to associate slavery with the South "to dissociate themselves from the taint of slavery" (149).

26. David A. Bateman, "Partisan Polarization on Black Suffrage, 1785–1868," *Perspectives on Politics* 18 (2019), 7.

27. Pasley, *Tyranny of the Printers*, 13, 50.

28. See Riley, *Slavery and the Democratic Conscience*, on the *Aurora*'s treatment of Jefferson in 1800 (80) and on the Louisiana Purchase (124–25).

29. Peskin, "How the Republicans Learned to Love Manufacturing," 251–52.

30. Pasley, *Tyranny of the Printers*, 208–9.

31. Pasley, *Tyranny of the Printers*, 9, 216–17, 301–10, 350.

32. Brooke, "Early Republic, 1789–1815," 54.

33. For example, New York Republicans were plagued by a factional fight between Clintonians and Van Buren-led Bucktails, "each claiming the Jeffersonian Republican mantle" (Kathleen Smith Kutolowski, "The Janus Face of New York's Local Parties: Genesee County, 1821–1827," *New York History* 59 [1978]: 145–72).

34. The Federalists' narrow regional base meant that they could not hope to win national power after 1800. The unpopularity of the Embargo Act of 1807 and Republican divisions over the War of 1812 did allow Federalists to make noteworthy gains from 1807–14. Amid these wartime gains, the Federalists' movement toward secession constituted a serious threat to stability. Following the war's end, however, "the Federalists found themselves wounded by Republican charges of treason and without an issue to rally their supporters around. As a result, the power of the Federalists noticeably began to wane, even within their base in New England" (Philip J. Lampi, "The Federalist Party Resurgence, 1808–1816: Evidence from the New Nation Votes Database," *Journal of the Early Republic* 33 [2013]: 277).

35. See Jennifer McCoy and Murat Somer, "Transformations through Polarizations and Global Threats to Democracy," *Annals of the Academy of Political and Social Sciences* 681 (2019): 8–22, for elaboration of the concept of a "formative divide."

36. Harry Watson, "Democrats and Whigs: The Second American Party System," in *The Oxford Handbook of American Political History*, ed. Paula Baker and Donald T. Critchlow (New York: Oxford University Press, 2020).

37. Joanne Freeman, *The Field of Blood: Violence in Congress and the Road to Civil War* (New York: Farrar, Straus, and Giroux, 2018), 178–79.

38. Freeman, *Field of Blood*, 170–73, 184.

39. Ariel Ron, "How Twitter Explains the Civil War (and Vice Versa): Political Violence and Communications Revolution," *The Strong Paw of Reason* (blog), January 6, 2022, https://bearistotle.substack.com/p/how-twitter-explains-the-civil-war.

40. See Ariel Ron, *Grassroots Leviathan: Northern Agricultural Reform in the Slaveholding Republic* (Baltimore: Johns Hopkins University Press, 2020), 211. See also Ron, "How Twitter Explains the Civil War"; and Corey Brooks, *Antislavery Third Parties and the Transformation of American Politics* (Chicago: University of Chicago Press, 2016).

41. Corey Brooks, "Stoking the 'Abolition Fire in the Capitol': Liberty Party Lobbying and Antislavery in Congress," *Journal of the Early Republic* 33 (2013): 541.

42. See Brooks, "Stoking the Abolition Fire," 546 on the Speakership fight of 1849. Slavery was not alone, of course, in disrupting the party system. Most notably, nativism played an important role in undermining the Whig Party in much of the North.

43. Ron, *Grassroots Leviathan*, 170.

44. For example, disagreements over slavery sparked sectional splits among Presbyterians, Methodists, and Baptists. See C. C. Goen, "Broken Churches, Broken Nation: Regional Religion and North–South Alienation in Antebellum America," *Church History* 52 (1983): 21–35. These splits "not only severed a bond of national unity and set a deceptive example for the states to follow; they also cast the sectional churches in an adversary relationship that actively furthered the alienation of North and South" (34).

45. Ron, *Grassroots Leviathan*, 94.

46. The second party system of Whigs and Democrats was not consolidated until 1840, when the Whigs first fielded a single presidential candidate. Although the parties initially took clearly different stands on economic policy, Democrats in several states soon drifted toward

Whiggish positions on various economic development issues, "such as Pennsylvania Democrats' embrace of tariff protection in 1844, midwestern Democrats' endorsement of internal improvements in the 1840s and 1850s, North Carolina Democrats' acquiescence in railroad aid after 1848, [and] Alabama Democrats' shift to a pro-banking stance in 1849" (Michael F. Holt, *The Rise and Fall of the American Whig Party* [New York: Oxford University Press, 1999], 955). Holt also cites "logrolling deals" between the parties in Virginia, Louisiana, and Maryland that blurred party differences, and observes that post-1848 prosperity "drove far more Democrats in a pro-banking, pro-business, pro-development direction," while railroad construction debates "divided both parties along regional and interest group lines."

47. James Oakes argues persuasively that opposition to slavery constituted the glue that held the Republican coalition together. Although Lincoln and other leading Republicans asserted that they lacked the constitutional authority to abolish slavery in existing southern states, Republicans' shared policy agenda—no slavery in the territories; abolition in Washington, DC; and no federal enforcement of the fugitive slave clause—promised to put a tight cordon around the slave states that both Republicans and southern slaveholders believed would put the nation on a path to abolition. Despite the range of positions Republicans adopted on the question of immediate abolition, this strategy—referred to as the "scorpion's sting"—united the party. However, it left open the divisive question of what would happen once slavery had been eliminated. See James Oakes, *The Scorpion's Sting: Antislavery and the Coming of the Civil War* (New York: Norton, 2014).

48. Important accounts emphasizing the centrality of party include Eric L. McKitrick, "Party Politics and the Union and Confederate War Efforts," in *American Party Systems: Stages of Development*, ed. William N. Chambers and Walter Dean Burnham (New York: Oxford University Press, 1967); and Nathan P. Kalmoe, *With Ballots and Bullets: Partisanship and Violence in the American Civil War* (New York: Cambridge University Press, 2020). For accounts emphasizing Lincoln's efforts to downplay partisanship, see Adam I. P. Smith, *No Party Now: Politics in the Civil War North* (New York: Oxford University Press, 2006); and Erik B. Alexander, "Politics of the Civil War and Reconstruction," in *Oxford Handbook of American Political History*, ed. Paula Baker and Donald T. Critchlow (New York: Oxford University Press, 2020).

49. There is considerable debate about Lincoln's role in the decision to select Johnson as vice president; state party leaders, who were focused on factional battles within their own states, evidently played a critical role in replacing Hannibal Hamlin with Johnson (see Don E. Fehrenbacher, "The Making of a Myth: Lincoln and the Vice-Presidential Nomination in 1864," *Civil War History* 41 (1995): 273–90). Intraparty dissension is also evident in the abortive effort among some Republicans to run a more radical ticket in 1864 headed by John C. Fremont.

50. Oakes, *Scorpion's Sting*, 81.

51. See Richard F. Bensel, *Yankee Leviathan: The Origins of Central State Authority in America, 1859–1877* (New York: Cambridge University Press, 1990); and Nicolas Barreyre, *Gold and Freedom: The Political Economy of Reconstruction* (Charlottesville: University of Virgina Press, 2015).

52. One might ask whether intense party polarization might have persisted for a long period of time—as it has today—if political elites had proven capable of enacting a compromise in 1861 that prevented the outbreak of war. In principle, this might have locked in the stacked cleavages that had developed in the 1850s for several more years. We are deeply skeptical of this counterfactual. The same societal pressures that led to partisan polarization around slavery meant that any such compromise between the parties would have been inherently unstable.

If the Republican Party sought to submerge debates about the future of slavery, many of its politicians would have found themselves under siege at the local level by opponents of the Slave Power. Similarly, southern Democrats would have faced intense pressure from slaveholding elites at home if they appeared to give any quarter to efforts to limit slavery's reach. With the admission of new states and abolitionist activism constantly bringing questions of slavery and freedom to the fore, it is not plausible that the two parties could have remained internally unified and polarized against one another even as they sidestepped the existential issue that most clearly underwrote the present partisan alignment.

53. Barreyre, *Gold and Freedom*, 217–18. See also Eric Foner's magisterial *Reconstruction: America's Unfinished Revolution, 1863-1877* (New York: Harper & Row, 1989).

54. *Chicago Tribune*, "The Negro Out of Politics," April 24, 1877, 4.

55. *The Nation*, "God's Will in Politics," November 14, 1867, 396–97. See also Foner, *Reconstruction*, 314–15 on the Republican reaction to the election results.

56. As quoted in Jeffery A. Jenkins and Justin Peck, *Congress and the First Civil Rights Era, 1861-1918* (Chicago: University of Chicago Press, 2021), 194.

57. Bensel, *Yankee Leviathan*. See also Barreyre, *Gold and Freedom*. David Martin argues that Bensel and Barreyre exaggerate the importance of finance capital's opposition to Reconstruction. Even so, Martin's account of diverse factional interests jockeying for power within the GOP—partly rooted in particular economic interests and partly rooted in differences in ideas—reinforces our broader argument that the GOP's incorporation of diverse, locally rooted interests severely undermined the party's unity of purpose in the Reconstruction era. See David Martin, "The Early Limits of Liberalism: Ideas and Interests in the Resumption of the Gold Standard in Postbellum America," paper presented at the Annual Meeting of the American Political Science Association, Los Angeles, CA, September 2023.

58. The new party also included prominent former Radicals who advocated civil service reform and claimed to be motivated by the corruption of the Grant administration. See Wilbert H. Ahern, "Laissez Faire vs. Equal Rights: Liberal Republicans and Limits to Reconstruction," *Phylon* 40 (1979): 52–65.

59. Jeffrey B. Rutenbeck, "Newspaper Trends in the 1870s: Proliferation, Popularization, and Political Independence," *Journalism of Mass Communication Quarterly* 72 (1995): 361–75.

60. Barreyre, *Gold and Freedom*, 185. Barreyre notes that "it made sense that the Liberal experiment began in Missouri" as it was a border state that shared many of the concerns of midwestern agrarians. "Two distinct political logics therefore converged: a midwestern sectional logic, which made the tariff question a major issue, and a southern partisan logic based on a Democratic centrist strategy, soon to be known as the 'New Departure'" (186).

61. Foner, *Reconstruction*, 504–5. See also W. E. B. Du Bois, *Black Reconstruction: An Essay toward a History of the Part which Black Folk Played in the Attempt to Reconstruct Democracy in America, 1860-1880* (Philadelphia: A. Saifer, 1935), 670–710.

62. Both platforms are reprinted in *Appletons' Annual Cyclopaedia and Register of Important Events of the Year 1876*, New Series, vol. I (New York: D. Appleton and Company, 1877).

63. We obtained twenty-seven state Republican platforms from 1876 and sorted them based on whether they included a clear statement against the violent suppression of Black voting in the South (or directly calling for federal action to protect the right to vote) or instead included a vague statement regarding Reconstruction. These generally consisted of taking credit for prior Republican actions in winning the Civil War and passing the Reconstruction amendments, and an abstract endorsement of the concept of equal rights with no statement that action must be

taken to secure those rights. Strong statements were included in the Connecticut, Delaware, Illinois, Louisiana, Mississippi, Nebraska, Pennsylvania, South Carolina, and Virginia platforms. Although somewhat less clear-cut, Massachusetts and Wisconsin can also be included in this category. The weaker statements were found in the Florida, Iowa, Kansas, Kentucky, Michigan, Missouri, New Hampshire, New Jersey, New York, Ohio, Oregon, Rhode Island, and West Virginia platforms. The strong statements in several Deep South platforms indicate that Republicans in these states had a clear understanding of the stakes. See *Appletons' Annual Cyclopaedia*, 1877.

64. Gregory P. Downs, "The Mexicanization of American Politics: The United States' Transitional Path from Civil War to Stabilization," *American Historical Review* 117 (2012): 407. On the Compromise of 1877, see Allan Peskin, "Was There a Compromise of 1877?" *Journal of American History* 60 (1973): 63–75.

65. Ron, *Grassroots Leviathan*, 221.

66. Ron, *Grassroots Leviathan*, 224. See pp. 222–24 on the USDA's strategy. The Grange's effort to unite northern and southern white farmers played a significant role in pushing Republicans away from Reconstruction. Its leaders promised to "bind again the North and South in one nation," leading the organization to oppose the Ku Klux Klan Act of 1871. Charles Postel, *Equality: An American Dilemma, 1866–1896* (New York: Farrar, Straus, and Giroux, 2019), 86, 90, 99.

67. Postel, *Equality*, 19; see also 89–96.

68. Greenbacks had been issued to help finance the war.

69. Barreyre, *Gold and Freedom*, 130, 139.

70. Foner, *Reconstruction*, 512–24.

71. On agrarian pressures for regulatory action, see especially Elizabeth M. Sanders, *The Roots of Reform: Farmers, Workers, and the American State, 1877–1917* (Chicago: University of Chicago Press, 1989). On Democratic divisions, see Alan Ware, *The Democratic Party Heads North, 1877–1962* (New York: Cambridge University Press, 2006). See Barreyre, *Gold and Freedom* (140) on the 1868 Democratic nomination contest.

72. See Sanders, *Roots of Reform*; Samuel DeCanio and Corwin D. Smidt, "Prelude to Populism: Mass Electoral Support for the Grange and Greenback Parties," *Party Politics* 19 (2011): 798–820; and James Sundquist, *Dynamics of the Party System* (Washington, DC: Brookings Institution, 1983). Postel analyzes the rise of the Knights of Labor and Women's Christian Temperance Union, demonstrating that they each—like the Grange—had ties to members of both parties and did not ultimately form an alliance with either the Democrats or Republicans (Postel, *Equality*).

73. Railroads charged low rates for many long-haul routes between major cities that featured intense competition, while levying exorbitant rates for the less competitive routes that connected many smaller cities.

74. See Sanders, *Roots of Reform*; and Stephen Skowronek, *Building a New American State: The Expansion of National Administrative Capacities, 1877–1920* (Cambridge, MA: Harvard University Press, 1982).

75. Drawing on Richard Bensel's summary of state platforms, we find that Republicans in eight states and Democrats in twelve states included a clear call for railroad rate regulation between 1877 and 1882 (in several states, the calls were included in multiple platforms). Seven of the eight GOP calls were in midwestern or western states (Iowa, Kansas, Nebraska, Wisconsin, Nevada, Oregon, and California); the sole exception was Pennsylvania, where independent oil producers were motivated to back regulation to combat high rates charged on their routes. Similarly,

Democratic calls were concentrated in areas of agrarian strength (Arkansas, Iowa, Kansas, Minnesota, Nevada, Ohio, Tennessee, Texas, Oregon, and California), with Pennsylvania and New York as exceptions. It is also worth noting that in several states, *both* parties adopted a similar position in support of railroad regulation. See Richard F. Bensel, *Political Economy of American Industrialization, 1877–1900* (New York: Cambridge University Press, 2001).

76. Mark W. Summers, *Party Games: Getting, Keeping, and Using Power in Gilded Age Politics* (Chapel Hill: University of North Carolina Press, 2004), 174.

77. Skowronek, *Building a New American State*, 141.

78. See Lee, "Patronage, Logrolls, and 'Polarization.'" McCarty ("In Defense of DW-NOMINATE") argues persuasively that significant differences between the parties persisted throughout the 1870s–80s, with Republicans, on average, more supportive of high tariffs, limited corporate regulation, and hard currency than were the Democrats. But his account also acknowledges the persistence of intraparty factionalism rooted in regional political economy. McCarty and Lee disagree about whether these divisions reflected an underlying "ideological" dimension, but for our purposes the critical point is that each party encompassed regionally based factions that often fought about key issues and, in important cases, found common ground with members of the out-party from their region.

Chapter Three

1. Julia Azari and Marc J. Hetherington, "Back to the Future? What the Politics of the Late Nineteenth Century Can Tell Us about the 2016 Election," *The Annals of the American Academy of Political and Social Science* 667 (2016): 93; Eric Foner, "The New Party Bosses," *The Nation*, June 1, 2021, https://www.thenation.com/article/politics/jon-grinspan-age-of-acrimony/. Numerous other scholars have noted the strong parallels between the two periods. See, e.g., John A. Aldrich, Mark M. Berger, and David Rohde, "The Historical Variability in Conditional Party Government, 1877–1994," in *Party, Process, and Political Change in Congress*, vol. 1, ed. David Brady and Mathew McCubbins (Stanford: Stanford University Press, 2002); Devin Caughey and Sara Chatfield, "Polarization Lost: Exploring the Decline of Ideological Voting in Congress after the Gilded Age," *Journal of Historical Political Economy* 1 (2021): 183–214; Steven S. Smith and Gerald Gamm, "The Dynamics of Party Government in Congress," in *Congress Reconsidered*, 12th ed., ed. Lawrence C. Dodd, Bruce I. Oppenheimer, and C. Lawrence Evans (Washington: CQ Press, 2021).

2. Richard F. Bensel, *Political Economy of American Industrialization, 1877–1900* (New York: Cambridge University Press, 2001); Elizabeth M. Sanders, *The Roots of Reform: Farmers, Workers, and the American State, 1877–1917* (Chicago: University of Chicago Press, 1989).

3. NOMINATE scores estimate each member of Congress's location in a two-dimensional space based on all non-unanimous roll-call votes in each Congress. The first NOMINATE dimension is generally interpreted to reflect members' location on an underlying economic policy dimension. We measured the degree of polarization in the House of Representatives within each decade along that first dimension (starting with the First Congress, 1789–91). The average distance between the two main parties (whether measured with party means or medians) is the highest in 1889–99, 1899–1909, 1999–2009, and 2009–2019. Note that new Congresses generally convened in December of each odd year prior to 1932; as a result, the Congress that started in 1889 did not convene until December of that year (hence the decision to refer to 1890, rather than 1889, as the start date), The most recent decade exceeds the polarization level in any prior

decade. NOMINATE scores have important limitations, but other indicators—such as party unity votes—tell a very similar substantive story. See also Smith and Gamm, "Dynamics of Party Government in Congress."

4. See, e.g., Eric Schickler, *Disjointed Pluralism: Institutional Innovation and the Development of the US Congress* (Princeton: Princeton University Press, 2021); and Ronald Peters, *The American Speakership: The Office in Historical Perspective* (Baltimore: Johns Hopkins University Press, 1990).

5. The changes allowed the Speaker to count non-voting members as present for purposes of establishing a quorum, eliminating the "disappearing quorum" tactic that had routinely stalled action. The rules also allowed the Speaker to rule motions out of order if they were purely dilatory. See Schickler, "Institutional Development, 1890–1910: An Experiment in Party Government," chap. 2 in *Disjointed Pluralism* on the Reed Rules.

6. Congress, "21 Congressional Record: vol. 21, part 1 (March 4, 1889, to February 3, 1890)," US Government Publishing Office, February 2, 1890, https://www.govinfo.gov/app/details/GPO -CRECB-1890-pt1-v21/.

7. *New York Times*, "Gag Disguised as Cloture," December 24, 1890, 1.

8. *New York Herald*, "Fighting Despotism in Both Houses," January 22, 1891, 3. On the boycott threats, see *Atlanta Constitution*, "To Meet the Force Bill," July 20, 1890, 14; *New York Tribune*, "Southern Threats Irritating to Northwestern Democrats," January 27, 1891, 7.

9. Bensel's magisterial study of late nineteenth–century political economy identifies the tariff, currency, and construction of the national market (i.e., corporate regulation and antitrust) as paramount (*Political Economy of American Industrialization*, 6–8). His examination of state party platforms shows that these issues, along with imperialism, were the most commonly discussed topics (184–87). Although imperialism was clearly a major issue, we focus on domestic policies. The Federal Elections Bill (race), immigration, and temperance were the top social or cultural issues in terms of platform attention (calculations by the authors based on the data in Bensel, 184–87). Similarly, David Mayhew's canvas of general histories of the US reveals that the policy areas that historians have most associated with "significant actions" by members of Congress during these years were the tariff, currency, antitrust, railroad regulation, imperialism, and the Federal Elections Bill (calculations by the authors based on Mayhew's dataset). See David R. Mayhew, *America's Congress: Actions in the Public Sphere* (New Haven: Yale University Press, 2002).

10. If we extended our time frame a few years after 1910, women's suffrage, for which attention peaked in 1910–20, would have made our list of highly salient issues that tapped into social cleavages. The suffrage movement fits well with the patterns we identify; suffrage organizations made their initial progress at the state level and were not closely tied to a single party. Instead, suffragists generally succeeded through forging coalitions with partner groups—such as farmers or labor—to wield influence with the majority party in a given state. Although parties thus played a significant role in specific contexts, there was no national-level alignment between the suffrage cause and either party. See Corrine M. McConnaughy, *The Woman Suffrage Movement in America: A Reassessment* (New York: Cambridge University Press, 2013); and Dawn L. Teele, *Forging the Franchise: The Political Origins of the Women's Vote* (Princeton: Princeton University Press, 2018).

11. Charles Stewart and Barry R. Weingast, "Stacking the Senate, Changing the Nation: Republican Rotten Boroughs, Statehood Politics, and American Political Development." *Studies in American Political Development* 6 (1992): 223–71.

12. On Republican divisions, see Nicolas Barreyre, *Gold and Freedom: The Political Economy of Reconstruction* (Charlottesville: University of Virgina Press, 2015), 96–109; and Edward Stanwood, "Protection Assailed and Maintained," chap. 14 in *American Tariff Controversies in the Nineteenth Century*, Boston: Houghton Mifflin, 1903. Randall's tariff stance led the Pennsylvania Republican chair to privately promise to protect him from a GOP gerrymander in the state (Mark W. Summers, *Party Games: Getting, Keeping, and Using Power in Gilded Age Politics* [Chapel Hill: University of North Carolina Press, 2004], 130). National Democrats allied with Cleveland eventually backed a successful challenge to Randall for leadership of the state party, but his replacement found that "the further [he] ranged from where rank-and-file Democrats stood, the more tenuous his hold upon them became" (158). See also Peters, *American Speakership*, on Randall.

13. Bensel, "Tariff Protection and the Republican Party," chap. 7 in *Political Economy of American Industrialization*.

14. The share of Republicans closer to the Democrats was 2 percent in 1879–89, as compared to 0.3 percent in 1889–1911.

15. *New York Tribune*, "Cleveland Brands His Party," July 20, 1894, 6.

16. The Coinage Act of 1873 essentially demonetized silver. Under the terms of the Bland-Allison Act of 1878, the Treasury Department coined a limited amount of silver, but the coins generally ended up held in government vaults because the value of silver was below that of gold. See Bensel, *Political Economy of American Industrialization*, 393–94 for a detailed explanation on the implications of bimetallism.

17. Democrats nominated a New Yorker for president in every election from 1868–92 except 1880, when the party selected Pennsylvanian Winfield Hancock.

18. Bensel, *Political Economy of American Industrialization*, 378–99; see also Gretchen Ritter, *Goldbugs and Greenbacks: The Antimonopoly Tradition and the Politics of Finance in America, 1865–1896* (New York: Cambridge University Press, 1997), 29.

19. Summers observes that "with so many causes having sectional, but not national appeal . . . third parties had to content themselves with enclaves." They used local leverage, however, to extract concessions from their major party competitors (*Party Games*, 202; see also 203, 267–68).

20. Just four state Republican parties and three state Democratic parties had included a free-silver plank in 1888–89.

21. We rely on the platform coding by Bensel, who provided us with his summary files for each year during this period. South Dakota Democrats and Republicans either straddled or stayed silent on the issue initially, but effectively endorsed free coinage by 1894. A number of southern Democratic platforms also endorsed free coinage during this period, as did Republicans in a handful of states outside the plains and West (e.g., Michigan in 1890). See "Platform Demands, Party Competition, and Industrialization," chap. 3 in *Political Economy of American Industrialization*.

22. Summers, *Party Games*, 267.

23. This is based on coding the newspaper excerpts in *Public Opinion* from fall 1989 through the end of 1890. *Public Opinion* presented capsule discussions of major issues from a wide range of newspapers across the US. It included few western Democratic papers—likely due to Democrats' limited strength in the region. The regional coding here defines the West as the twelve coastal, Mountain, and Plains states.

24. See Sanders, *Roots of Reform*.

25. *New York Tribune,* "Mr. Hoar on the Election Bill," January 30, 1891; George F. Hoar, "The Fate of the Election Bill," *Forum* 11 (April 1891): 127–36.

26. Seven of the eight had signed the pledge to pass the bill just five months earlier. Six voted against their party; a seventh paired against it, while the eighth was absent on the day of the key vote but made clear he would oppose reconsideration. See Vincent DeSantis, *Republicans Face the Southern Question* (New York: Greenwood Press, 1969), 212.

27. Just days before the key vote, the Democratic *New York Herald* noted that if the "Republicans from the mining states really care for a silver bill they may learn that the only way to get it is to vote against the Force bill. . . . The fate of the two measures is likely to be inextricably intermingled from now until the end of the session" (*New York Herald,* "Nearing a Vote on the Force Bill," January 17, 1891, 4; see also DeSantis, *Republicans Face the Southern Question,* 212–14).

28. *Boston Journal,* January 27, 1891, as quoted in *Public Opinion,* January 31, 1891, 391.

29. *Ohio State Journal,* January 27, 1891, as quoted in *Public Opinion,* January 31, 1891, 391.

30. Summers, *Party Games,* 268.

31. See Joseph Cooper and David W. Brady, "Institutional Context and Leadership Style: The House from Cannon to Rayburn," *American Political Science Review* 75 (1981): 411–25.

32. Bensel, *Political Economy of American Industrialization,* 434.

33. Richard McCormick writes that the merger wave "had barely been raised" in 1896 (*The Party Period and Public Policy American Politics from the Age of Jackson to the Progressive Era* [New York: Oxford University Press, 1986], 82). On the importance of these issues after 1896, see John Milton Cooper Jr., *Pivotal Decades: The United States 1900–1920* (New York: W. W. Norton, 1990).

34. Paula Baker, "Politics in the Gilded Age and Progressive Era," in *Oxford Handbook of American Political History,* ed. Paula Baker and Donald T. Critchlow (New York: Oxford University Press, 2020).

35. On the state-level victories, see George E. Mowry, *The Era of Theodore Roosevelt* (New York: Harper & Brothers, 1958), 72–75; see also Cooper, *Pivotal Decades*; and Sanders, *Roots of Reform.*

36. See Mowry, *Era of Theodore Roosevelt,* 127 on Idaho, Minnesota, and Nebraska. Wisconsin Republicans endorsed the Iowa Idea in their 1904 platform (*Wisconsin Blue Book,* 1905, 1018).

37. We obtained Republican platforms in fourteen states with coverage in both 1900–1902 and 1906–8. Four states included a call for railroad regulation in 1900–1902, but each was weak or vague. In 1906–8, eleven states included a call for regulation, with eight of those endorsing strong action. We code a platform as "weak" when it only included a call to end special privileges (e.g., land grants, free passes) or a vague denunciation of high rates; a platform is coded as "strong" when it calls for specific legislation to restrict railroad rates. The strong calls were in Illinois, Indiana, Missouri, Nebraska, North Carolina, Pennsylvania, Washington, and Wisconsin.

38. On the state reform movement, see Mowry, *Era of Theodore Roosevelt,* 198–99. See Sanders, "The Transportation System," chap. 6 in *Roots of Reform,* on the congressional dynamics.

39. Cooper, *Pivotal Decades,* 26–27.

40. Mowry, *Era of Theodore Roosevelt,* 128; Stephen Skowronek, *The Politics Presidents Make* (Cambridge, MA: Harvard University Press, 1993), 237–43.

41. For the "malefactors of great wealth" speech, see "Address of President Roosevelt on the Occasion of the Laying of the Corner Stone of the Pilgrim Memorial Monument," August 20, 1907, Provincetown, MA, https://archive.org/details/addressofpresideooroo/page/n1/mode/2up.

On Roosevelt's January 1908 speech, see *New York Times*, "Message Dazes Party Leaders," February 1, 1908, 1; see also Mowry, *Era of Theodore Roosevelt*, 221–22.

42. See Elisabeth S. Clemens, *The People's Lobby: Organizational Innovation and the Rise of Interest Group Politics in the United States, 1890–1925* (Chicago: University of Chicago Press, 1997), 7–9; see also McCormick, *Party Period and Public Policy*, 223. Postel dates the growth of movements lobbying for policy change to the last third of the nineteenth century. Each of the groups he highlights—the Grange, Women's Christian Temperance Union, and Knights of Labor—adopted a formally nonpartisan stance and avoided an alliance with either national Democrats or Republicans. The organizational strategies developed by these groups clearly influenced several of the interest groups most active in the early 1900s, such as the Farmers' Union. See Charles Postel, *Equality: An American Dilemma, 1866–1896* (New York: Farrar, Straus, and Giroux, 2019).

43. The Farmers' Union's record-keeping was uneven, giving rise to varied membership estimates. Sanders places the membership in the five hundred thousand to nine hundred thousand range (*Roots of Reform*, 150).

44. Sanders, *Roots of Reform*, 152.

45. See Clemens, *People's Lobby*, 113–27 on labor, and 191–93 on temperance; see McConnaughy, *Woman Suffrage Movement*, on suffrage advocates' strategy; see Daniel J. Tichenor and Richard A. Harris, "Organized Interests and American Political Development," *Political Science Quarterly* 117 (2002): 587–612, on immigration; and see Daniel Okrent, *Last Call: The Rise and Fall of Prohibition* (New York: Scribner, 2010), 36 on temperance.

46. Sanders, *Roots of Reform*, 413.

47. Ruth Bloch Rubin, "Organizing for Insurgency: Intraparty Organization and the Development of the House Insurgency, 1908–1910," *Studies in American Political Development* 27 (2013): 86–110.

48. Cooper, *Pivotal Decades*, 86.

49. Ruth Bloch Rubin, *Building the Bloc: Intraparty Organization in the US Congress* (New York: Cambridge University Press, 2017), 47. See also Schickler, "Institutional Development, 1890–1910," chap. 2 in *Disjointed Pluralism*.

50. Bloch Rubin, *Building the Bloc*, 88.

51. As quoted in Bloch Rubin, *Building the Bloc*, 107.

52. Sanders, *Roots of Reform*, 168.

53. See Cooper and Brady, "Institutional Context and Leadership Style"; and Schickler, "Institutional Development, 1890–1910."

54. See Lee Benson, *The Concept of Jacksonian Democracy: New York as a Test Case* (Princeton: Princeton University Press, 1961); Paul Kleppner, *The Third Electoral System, 1853–1892: Parties, Voters, and Political Cultures* (Chapel Hill: University of North Carolina Press, 1979). For a critical assessment, see Ronald P. Formisano, "The Invention of the Ethnocultural Interpretation," *The American Historical Review* 99 (1994): 453–77.

55. See Richard Jensen, *The Winning of the Midwest: Social and Political Conflict, 1888–1896* (Chicago: University of Chicago Press, 1971), for a thorough account of these dynamics.

56. Jensen, *Winning of the Midwest*, 153.

57. Daniel J. Tichenor, *Dividing Lines: The Politics of Immigration Control in America* (Princeton: Princeton University Press, 2009), 74–75.

58. Arguably, Donald Trump tested this proposition during the 2024 primary season, as he sought to determine whether his tremendous popularity with GOP base voters (and his delivery

of a Supreme Court majority that overturned *Roe*) would allow him to step away from strict abortion commitments that were clearly damaging the party with swing voters.

59. See Jensen, *Winning of the Midwest*, 291–304; and James Sundquist, *Dynamics of the Party System* (Washington, DC: Brookings Institution, 1983), 154–64.

60. John Gerring, "Culture versus Economics: An American Dilemma," *Social Science History* 23 (1999): 129–72; see also Summers, *Party Games*, 186–91.

61. Frederick Luebke, *Germans in the New World: Essays in the History of Immigration* (Urbana: University of Illinois Press, 1990), 85–86; Jensen, *Winning of the Midwest*.

62. Aaron J. Ley and Cornell W. Clayton, "Constitutional Choices: Political Parties, Groups, and Prohibition Politics in the United States," *Journal of Policy History* 30 (2018): 610, 615. See also Gerring, "Culture versus Economics," 143–49.

63. Andrew Sinclair notes that as of 1913, both parties opposed Prohibition in California, Nevada, Illinois, New Hampshire, New Jersey, New York, Rhode Island, and Wisconsin. Both supported Prohibition throughout the Deep South. Even when the parties took opposing positions, it was not always the case that the GOP backed the "dry," pro-temperance side (e.g., in Oklahoma, Democrats were dry and Republicans wet). See Andrew Sinclair, *Prohibition: The Era of Excess* (Boston: Little, Brown, 1962), 91; see also Gerring, "Culture Versus Economics," 144–48.

64. Ley and Clayton, "Constitutional Choices," 618.

65. Tichenor, *Dividing Lines*, 76.

66. Adam Silver, "Elites and Masses: The Prevalence of Economics and Culture in Nineteenth-Century American Party Platforms," *American Nineteenth Century History*, 20 (2019): 41–64.

67. John Higham, *Strangers in the Land: Patterns of American Nativism, 1860–1925* (New Brunswick, NJ: Rutgers University Press, 2002), 164.

68. See Paula Baker, "The Culture of Politics in the Late Nineteenth Century: Community and Political Behavior in Rural New York," *Journal of Social History* 18 (1984–85): 167–93; Alan Ware, *The Democratic Party Heads North, 1877–1962* (New York: Cambridge University Press, 2006), 51; Frederick Luebke, *Bonds of Loyalty: German-Americans and World War I* (Dekalb: Northern Illinois University Press, 1974); David R. Mayhew, *Placing Parties in American Politics: Organization, Electoral Settings, and Government Activity in the Twentieth Century* (Princeton: Princeton University Press, 1986); Philip A. Bean, "The Irish, the Italians, and Machine Politics, A Case Study: Utica, New York (1870–1960)," *Journal of Urban History* 20 (1994): 205–39. The main exception were Irish voters, who were typically strongly associated with Democratic machines. But even the Irish vote was split in GOP-run Philadelphia and Pittsburgh in the 1880s–1910s and in Chicago prior to the rise of the modern Democratic machine in the 1930s. Steven Erie also notes that Irish-run Democratic machines repeatedly faced opposition from Jews and Italians, who at times organized through other parties. See Erie, *Rainbow's End* (Berkeley: University of California Press, 1990), 11–12, 21–22, 28–29, and 43–44.

69. Baker, "Culture of Politics," 181.

70. See Richard M. Valelly, "The Reed Rules and Republican Party Building: A New Look," *Studies in American Political Development* 23 (2009): 115–42.

71. Racial divisions also loomed large in preventing the development of a more coherent class politics that might have bridged sectional divisions. Populists' efforts to build a biracial coalition of southern have-nots in the early 1890s—which might, in principle, have served as the basis for a broader national alignment—ran aground in the face of intense violent repression and broad-based white racism.

72. Given the prevalence of northern racism and the different class positions of southern Black Republicans and northern white Republicans, it is not clear that southern Black enfranchisement would have coincided with increased national party polarization in the early twentieth century. Rather, the Republicans' coalition would have had significant race and class-based divisions. But this speaks to the broader point, that neither party believed its electoral interests would be served by promoting racial equality; as a result, party polarization on racial issues was limited. This would only change when Black activists and the Great Migration began to transform the electoral calculus for northern Democratic politicians. See Eric Schickler, *Racial Realignment: The Transformation of American Liberalism, 1932–1965* (Princeton: Princeton University Press, 2016); and Keneshia N. Grant, *The Great Migration and the Democratic Party: Black Voters and the Realignment of American Politics in the 20th Century* (Philadelphia: Temple University Press, 2020).

73. Stewart and Weingast, "Stacking the Senate, Changing the Nation." Nineteenth-century parties also manipulated electoral rules and processes as a deck-stacking strategy. This was most notable in the case of the disenfranchisement of Black voters and many poor whites in the South, but also in the case of northern voter eligibility and registration laws and gerrymanders. These practices had a major impact within the states, which in turn had implications for the national balance of power. But the focus of the efforts was primarily control at the state level, rather than the competition for majorities in Washington, DC. By contrast, deck-stacking today is focused as much on the contest for national power as it is on state-level concerns.

74. See David Mayhew, *Partisan Balance: Why Political Parties Don't Kill the US Constitutional System* (Princeton: Princeton University Press, 2011). Mayhew identifies five GOP state admissions in the Civil War era (Kansas, West Virginia, Nevada, Nebraska, and Colorado) and five in 1889–90 (Washington, North Dakota, South Dakota, Idaho, and Wyoming). Washington and the Dakotas were admitted in 1889 as part of a compromise under divided government; the package also included the Democratic-leaning state of Montana. With Republicans taking full control of the government after March 1889, the compromise leaned heavily in the GOP's favor. (Montana is not counted here as a Republican admission because it was expected to vote Democratic at the time. This assumption's basis also proved to be mistaken: Republicans won the state in half of the presidential elections from 1892–1912).

75. See Mayhew's *Partisan Balance* more generally on this point. This was not the case for *all* deck-stacking strategies. When deck-stacking involved systematically depriving groups of voters of the franchise—as was the case in the Jim Crow South—the resulting non-democratic rules of the game enabled one-party entrenchment that required national intervention to undo. One-party dominance in the South often gave rise to factionalism, but racial exclusion remained near-constant in most states. See Robert Mickey, *Paths Out of Dixie : The Democratization of Authoritarian Enclaves in America's Deep South, 1944–1972* (Princeton: Princeton University Press, 2015); and; V. O. Key, *Southern Politics in State and Nation* (New York: Vintage, 1949).

76. As noted above, party voting declined gradually in the first decades of the twentieth century, rather than suddenly. But the Cannon revolt marked a critical shift from the centralized party government in Congress that had been enabled by high levels of polarization.

77. It should be noted that this was responsiveness to the median in a highly restricted electorate (i.e., women and most Black voters were disenfranchised).

78. See Kathleen Bawn et al., "A Theory of Parties," *Perspectives on Politics* 10 (2012): 571–97; and Jacob S. Hacker and Paul Pierson, "After the 'Master Theory': Downs, Schattschneider, and the Rebirth of Policy-Focused Analysis," *Perspectives on Politics* 12 (2014): 643–62.

79. Northern Civil War veterans' connection to the GOP offers a third possible example. The Grand Army of the Republic officially proclaimed its nonpartisanship throughout most of the late nineteenth century, but it generally had close ties to the Republican Party (see Mary R. Dearing, *Veterans in Politics: The Story of the GAR* [Baton Rouge: Louisiana State University Press, 1952]). The need for funds to pay for high pensions gave the group a vested interest in backing Republicans' high tariff stance, which further bolstered the party-group alliance. See Bensel, *Political Economy of American Industrialization* 9–10, 457–63, 495–96; and Theda Skocpol, *Protecting Soldiers and Mothers: The Political Origins of Social Policy in the United States* (Cambridge, MA: Belknap Press of Harvard University, 1992). Nonetheless, the GAR aggressively lobbied Democrats in Congress and both parties competed hard for veterans' support. Indeed, northern Democrats often supported the drive for generous pensions; for example, a large majority of non-southern Democrats voted for the Dependent Pensions Act of 1890, which greatly expanded the pension system (Bensel, *Political Economy of American Industrialization*, 502–3; and Scott Ainsworth, "Electoral Strength and the Emergence of Group Influence in the Late 1800s: The Grand Army of the Republic," *American Politics Quarterly* 23 [1995]: 319–38). The alliance with the GOP frayed by the end of the nineteenth century, as western veterans, in particular, "were abandoning their alliance with the party of big business to join a pressure group that expressed their economic grievances" (Dearing, *Veterans in Politics*, 423). Once veterans had achieved most of their pension goals, the Republican party "was unable to combat the interest of western members in low-tariff and free-silver issues" (496). The veterans case thus fits the more general pattern of party-group linkages being less far-reaching and durable in the nineteenth century.

80. Bensel's analysis of state party platforms from 1877–1901 demonstrates that the tariff was the single prominent issue on which Republicans achieved the highest level of unity ("Platform Demands, Party Competition, and Industrialization").

Chapter Four

1. Ira Katznelson, *Fear Itself: The New Deal and the Origins of Our Time* (New York: Liveright Publishing, 2013), 54. See 53–57 on communist and right-wing movements in this period.

2. See Robert W. Mickey, "The Beginning of the End for Authoritarian Rule in America: Smith v. Allwright and The Abolition of the White Primary in the Deep South, 1944–1948," *Studies in American Political Development* 22 (2008): 171; and Eric Schickler, *Disjointed Pluralism: Institutional Innovation and the Development of the US Congress* (Princeton: Princeton University Press, 2021), 168–74. Ironically, Samuel Dickstein, a New York Jewish Democrat, helped Dies win approval for his investigation. Dickstein worked assiduously to expose German Bund activity in the US and believed Dies would focus his committee on Nazi sympathizers. But Dies immediately turned his attention to alleged communists. See Walter Goodman, *The Committee* (New York: Farrar, Straus, and Giroux, 1968).

3. Anthony D. Di Biase, *Labor's Non-Partisan League, 1936–1941* (master's thesis, University of Wisconsin, 1962).

4. In accusing the New Deal of communism, the Republicans increasingly found allies in southern Democratic conservatives, such as Dies, Howard Smith (D-VA), and Harry Byrd (D-VA) (see Schickler, "Institutional Development, 1937–1952: The Conservative Coalition, Congress against the Executive, and Committee Government," chap. 4 in *Disjointed Pluralism*).

5. Henry Lee Moon, *Balance of Power: The Negro Vote* (Garden City, NY: Country Life Press, 1948); Keneshia N. Grant, *The Great Migration and the Democratic Party: Black Voters and the Realignment of American Politics in the 20th Century* (Philadelphia: Temple University Press, 2020).

6. Moon, *Balance of Power*, 21.

7. Eric Schickler, *Racial Realignment: The Transformation of American Liberalism, 1932–1965* (Princeton: Princeton University Press, 2016), 45–80.

8. See Robert H, Zieger, *The CIO: 1935–1955* (Chapel Hill: University of North Carolina Press, 1995); and Michael Goldfield, "Race and the CIO: The Possibilities for Racial Egalitarianism During the 1930s and 1940s," *International Labor and Working-Class History* 44 (1993): 1–32.

9. Schickler, *Racial Realignment*, 52–65.

10. Sean Farhang and Ira Katznelson, "The Southern Imposition: Congress and Labor in the New Deal and Fair Deal," *Studies in American Political Development* 19 (2005): 1–30. The act's exclusion of agricultural and domestic workers helped ensure southern support. Many southerners were still deeply skeptical of the bill, but chose not to oppose it, in part due to the expectation the Supreme Court would invalidate it (see Irving Bernstein, *The New Deal Collective Bargaining Policy* [Berkeley: University of California Press, 1950], 116).

11. Schickler, *Racial Realignment*, 45–80.

12. Brian D. Feinstein and Eric Schickler, "Platforms and Partners: The Civil Rights Realignment Reconsidered," *Studies in American Political Development* 22 (2008): 1–31.

13. Anthony Chen, *The Fifth Freedom: Jobs, Politics, and Civil Rights in the United States, 1941–1972* (Princeton: Princeton University Press, 2009). The push for fair employment laws started with A. Philip Randolph's March on Washington Movement, which forced a reluctant Roosevelt to issue an executive order creating a temporary wartime FEPC to fight discrimination in the defense industry.

14. See Eric Schickler, Kathryn Pearson, and Brian Feinstein, "Shifting Partisan Coalitions: Support for Civil Rights in Congress from 1933–1972," *Journal of Politics* 72 (2009): 672–89; and Schickler, *Racial Realignment*, 150–75, for details.

15. As quoted in Schickler, *Racial Realignment*, 249.

16. Sam Rosenfeld, *The Polarizers: Postwar Architects of Our Partisan Era* (Chicago: University of Chicago Press, 2018).

17. Schickler, *Racial Realignment*, 238–45.

18. Mary L. Dudziak, *Cold War Civil Rights: Race and the Image of American Democracy* (Princeton: Princeton University Press, 2001).

19. Schickler, *Racial Realignment*, 8, 231–33.

20. Schickler, *Racial Realignment*, 270; see also Timothy Thurber, "Goldwaterism Triumphant? Race and the Republican Party, 1965–1968," *Journal of the Historical Society* 7 (2007): 371–73. Segregationist George Wallace's relatively strong showing in his 1968 third-party campaign for president underscored the case advocates of a GOP "southern strategy" were making—that there were more votes to be won for the party if it doubled down on appeals to Jim Crow defenders. (Wallace won forty-six electoral votes—all in the South—and 13.5 percent of the popular vote.)

21. Neil O'Brian, *The Roots of Polarization: From the Racial Realignment to the Culture Wars* (Chicago: University of Chicago Press, 2024).

22. Lilliana Mason, *Uncivil Agreement: How Politics Became Our Identity* (Chicago: University of Chicago Press, 2018).

23. Angie Maxwell and Todd Shields, *The Long Southern Strategy: How Chasing White Voters in the South Changed American Politics* (New York: Oxford University Press, 2019).

24. Wallace lobbed this charge as he prepared to enter the presidential race as a left-wing, third-party candidate (*Baltimore Sun*, "Wallace Assaults Democrats' Stand: Only Tweedledum Version of GOP Tweedledee," July 16, 1948, 2). The charge would be echoed in the American Political Science Association's 1950 report, "Toward a More Responsible Two-Party System," which called for greater clarity in the parties' respective stands.

25. See David R. Mayhew, *Divided We Govern: Party Control, Lawmaking, and Investigations* (New Haven: Yale University Press, 1991); Matthew Grossmann, *Artists of the Possible: Governing Networks and American Policy Change since 1945* (New York: Oxford University Press, 2014); and Theda Skocpol, *Diminished Democracy: From Membership to Management in American Civic Life* (Norman: University of Oklahoma Press, 2003).

26. Paul Pierson, "Fragmented Welfare States: Federal Institutions and the Development of Social Policy," *Governance* 8 (1995): 449-78, https://doi.org/10.1111/j.1468-0491.1995.tb00223.x.

27. There were, of course, important exceptions, such as the Food and Drug Administration. See Daniel Carpenter, *Reputation and Power: Organizational Image and Pharmaceutical Regulation at the FDA* (Princeton: Princeton University Press, 2010).

28. David Vogel, *Fluctuating Fortunes: The Political Power of Business in America* (New York: Basic Books, 1989).

29. Paul Pierson, "The Rise and Reconfiguration of Activist Government," in *The Transformation of American Politics: Activist Government and the Rise of Conservatism*, ed. Paul Pierson and Theda Skocpol (Princeton: Princeton University Press, 2007), 24-25.

30. Vogel, *Fluctuating Fortunes*; Benjamin C. Waterhouse, *The Land of Enterprise: A Business History of the United States* (New York: Simon & Schuster, 2019).

31. Jacob Hacker and Paul Pierson, *Winner-Take-All-Politics: How Washington Made the Rich Richer and Turned Its Back on the Middle Class* (New York: Simon & Schuster, 2010), 126-34.

32. Robert Kagan, *Adversarial Legalism: The American Way of Law* (Cambridge, MA: Harvard University Press, 2001), 47.

33. Charles R. Epp, *The Rights Revolution: Lawyers, Activists, and Supreme Courts in Comparative Perspective* (Chicago: University of Chicago Press, 1998), 28.

34. Mayhew, *Divided We Govern*, 162.

35. Grossmann, *Artists of the Possible*, 128.

36. Doug McAdam and Karina Kloos, *Deeply Divided: Racial Politics and Social Movements in Postwar America* (New York: Oxford University Press, 2014), 65-120.

37. The civil rights movement's success also rested in part on increased national governmental capacity to enforce uniform standards on the states. This increased capacity, in turn, proved useful for aggressive national policy action in other policy areas. See Desmond King and Robert C. Lieberman, "'The Latter-Day General Grant': Forceful Federal Power and Civil Rights," *Journal of Race, Ethnicity, and Politics* 6 (2021): 529-64.

38. James Q. Wilson, "American Politics, Then & Now," *Commentary*, February 1979, https://www.commentary.org/articles/james-wilson/american-politics-then-now/.

39. Eugene C. Steuerle and Masahiro Kawai, *The New World Fiscal Order: Implications for Industrialized Nations.* (Washington, DC: The Urban Institute, 1996).

40. Ronald Inglehart, *The Silent Revolution: Changing Values and Political Styles among Western Publics* (Princeton: Princeton University Press, 1977).

41. Grossmann, *Artists of the Possible*, 102.

42. Mayhew, *Divided We Govern*, 89.

43. Grossmann, *Artists of the Possible*, 114–17.

44. Kim Phillips-Fein, *Invisible Hands: The Making of the Conservative Movement from the New Deal to Reagan* (New York: Norton, 2009), 158–61.

45. Bryan D. Jones, Sean M. Theriault, and Michelle Whyman, *The Great Broadening: How the Vast Expansion of the Policymaking Agenda Transformed American Politics* (Chicago: University of Chicago Press, 2019), 11. State governments also expanded their capacity to act in these decades, but an increased share of state activity depended on federal funds or was partly guided by federal mandates. See Jon C. Teaford, *The Rise of the States: Evolution of American State Government* (Baltimore: Johns Hopkins University Press, 2002).

46. Jacob Hacker, Paul Pierson, and Sam Zacher, "Why So Little Sectionalism in the United States? The Under-Representation of Place-Based Interests," in *Unequal Democracies*, ed. Noam Lupu and Jonas Pontusson (Cambridge, UK: Cambridge University Press, 2024), 98–129.

47. Enrico Moretti, *The New Geography of Jobs* (Boston: Houghton Mifflin Harcourt, 2012).

48. Jacob Grumbach, Jacob Hacker, and Paul Pierson, "The Political Economies of Red States," in *American Political Economy: Politics, Markets, and Power*, ed. Jacob S. Hacker et al. (New York: Cambridge University Press, 2021).

49. Neil Fligstein, *The Architecture of Markets: An Economic Sociology of Twenty-First Century Capitalist Economies* (Princeton: Princeton University Press, 2001); Greta Krippner, *Capitalizing on Crisis: The Political Origins of the Rise of Finance* (Harvard: Harvard University Press, 2011).

50. Mark S. Mizruchi, *The Fracturing of the American Corporate Elite* (Cambridge, MA: Harvard University Press, 2013); Neil Fligstein and Adam Goldstein, "The Legacy of Shareholder Value Capitalism," *Annual Review of Sociology* 48 (2022): 193–211; Gustavo Grullon, Yelena Larkin, and Roni Micaely, "Are US Industries Becoming More Concentrated?" *Review of Finance* 23, no. 4 (2019): 697–743; Matais Covarrubias, Germán Gutiérrez, and Thomas Philippon, "From Good to Bad Concentration? US Industries Over the Past Thirty Years," *NBER Macroeconomics Annual* 34 (2020): 1–46.

51. Josh Pacewicz, *Partisans and Partners: The Politics of the Post-Keynesian Society* (Chicago: University of Chicago Press, 2016), 121, 280.

52. Hacker and Pierson, *Winner-Take-All-Politics*, 24.

53. Jacob S. Hacker and Paul Pierson, *American Amnesia: How the War on Government Led Us to Forget What Made America Prosper* (New York: Simon and Schuster, 2016), 181.

54. Adam Bonica et al., "Why Hasn't Democracy Halted Rising Inequality?" *Journal of Economic Perspectives* 27, no. 3 (Summer 2013): 103–24.

55. Alexander Hertel-Fernandez, Theda Skocpol, and Jason Sclar, "Donor Consortia and American Politics," *Studies in American Political Development* 32 (2018): 127–65.

56. The agglomerations mentioned earlier constitute an important if partial exception. Iversen and Soskice, as well as Ogorzalek, have argued that reliance on dense labor markets of highly skilled workers now limits the mobility of knowledge economy firms. Torben Iversen and David Soskice, *Democracy and Prosperity: Reinventing Capitalism through a Turbulent Century* (Princeton: Princeton University Press), 2019; Thomas K. Ogorzalek, "The City Recentered? Local Inequality Mitigation in the Twenty-First Century," in *The American Political Economy: Politics, Markets and Power*, ed. Jacob Hacker, Alexander Hertel-Fernandez, Paul Pierson and Kathleen Thelen (Cambridge, UK: Cambridge University Press, 2021), 181–208.

57. Hacker, Pierson, and Zacher, "Why So Little Sectionalism in the United States?"

58. Hacker and Pierson, *Winner-Take-All-Politics*; Thomas W. Volscho and Nathan J. Kelly "The Rise of the Super-Rich: Power Resources, Taxes, Financial Markets, and the Dynamics of the Top 1 Percent, 1949 to 2008," *American Sociological Review* 77, no. 5 (2012): 679–99.

Chapter Five

1. See Jacob M. Grumbach, *Laboratories against Democracy: How National Parties Transformed State Politics* (Princeton: Princeton University Press, 2022); see also chap. 6.

2. Peter H. Argersinger, "A Place on the Ballot: Fusion Politics and Antifusion Laws," *The American Historical Review* 85 (1980): 287–306. A handful of states continued to allow candidates to run on multiple party ballot lines. Seth Masket demonstrates that the persistence of fusion in California allowed individual elected officials to be more independent of their parties. The elimination of fusion in 1959 empowered ideological activists to gain the upper hand in selecting candidates and shaping state party positioning. See Seth E. Masket, "It Takes an Outsider: Extralegislative Organization and Partisanship in the California Assembly, 1849–2006," *American Journal of Political Science* 51 (2009): 482–97.

3. Hirano and Snyder show that the adoption of direct primaries did not, on its own, generate increased polarization. Instead, primary competition tended to increase the quality of elected officials, particularly in areas that were safe for one party (and therefore lacked competition in the general election). See Shigeo Hirano and James M. Snyder, Jr., *Primary Elections in the United States* (New York: Cambridge University Press, 2019).

4. See David R. Mayhew, *Placing Parties in American Politics: Organization, Electoral Settings, and Government Activity in the Twentieth Century* (Princeton: Princeton University Press, 1986); and James Q. Wilson, *The Amateur Democrat: Club Politics in Three Cities* (Chicago: University of Chicago Press, 1962). Recent studies have shown that states with a legacy of traditional party organization strength (that is, political machines or machine-like organizations) remain somewhat less polarized even in the postreform era (see Katherine Krimmel, *The Transformation of American Political Parties*, PhD Dissertation, Columbia University, 2013; and Nolan M. McCarty, "Reducing Polarization by Making Parties Stronger," in *Solutions to Political Polarization in America*, ed. Nathaniel Persily (New York: Cambridge University Press, 2015), 140–43.

5. Rising education levels and changes in the labor movement also contributed to the increased role of ideological activists. The college educated tend to be more focused on issues than bread-and-butter politics, while having the resources to dominate state and local party structures. Democrats' increased dependence on public-sector unions has also helped tip the balance in favor of college educated, ideologically oriented activists.

6. Ken Kollman and Pradeep Chhibber, *The Formation of National Party Systems: Federalism and Party Competition in Canada, Great Britain, India, and the United States* (Princeton: Princeton University Press, 2004); see also Daniel J. Hopkins, *The Increasingly United States: How and Why American Political Behavior Nationalized* (Chicago: University of Chicago Press, 2018).

7. Nelis Saunders, "We Should Know," *Michigan Chronicle*, August 3, 1968, C8; Robert Mickey, *Paths Out of Dixie: The Democratization of Authoritarian Enclaves in America's Deep South, 1944–1972* (Princeton: Princeton University Press, 2015), 279; Adam Hilton, *True Blues: The Contentious Transformation of the Democratic Party* (Philadelphia: University of Pennsylvania Press, 2021), 46–56.

8. On the nationalizing impact of the reforms, see Jaime Sanchez, "Revisiting McGovern–Fraser: Party Nationalization and the Rhetoric of Reform," *Journal of Policy History* 32 (2020): 1–24; William Lunch, *The Nationalization of American Politics* (Berkeley: University of California Press, 1987); and Nelson W. Polsby, *Consequences of Party Reform* (New York: Oxford University Press, 1983).

9. See Marty Cohen et al., *The Party Decides: Presidential Nominations before and after Reform* (Chicago: University of Chicago Press, 2009); Jonathan Rauch and Raymond J. La Raja, "Re-Engineering Politicians: How Activist Groups Choose Our Candidates—Long before We Vote," Brookings Report, December 7, 2017, https://www.brookings.edu/articles/re-engineering-politicians-how-activist-groups-choose-our-politicians-long-before-we-vote/.

10. Robert J. Huckshorn et al., "Party Integration and Party Organizational Strength," *The Journal of Politics* 48 (1986): 976–91; see Margaret M. Conway, "Republican Political Party Nationalization, Campaign Activities, and Their Implications for the Party System" *Publius: The Journal of Federalism* 13 (1983): 1–17.

11. Raymond J. La Raja and Brian F. Schaffner, *Campaign Finance and Political Polarization: When Purists Prevail* (Ann Arbor: University of Michigan Press, 2015).

12. Hopkins, *Increasingly United States*, 76. According to Open Secrets, the share of funds raised by House candidates from within their states has fallen from about 75 percent in the early 2000s to below 62 percent in 2020–22. For Senate candidates, the share of in-state funds has fallen from 62 percent in 2000 to 33 percent in 2020 and 42 percent in 2022 (see Sarah Bryner, "The Nationalization of Political Contributions and the Rising Role of Out-of-State Donations," *Open Secrets Report*, May 31, 2023, https://www.opensecrets.org/news/reports/out-of-state-donations).

13. ActBlue was founded in 2004. Its fundraising skyrocketed from $19 million in its first three years to more than $3 billion in 2020 alone. WinRed was founded much later and raised $1.9 billion in 2020 (see Matthew Mosk, "Donations Pooled Online Are Getting Candidates' Attention," *Washington Post*, March 11, 2007, https://www.washingtonpost.com/wp-dyn/content/article/2007/03/10/AR2007031001185_pf.html; Melissa Holzberg, "ActBlue Still Outraises WinRed, But the GOP Platform is Catching Up," Opensecrets.org, August 4, 2021, https://www.opensecrets.org/news/2021/08/actblue-outraises-winred-gop-catching-up/).

14. Brandice Canes-Wrone and Kenneth M. Miller, "Out-of-District Donors and Representation in the US House," *Legislative Studies Quarterly* 47 (2022): 361–95, https://doi.org/10.1111/lsq.12336. According to Open Secrets, the share of funds raised for House campaigns from within candidates' congressional district has fallen from 37 percent in 2012 to 26 percent in 2022 (Bryner, "Nationalization of Political Contributions").

15. Bryner, "Nationalization of Political Contributions." By raising the contribution limits for individuals while not changing the limits on PAC contributions, the McCain-Feingold Act (2002) shifted the fundraising balance in favor of ideologically oriented donors over the more access-oriented PACs. On the impact of individual and PAC contribution limits on state-level polarization, see Michael Barber, "Ideological Donors, Contribution Limits, and the Polarization of American Legislatures," *Journal of Politics* 78 (2016): 296–310.

16. See Keith E. Hamm et al., "Independent Spending in State Elections, 2006–2010: Vertically Networked Political Parties Were the Real Story, Not Business." *Forum* 12 (2014): 305–28; and Charles R. Hunt et al., "Assessing Group Incentives, Independent Spending, and Campaign Finance Law by Comparing the States" *Election Law Journal* 19 (2020): 374–91.

17. See Jaclyn J. Kettler et al., "State Party Organizations, Independent Expenditures, and Spending Strategies" (unpublished manuscript, spring 2021); and Cory Manento, "Party Crashers: Interest Groups as a Latent Threat to Party Networks in Congressional Primaries," *Party Politics* 27 (2021): 137–48. Connor Phillips shows that ideologically oriented PACs have played an increasing role in state legislative elections since 2000 and provides suggestive evidence that as the share of ideological PAC spending rises relative to access-oriented PACs, state-level polarization tends to increase ("Interest Group Strategy and State Legislative Polarization," Paper presented at the Annual Meeting of the American Political Science Association, Montreal, September 2021).

18. Joel W. Paddock, "Local and State Political Parties," in *Oxford Handbook of State and Local Government*, ed. Donald P. Haider-Markel (New York: Oxford University Press, 2014), 165.

19. Seth Hill and Chris Tausanovitch, "Southern Realignment, Party Sorting, and the Polarization of American Primary Electorates, 1958–2012," *Public Choice* 176, no. 1–2 (2018): 107–32, https://doi.org/10.1007/s11127-017-0478-0.

20. Cassandra Handan-Nader, Andrew C. W. Myers, and Andrew B. Hall, "Polarization and State Legislative Elections," Working paper, Stanford University, 2022, https://stanforddpl .org/papers/handan-nader_myers_hall_polarization_2022/handan-nader_myers_hall_po larization_2022.pdf; Connor H. Phillips, James M. Snyder, and Andrew Hall, "Who Runs for Congress? A Study of State Legislators and Congressional Polarization" (unpublished working paper, 2021).

21. Danny Vinik, "Immigration Reform Died with Eric Cantor's Shocking Loss to a Tea Party Challenger," *The New Republic*, June 10, 2014, https://newrepublic.com/article/118092/eric -cantors-primary-loss-dave-brat-mean-immigration-reforms-dead.

22. Sarah E. Anderson, Daniel M. Butler, and Laurel Harbridge-Yong, *Rejecting Compromise: Legislators' Fear of Primary Voters* (New York: Cambridge University Press, 2020).

23. Rauch and La Raja, "Re-Engineering Politicians."

24. Rachel Porter and Tyler S. Steelman, "No Experience Required: Early Donations and Amateur Candidate Success in Primary Elections," *Legislative Studies Quarterly* 48 (2022): 455–66. Danielle Thomsen and Andrew Hall show that moderate state legislators are less likely to run for Congress today and that centrists are more likely to retire if they are elected. They each argue that the increased strength of national parties makes congressional service less satisfying for moderates. See Thomsen, *Opting Out of Congress: Partisan Polarization and the Decline of Moderate Candidates* (New York: Cambridge University Press, 2017); and Hall, *Who Wants to Run? How the Devaluing of Political Office Drives Polarization* (Chicago: University of Chicago Press, 2019).

25. Rauch and La Raja, "Re-Engineering Politicians," section 3.

26. The 1979–80 results are from Cornelius P. Cotter et al., *Party Organizations in American Politics* (Pittsburgh: University of Pittsburgh Press, 1984), 42. On the 2013 survey, see David Broockman et al., "Why Local Party Leaders Don't Support Nominating Centrists," *British Journal of Political Science* 51 (2021): 724–49. While the question wording and response options are not identical, we have explored a series of surveys of county party leaders from 1979 through 2019. The results are consistent in showing a dramatic increase in the extent to which county chairs have ideologically sorted and become more extreme. The evidence suggests that this process took hold more firmly among Republicans in the 1990s, while the Democratic shift is more noteworthy after 2000.

27. On the preference for extremists, see Broockman et al., "Why Local Party Leaders Don't Support Nominating Centrists." The 2019 survey was conducted by Shannon Jenkins and Douglas Roscoe. We thank them for providing the frequency distribution and regional breakdown. See also David Doherty, Conor M. Dowling, and Michael G. Miller, *Small Power: How Local Parties Shape Elections* (New York: Oxford University Press, 2022).

28. We were unable to obtain the distribution of ideology by region in the 1980 survey summarized in table 5.1. The survey was conducted by Cornelius Cotter and collaborators, but the original data have been lost. However, a separate survey of party elites that same year included a sizable sample of county chairs, asking them whether they are liberal, moderate, or conservative (without response options for "slightly" or "somewhat"). In that sample, 63 percent of southern Democratic chairs identified as moderate and 15 percent as conservative. By 2019, just 8 percent of southern chairs identify as moderate or conservative. Among Republicans, 55 percent of northeastern chairs identified as moderate and 3 percent as liberal in 1980. Thirty-nine years later, 10 percent of northeastern GOP chairs identified as moderate or liberal. For the 1980 survey. See John S. Jackson, III, and Barbara Leavitt Brown, "Party Elites in the United States, 1980: Republican and Democratic Party Leaders," Data set, *ICPSR Data Holdings*, February 9, 1996, https://doi.org/10.3886/ICPSR08209.v1.

29. This is consistent with Wilson's prediction that the rise of "amateur democrats" would lead to more ideological party stances. Indeed, Paddock's survey of state and local party activists shows that they generally favor a "purist" ideological platform and are not concerned with direct material incentives. See Joel W. Paddock, *State & National Parties & American Democracy* (New York: Peter Lang, 2005). Doherty et al. report that county chairs are almost always volunteers and that they "tend to, personally, be ideologically 'pure' " (Doherty, Dowling, and Miller, *Small Power*, 41, 227). Republican chairs were especially likely to believe that their voters prefer rigid candidates opposed to compromise, leading to recruitment practices that may further polarization (233, 250). Walters and her coauthors' innovative study of state party chair elections suggests that they have been an important pathway through which ideological movements have captured state parties (Kirsten Walters, Ben TerMaat, June Park, and Theda Skocpol, "Party Organizations in a Polarizing Era: New Research on US State Party Chairs, 1980–2022," Paper presented at the Annual Meeting of the American Political Science Association, Montreal, September 2022). See also Adrian Elimian's collection of biographical information on GOP state party chairs, which supports the conclusion that chairs generally lack prior experience in elective office and often enter politics through ideologically oriented groups ("GOP State Party Chairs," *Medium*, September 5, 2023, https://medium.com/@adrianelimian/gop-state-party-chairs-4ca5da18b5).

30. Daniel J. Hopkins, Eric Schickler, and David L. Aziz, "From Many Divides, One? The Polarization and Nationalization of American State Party Platforms, 1918–2017," *Studies in American Politics* 36 (2022): 1–20, https://doi.org/10.1017/S0898588X22000013.

31. Paddock, *State & National Parties*.

32. Gerald Gamm, Justin Phillips, Matthew Carr, and Michael Auslen, "The Culture War and Partisan Polarization: State Political Parties, 1960–2018," Paper presented at the Annual Meeting of the American Political Science Association, Montreal, September 2022. The authors argue that the state-level polarization on social issues occurred gradually, with no particular year standing out as a critical juncture. Feinstein and Schickler ("Platforms and Partners") identify a similar pattern decades earlier in the case of civil rights, with northern state parties gradually moving apart from each other in the 1940s–50s, with the national parties following in the 1960s.

33. Alexander Burns, "11 Dem State Chairs Endorsing 'Freedom to Marry,'" *Politico*, May 3, 2012, https://www.politico.com/blogs/burns-haberman/2012/05/11-dem-state-chairs-endorsing -freedom-to-marry-122373.

34. Lara Korte, "California GOP Rejects Effort to Strip Abortion, Same Sex Marriage from Platform," *Politico*, September 30, 2023, https://www.politico.com/news/2023/09/30/california -gop-rejects-effort-to-strip-abortion-same-sex-marriage-from-platform-00119299.

35. Daniel J. Coffey, "State Party Activism in 2016," in *The State of the Parties*, 8th ed., ed. John Green, Daniel Coffey, and David Cohen (Lanham, MD: Rowman & Littlefield, 2018), 94. Along these lines, Gamm et al. ("The Culture War and Partisan Polarization") report that 100 percent of state Democratic parties took a pro-choice and pro-gay rights position by 2016. Republicans were unified in opposition to abortion by 2012 and have become nearly unanimous in refusing to support gay rights.

36. Hopkins, *Increasingly United States*, 238.

37. Hopkins, *Increasingly United States*. On state legislative outcomes, David R. Jones, "Partisan Polarization and the Effect of Congressional Performance Evaluations on Party Brands and American Elections," *Political Research Quarterly* 68 (2015): 785–801; Joshua N. Zingher and Jesse Richman, "Polarization and the Nationalization of State Legislative Elections," *American Politics Research* 47 (2019): 1036–54, https://doi.org/10.1177/1532673X18788050; and Steven Rogers, "Electoral Accountability for State Legislative Roll Calls and Ideological Representation," *American Political Science Review* 111 (2017): 555–71.

38. On state legislative polarization, see Boris Shor and Nolan McCarty, "Two Decades of Polarization in American State Legislatures," *Journal of Political Institutions and Political Economy* 3 (2022): 343–70. On state policy choices, see Grumbach, *Laboratories against Democracy*; and Devin Caughey and Christopher Warshaw, *Dynamic Democracy: Citizens, Parties, and Policymaking in the American States* (Chicago, University of Chicago Press, 2022).

39. See, e.g., Hank Stephenson and Jennifer Medina, "Arizona GOP Rebukes 3 Influential Figures," *New York Times*, January 24, 2021, A15; Sewell Chan and Eric Neugeboren, "Texas Republican Convention Calls Biden Win Illegitimate and Rebukes Cornyn over Gun Talks," *Texas Tribune*, June 18, 2022, https://www.texastribune.org/2022/06/18/republican-party-texas -convention-cornyn/; Penelope Overton, "Maine Republicans Adopt Platform to Ban Sexually Based Material, Transgender Identity in Schools." *Portland Press Herald*, April 29, 2022, https:// www.pressherald.com/2022/04/29/platform-amendments-spark-debate-at-maine-republican -convention/; and Trip Gabriel, "After Roe, Republicans Sharpen Attacks on Gay and Transgender Rights," *New York Times*, July 22, 2022, https://www.nytimes.com/2022/07/22/us/politics/after-roe -republicans-sharpen-attacks-on-gay-and-transgender-rights.html.

40. Daniel Schlozman and Sam Rosenfeld, *The Hollow Parties: The Many Pasts and Disordered Present of American Party Politics* (Princeton: Princeton University Press, 2024), 246.

41. See Todd Richmond and David A. Leib, "Trump-Aligned Challengers Ousting GOP Legislative Incumbents," Associated Press, August 4, 2022, https://apnews.com/article/2022-mid term-elections-wisconsin-donald-trump-gun-politics-b892a5eb2bf1dfa3ad148f8cb0119b31.

42. Schlozman and Rosenfeld, *Hollow Parties*, 265.

43. Robert A. Dahl, *A Preface to Democratic Theory* (Chicago: University of Chicago Press, 1956). Dahl was no fan of the Constitution, arguing that it went too far in empowering minorities to block action. He asserted that "to assume that this country has remained democratic because of its Constitution seems to me an obvious reversal of the relation; it is much more plausible to suppose that the Constitution has remained because our society is essentially democratic" (143).

In Dahl's view, societal pluralism—reflected in the diversity of active organized groups—was the foundation of American democracy's robustness.

44. Dahl, *Preface to Democratic Theory*, 150–51.

45. As discussed in chapter 1, this pluralist view also included important blind spots. Most notably, it underestimated the extent to which certain groups—in particular, racial minorities and the poor—could be excluded from effective influence for long spans of time.

46. John Mark Hansen develops this logic in his study of the bipartisan farm lobby, which dominated agricultural policymaking for much of the twentieth century (*Gaining Access: Congress and the Farm Lobby, 1919–1981* [Chicago: University of Chicago Press, 1981]). He notes that rather than "fight battles on all possible fronts," Democrats and Republicans "choose their conflicts carefully" (224). In a highly pluralistic society, party "dominance is necessarily rare . . . political parties structure a few important social conflicts, but they fail to structure many more" (226).

47. See Theda Skocpol, *Diminished Democracy: From Membership to Management in American Civic Life* (Norman: University of Oklahoma Press, 2003); Charles M. Cameron et al., "From Textbook Pluralism to Modern Hyperpluralism: Interest Groups and Supreme Court Nominations, 1930–2017," *Journal of Law and Courts* 8, no. 2 (2022): 301–32, https://doi.org/10.1086/709912; and Frank Baumgartner and Bryan D. Jones, *Agendas and Instability in American Politics* (Chicago: University of Chicago Press, 1993). Hugh Heclo's analysis of "issue networks" is consistent with these other studies, suggesting that interest group participation typically worked through loose "networks of people who regard each other as knowledgeable, or at least as needing to be answered" ("Issue Networks and the Executive Establishment," in *The New American Political System*, ed. Anthony King [Washington, DC: American Enterprise Institute, 1978], 104).

48. Jack L. Walker, *Mobilizing Interest Groups in America: Patrons, Professions, and Social Movements* (Ann Arbor: University of Michigan Press, 1991), 72.

49. Skocpol, *Diminished Democracy*, 139. The 2018 edition of the *Encyclopedia* listed more than 24,100 nonprofit membership associations of national scope in the US.

50. On the Sierra Club's growth, see David Karol, *Red, Green, and Blue: The Partisan Divide on Environmental Issues*, 2019, https://doi.org/10.1017/9781108673266, 3. On Greenpeace, see Jeffrey M. Berry, *The New Liberalism and the Rising Power of Citizen Groups* (Washington, DC: Brookings Institution, 1999), 145. On the growth of staff, see Baumgartner and Jones, *Agendas and Instability*, 186–87.

51. Theda Skocpol, "Activist Government and the Reorganization of American Civic Democracy," in *The Transformation of American Politics*, ed. Paul Pierson and Theda Skocpol (Princeton: Princeton University Press, 2007), 48. See also Beth Leech, Frank Baumgartner, Tim La Pira, and Nicholas Semanko, "Drawing Lobbyists to Washington: Government Activity and the Demand for Advocacy," *Political Research Quarterly*, 58 (2005): 19–30.

52. On public-sector unions, see Sarah Anzia and Terry Moe, "Do Politicians Use Policy to Make Politics? The Case of Public-Sector Labor Laws," *American Political Science Review* 110 (2016): 763–77. On litigation, see Sean Farhang, *The Litigation State: Public Regulation and Private Lawsuits in the US* (Princeton: Princeton University Press, 2010).

53. Leech et al., "Drawing Lobbyists to Washington," 28.

54. David Vogel, *Kindred Strangers: The Uneasy Relationship between Politics and Business in America* (Princeton: Princeton University Press, 1996); and Jacob Hacker and Paul Pierson, *Winner-Take-All-Politics: How Washington Made the Rich Richer and Turned Its Back on the Middle Class* (New York: Simon & Schuster, 2010), 126–34.

55. Skocpol, *Diminished Democracy*, 224.

56. Skocpol, *Diminished Democracy*, 210.

57. Kathleen Bawn et al., "A Theory of Parties," *Perspectives on Politics* 10 (2012): 571–97.

58. Hansen, *Gaining Access*; David R. Mayhew, *Divided We Govern: Party Control, Lawmaking, and Investigations* (New Haven: Yale University Press, 1991).

59. David Karol, *Party Position Change in American Politics: Coalition Management* (New York: Cambridge University Press, 2009).

60. Frances E. Lee, *Insecure Majorities: Congress and the Perpetual Campaign* (Chicago: University of Chicago Press, 2016).

61. As we discuss in chapter 6, bipartisan legislation has not disappeared. However, the constraints facing efforts to build bipartisan coalitions have grown considerably, and party-based legislative strategies have become much more common, particularly when it comes to the most salient, highly visible (and consequential) policy issues.

62. Jesse M. Crosson, Alexander C. Furnas, and Geoffrey M. Lorenz, "Polarized Pluralism: Organizational Preferences and Biases in the American Pressure System," *American Political Science Review* 114 (2020): 1117–37.

63. Crosson, Furnas, and Lorenz, "Polarized Pluralism"; E. J. Fagan, Zachary A. McGee, and Herschel F. Thomas, "The Power of the Party: Conflict Expansion and the Agenda Diversity of Interest Groups," *Political Research Quarterly* 74 (2019): 90–102, https://doi.org/10.1177/1065912919867142.

64. Michael Barber and Mandi Eatough, "Industry Politicization and Interest Group Campaign Contribution Strategies," *The Journal of Politics* 82 (2021): 1008–25.

65. Cameron et al., "From Textbook Pluralism to Modern Hyperpluralism."

66. Matthew J. Lacombe, *Firepower: How the NRA Turned Gun Owners into a Political Force* (Princeton: Princeton University Press, 2021).

67. Lacombe, *Firepower*.

68. See Hacker and Pierson, *Winner-Take-All-Politics*, on the NRA's growth. On the group's 1994 role, see Dan Balz and Ronald Brownstein, *Storming the Gates: Protest Politics and the Republican Revival* (Boston: Little, Brown, 1996).

69. Neil O'Brian, *The Roots of Polarization: From Racial Realignment to the Culture Wars* (Chicago: University of Chicago Press, 2024).

70. Daniel Schlozman, *When Movements Anchor Parties: Electoral Alignments in American History* (Princeton: Princeton University Press, 2015), 101–6. Evangelical voters had conservative views on abortion even in the early 1970s, but political mobilization on the issue was quite limited (Neil O'Brian, "Before Reagan: The Development of Abortion's Partisan Divide," *Perspectives on Politics* 18 [2020]: 1031–47).

71. See Amy Lakeman, *When Theology Responds: How Politics Shapes Religious Belief*, PhD Dissertation, Harvard University, 2022, on the changing Protestant–Catholic relationship; on the Moral Majority, see Doug Banwart, "Jerry Falwell, the Rise of the Moral Majority, and the 1980 Election." *Western Illinois Historical Review* 5 (2013): 133–57.

72. The party's 1976 platform had avoided a clear stance on abortion.

73. See Karol, *Party Position Change*; Schlozman, *When Movements Anchor Parties*; Greg D. Adams, "Abortion: Evidence of an Issue Evolution," *American Journal of Political Science* 41 (1997): 718–37; and Neil O'Brian, "Before Reagan," 1031–47. O'Brian shows that Republican vote choice was associated with antiabortion views among white voters in the 1970s–80s, but the relationship with party identification was negligible. Conservatism on a range of other non-economic

issues—racial equality, marijuana legalization, women's equality, and the rights of the accused, among others—was associated with antiabortion views by the 1970s.

74. Angie Maxwell and Todd Shields, *The Long Southern Strategy: How Chasing White Voters in the South Changed American Politics* (New York: Oxford University Press, 2019), 262.

75. Gamm, Phillips, Carr, and Auslen, "The Culture War and Partisan Polarization."

76. David Lesher, "Abortion is Litmus Test, Casey Says," *Los Angeles Times*, July 14, 1992, WA6. Casey's son, Robert Casey Jr., was elected to the Senate in 2007. Although Casey has called himself a pro-life Democrat, he gradually became a reliable pro-choice vote during his time in the Senate (Jennifer Haberkorn, "The Truth Behind Bob Casey's 'Pro-Life' Stand," *Politico*, July 2, 2018, https://www.politico.com/story/2018/07/02/casey-abortion-pennsylvania-midterms-689505).

77. Karol, "Red, Green, and Blue."

78. Karol, "Red, Green, and Blue," 6.

79. Karol, "Red, Green, and Blue," 23–24.

80. Karol, "Red, Green, and Blue," 32, 54.

81. Karol, "Red, Green, and Blue," 33, 54.

82. Vogel, *Kindred Strangers*; Jacob S. Hacker and Paul Pierson, *American Amnesia : How the War on Government Led Us to Forget What Made America Prosper* (New York: Simon and Schuster, 2016).

83. Hacker and Pierson, *American Amnesia*. Tensions between the GOP and Chamber would emerge in 2022 when Republican House leader Kevin McCarthy called on the Chamber to remove its president, Suzanne Clarke, after the Chamber endorsed more than a dozen House Democrats in the midterm elections. Given that the overwhelming majority of Chamber endorsements and campaign spending continued to go to Republicans in 2022, the rift indicates the heightened expectations of party loyalty in the contemporary era. Laura Davison, "House Republicans Target US Chamber of Commerce as GOP Battle against 'Woke Capitalism' Heats Up," *Fortune*, November 27, 2022, https://fortune.com/2022/11/27/chamber-of-commerce-gop-crosshairs-republican-house-lawmakers-target-woke-capitalism/.

84. Jacob S. Hacker and Paul Pierson, *Let Them Eat Tweets: How the Right Rules in an Age of Extreme Inequality* (New York: Norton, 2020).

85. On the development of partisan newspapers, see Maria Petrova, "Newspapers and Parties: How Advertising Revenues Created an Independent Press," *American Political Science Review*, 105 (2011): 790–808. For an analysis of party bias, see Shigeo Hirano and James M. Snyder Jr., "Measuring the Partisan Behavior of US Newspapers, 1880–1980," *Journal of Economic History*, forthcoming.

86. See Petrova, "Newspapers and Parties"; and Matthew Gentzkow, Edward L. Glaeser, and Claudia Goldin, "The Rise of the Fourth Estate," in *Corruption and Reform: Lessons from America's Economic History*, ed. Glaeser and Goldin (Chicago: University of Chicago Press, 2014), 210, 212.

87. Gentzkow, Glaeser, and Goldin, "Rise of the Fourth Estate."

88. Hirano and Snyder, "Measuring the Partisan Behavior US Newspapers." On the rise of an independent press, see also Michael Schudson, *Discovering the News: A Social History of American Newspapers* (New York: Basic Books, 1978). On the importance of local monopolies, see Milena Djourelova, Ruben Durante, and Gregory Martin, "The Impact of Online Competition on Local Newspapers: Evidence from the Introduction of Craigslist," May 1, 2021, https://ssrn.com/abstract=3846243.

89. On the decline in staffing and coverage, see Pew Research Center, "State of the News Media 2016," June 15, 2016, https://assets.pewresearch.org/wp-content/uploads/sites/13/2016/06/3014

3308/state-of-the-news-media-report-2016-final.pdf. See also Hopkins, *Increasingly United States*; and Gregory A. Huber and Patrick Tucker, "Congressional Accountability in the Contemporary Media Environment: Arguments, Data, and Method," in *Accountability Reconsidered: Voters, Interests, and Information in US Policymaking*, ed. Charles M. Cameron et al. (New York: Cambridge University Press, 2023).

90. Daniel J. Moskowitz, "Local News, Information, and the Nationalization of US Elections." *American Political Science Review* 115 (2021): 1–16.

91. Moskowitz, "Local News, Information, and the Nationalization of US Elections"; Hopkins, *Increasingly United States.*

92. Danny Hayes and Jennifer L. Lawless, *News Hole: The Demise of Local Journalism and Political Engagement* (New York: Cambridge University Press, 2021). See also Marc Trussler, "Get Information or Get in Formation: The Effects of High-Information Environments on Legislative Elections," *British Journal of Political Science* 51 (2021): 1529–49; James M. Snyder Jr. and David Strömberg, "Press Coverage and Political Accountability," *Journal of Political Economy* 118 (2010): 355–40; Brandice Canes-Wrone and Michael R. Kistner, "Local Newspapers and Ideological Accountability in US House Elections," in *Accountability Reconsidered.*

93. Even local TV news is subject to a form of delocalization through consolidation. Sinclair Broadcasting, for instance, has built an empire of nearly 200 local stations. Martin and McCrain document that stations purchased by Sinclair increased their focus on national news at the expense of local news and shifted political coverage to the right. Gregory J. Martin and Joshua McCrain, "Local News and National Politics," *American Political Science Review* 113 (2019): 372–84.

94. Yochai Benkler, Robert Faris, and Hal Roberts, *Network Propaganda: Manipulation, Disinformation and Radicalization in American Politics* (Oxford: Oxford University Press, 2018).

95. Nicole Hemmer, *Messengers of the Right: Conservative Media and the Transformation of American Politics* (Philadelphia: University of Pennsylvania Press, 2016), 258–60.

96. Jeffrey M. Berry and Sarah Sobieraj, *The Outrage Industry: Political Opinion Media and the New Incivility* (Oxford: Oxford University Press, 2013).

97. Markus Prior, *Post-Broadcast Democracy: How Media Choice Increases Inequality in Political Involvement and Polarizes Elections* (Cambridge, UK: Cambridge University Press, 2007).

98. Benkler, Faris, and Roberts, *Network Propaganda*; Matt Grossmann and David A. Hopkins, "Placing Media in Conservative Culture," in *Conservative Political Communication*, ed. Sharon E. Jarvis (New York: Routledge, 2021).

99. See Matthew Levendusky, *How Partisan Media Polarize America* (Chicago: University of Chicago Press, 2013). Broockman and Kalla (2023) show that viewership for partisan news is higher than some earlier studies suggested. Approximately one in seven Americans consume at least eight hours per month of partisan television, and few of these individuals consume cross-cutting television channels. See Broockman, David, and Joshua Kalla, "Selective Exposure and Partisan Echo Chambers in Television News Consumption: Evidence from Linked Viewership, Administrative, and Survey Data," OSF Preprints, April 14, 2023, https://osf.io/b54sx/.

100. For studies of the impact of Fox on vote share, see Gregory J. Martin and Ali Yurukoglu, "Bias in Cable News: Persuasion and Polarization." *American Economic Review*, 107 (2017): 2565–99; and Elliot Ash et al., "The Effect of Fox News Channel on US Elections: 2000–2020," May 2022, https://papers.ssrn.com/sol3/papers.cfm?abstract_id=3837457. On Fox's impact on viewers' policy views, see David Broockman and Josh Kalla, "Consuming Cross-Cutting Media Causes Learning and Moderates Attitudes: A Field Experiment with Fox News Viewers," *Journal of Politics*, forthcoming. On Fox's impact on congressional roll-call voting, see Kevin Arceneaux

et al., "The Influence of News Media on Political Elites: Investigating Strategic Responsiveness in Congress," *American Journal of Political Science*, 60 (2016): 5–29.

101. Zhao Li and Gregory J. Martin, "Media and Ideological Movements: How Fox News Built the Tea Party" (unpublished manuscript, April 2021), 2–3, https://as.nyu.edu/content/dam/nyu-as/politics/documents/fox_news_tea_party.pdf. See also Levendusky, *How Partisan Media Polarize America*.

102. Grossmann and Hopkins, "Placing Media in Conservative Culture," 18.

103. Broockman and Kalla, "Consuming Cross-Cutting Media."

104. Djourelova, Durante, and Martin, "The Impact of Online Competition on Local Newspapers," 1n2.

105. Djourelova, Durante, and Martin, "The Impact of Online Competition on Local Newspapers." See also Hayes and Lawless, *News Hole*; Moskowitz, "Local News, Information, and the Nationalization of US Elections"; Trussler, "Get Information or Get in Formation"; and Joshua P. Darr, Matthew P. Hitt, and Johanna L. Dunaway, "Newspaper Closures Polarize Voting Behavior," *Journal of Communication* 68 (2018): 1007–28.

106. Carrie Levine and Chris Zubak-Skees, "How ActBlue is Trying to Turn Small Donations into a Blue Wave," *Center for Public Integrity*, October 25, 2018, https://publicintegrity.org/politics/how-actblue-is-trying-to-turn-small-donations-into-a-blue-wave/.

107. See David W. Rohde, *Parties and Leaders in the Postreform House* (Chicago: University of Chicago Press, 1991); and John M. Barry, *The Ambition and the Power* (New York: Penguin Books, 1989).

108. As quoted in Barry, *Ambition and the Power*, 166.

109. Matthew N. Green and Jeffrey Crouch, *Newt Gingrich: The Rise and Fall of a Party Entrepreneur* (Lawrence: University Press of Kansas, 2022), 65. Gingrich worked closely with the conservative editorial boards of the *Wall Street Journal* and *Washington Times* to push the scandals. He also collaborated with conservative activists on the ground to push local news stories on Wright, which he then passed along to national reporters to create momentum for increased coverage. See Barry, *Ambition and the Power*, 531, 605–18; and Eric Schickler, *Disjointed Pluralism: Institutional Innovation and the Development of the US Congress* (Princeton: Princeton University Press, 2021), 242–46.

110. Julian E. Zelizer, *Burning Down the House: Newt Gingrich, the Fall of a Speaker, and the Rise of the New Republican Party* (New York: Penguin, 2020), 174.

111. As quoted in Balz and Brownstein, *Storming the Gates*, 140.

112. As quoted in Balz and Brownstein, *Storming the Gates*, 135.

113. Balz and Brownstein, *Storming the Gates*, 31. On depriving Clinton of a record to promote, see p. 46. See Mel Steely, *The Gentleman from Georgia: The Biography of Newt Gingrich* (Macon, GA: Mercer University Press, 2000), 256, on Gingrich's use of talk radio.

114. Green and Crouch, *Newt Gingrich: The Rise and Fall of a Party Entrepreneur*, 58; see also Steely, *Gentleman from Georgia*, 186–87; and Balz and Brownstein, *Storming the Gates*, 145.

115. For example, as an Ohio state legislator future Speaker John Boehner became "addicted" to Gingrich's vision after receiving the unsolicited tapes (Balz and Brownstein, *Storming the Gates*, 146).

116. Balz and Brownstein, *Storming the Gates*, 152.

117. Heather Cox Richardson, "When Republicans Went Insane: Newt Gingrich, Fox News, Grover Norquist and the Roots of Today's Shameful Intransigence," *Salon*, September 20, 2014;

David Maraniss and Michael Weisskopf, *"Tell Newt to Shut Up!"* (New York: Simon & Schuster, 1996), 10, 139.

118. Nick Confessore, "Welcome to the Machine," *Washington Monthly*, July 1, 2003, https://washingtonmonthly.com/2003/07/01/welcome-to-the-machine/. The National Republican Congressional Campaign Committee also began to grade "every single PAC, sorted by industry, with special marks for giving to freshman Republicans on committees with relevant jurisdiction" (Schlozman and Rosenfeld, *Hollow Parties*, 225).

119. Maraniss and Weisskopf, *"Tell Newt to Shut Up!"*, 139.

Chapter Six

1. Steven L. Taylor, Matthew S. Shugart, Arend Lijphart, and Bernard Grofman, *A Different Democracy: American Government in a 31-Country Perspective* (New Haven: Yale University Press, 2014).

2. See Rufus E. Miles, "The Origin and Meaning of Miles' Law," *Public Administration Review* 38 (1978): 399–403, https://doi.org/10.2307/975497.

3. Alfred Stepan and Juan J. Linz, "Comparative Perspectives on Inequality and the Quality of Democracy in the United States," *Perspectives on Politics* 9 (2011): 841–56.

4. Alex Isenstadt, "The Extreme Measure One House Republican is Taking to Win Over Donald Trump," *Politico*, January 31, 2020, https://www.politico.com/news/2020/01/31/thomas-massie-trump-110136.

5. Jacob M. Grumbach, *Laboratories against Democracy: How National Parties Transformed State Politics* (Princeton: Princeton University Press, 2022); and Devin Caughey and Christopher Warshaw, *Dynamic Democracy: Citizens, Parties, and Policymaking in the American States* (Chicago, University of Chicago Press, 2022).

6. Jonathan A. Rodden, *Why Cities Lose: The Deep Roots of the Urban-Rural Political Divide* (New York: Basic Books, 2018); Suzanne Mettler and Trevor Brown, "The Growing Rural–Urban Political Divide and Democratic Vulnerability," *The Annals of the American Academy of Political and Social Science* 99 (2022): 130–42, https://doi.org/10.1177/00027162211070061.

7. C. Lawrence Evans, "The Counter-Majoritarian Senate" (unpublished working paper, March 2023). In 1997–98, the GOP majority represented 50.2 percent of the population. In each subsequent Congress, the GOP represented less than half of the population. In Evans's analysis, each senator from a state is assigned half of its population; that is, if there is a split party delegation, each party is credited with half of the population, while one party receives credit for the full population if both senators are from that party.

8. Gregory Elinson and Jonathan Gould, "The Politics of Deference," *Vanderbilt Law Review* 75 (2022): 477–78.

9. Among the first to take stock of the changes were Roger H. Davidson, "The New Centralization on Capitol Hill," *Review of Politics* 50 (1988): 345–64; and David W. Rohde, *Parties and Leaders in the Postreform House* (Chicago: University of Chicago Press, 1991). On "partisan warfare," see Eric Schickler and Kathryn Pearson, "The House Leadership," in *Congress Reconsidered*, 8th ed., ed. Lawrence C. Dodd and Bruce Oppenheimer (Washington: CQ Press, 2005); and Sean Theriault, *The Gingrich Senators: The Roots of Partisan Warfare in Congress* (New York: Oxford University Press, 2013). On rising dysfunction, see Thomas E. Mann and Norman J. Ornstein, *It's Even Worse than It Looks: How the American Constitutional System Collided with the New Politics of Extremism* (New York: Basic Books, 2012).

10. Important exceptions include Frances E. Lee, "How Party Polarization Affects Governance," *Annual Review of Political Science*, 18 (2015):261–82; Nolan McCarty, "How Congressional Polarization is Transforming the Separation of Powers," in *Congress Reconsidered*, 12th ed., ed. Lawrence C. Dodd, Bruce I. Oppenheimer, and C. Lawrence Evans (Washington, DC: CQ Press, 2021); Sarah A. Binder, "The Dysfunctional Congress," *Annual Review of Political Science*, 18 (2015): 85–101; and Sarah A. Binder, *Stalemate: Causes and Consequences of Legislative Gridlock* (Washington, DC: Brookings Institution Press, 2004).

11. See McCarty, "How Congressional Polarization is Transforming the Separation of Powers"; and Sarah A. Binder, "Assessing Presidential and Congressional Rivalry in an Era of Polarization," in *Rivals for Power: Presidential-Congressional Relations*, 7th ed., ed. James Thurber (Lanham, MD: Rowman & Littlefield, 2022).

12. Steven S. Smith, *The Senate Syndrome: The Evolution of Procedural Warfare in the Modern US Senate* (Norman: University of Oklahoma Press, 2014).

13. See Frances E. Lee, *Insecure Majorities: Congress and the Perpetual Campaign* (Chicago: University of Chicago Press, 2016); and C. Lawrence Evans, "Committees, Leaders, and Message Politics," in *Congress Reconsidered*, 7th ed., ed. Lawrence Dodd and Bruce Oppenheimer (Washington, DC: CQ Press, 2001).

14. McCarty, "How Congressional Polarization is Transforming the Separation of Powers," 437.

15. Michael Grunwald, *The New New Deal: The Hidden Story of Change in the Obama Era* (New York: Simon and Schuster, 2012), 19.

16. Even where the filibuster is unavailable, unified minority opposition means that even a small number of majority party defections will sink a measure. See James M. Curry and Frances E. Lee, *The Limits of Party: Congress and Lawmaking in a Polarized Era*. (Chicago: University of Chicago Press, 2021).

17. See Binder, *Stalemate*; and Binder, "Assessing Presidential and Congressional Rivalry in an Era of Polarization." Drawing on David Mayhew's coding of "landmark" laws, McCarty finds that the ten least polarized Congresses since World War II produced an average of nearly sixteen highly significant enactments, while the ten most polarized produced just over ten such laws (McCarty, "How Congressional Polarization is Transforming the Separation of Powers," 437–38.

18. See Molly E. Reynolds, "The Politics of the Budget and Appropriations Process in a Polarized Congress," in *Congress Reconsidered*, 12th ed. In their debt-ceiling fight with President Biden in 2023, House Republicans chose not to pass a budget resolution, which would have required greater specificity about the areas of spending they wished to cut. Instead, they passed a messaging bill that set out general targets for cuts, but avoided specifics about which program areas would be subject to reductions.

19. Mark Strand and Tim Lang, "The Sausage Factory: Fixing the Authorization Process: Restoring Checks and Balances," *Congressional Institute*, October 19, 2017, https://www.congressionalinstitute.org/2017/10/19/fixing-the-authorization-process-restoring-checks-and-balances/.

20. Peter Hanson, *Too Weak to Govern: Majority Party Power and Appropriations in the US Senate* (New York: Cambridge University Press, 2014); and McCarty, "How Congressional Polarization is Transforming the Separation of Powers."

21. Reynolds, "The Politics of the Budget and Appropriations Process in a Polarized Congress."

22. See Lee and Curry, *Limits of Party*, 33–34.

23. In responding to two recent crises—the financial system bailout addressing the 2008 economic crash and the series of coronavirus relief bills enacted in 2020—divided party control facilitated bipartisan compromise as each party sought to avoid blame for the catastrophe that would have resulted from inaction. See Sarah A. Binder, "The Struggle to Legislate in Polarized Times," in *Congress Reconsidered*, 12th ed.; and Binder, "Assessing Presidential and Congressional Rivalry in an Era of Polarization.").

24. Binder, "The Struggle to Legislate in Polarized Times." Similarly, passing a long-term highway funding authorization bill used to be routine. Starting in 2009, however, such bills became more precarious. A short, two-year extension enacted in 2012 qualifies as a success based on Binder's gridlock measure, yet this meant punting on the longer-term extension that previously had been the norm (258).

25. See McCarty, "How Congressional Polarization is Transforming the Separation of Powers," 439.

26. Binder, "The Struggle to Legislate in Polarized Times," 269.

27. Lee and Curry, *Limits of Party*, 190.

28. Sarah A. Binder, "Assessing Presidential and Congressional Rivalry in an Era of Polarization," in *Rivals for Power: Presidential-Congressional Relations*, 7th ed., ed. James Thurber (Lanham: Rowman & Littlefield, 2022), 97.

29. Lee, "How Party Polarization Affects Governance," 276.

30. McCarty, "How Congressional Polarization is Transforming the Separation of Powers," 432.

31. The Act fell five votes short of the sixty-vote threshold to break a filibuster. It was not quite a party-line vote, as five moderate Democrats voted against it while three moderate Republicans voted for it.

32. Franklin Foer, "How Trump Radicalized ICE," *The Atlantic*, September 2018, https://www.theatlantic.com/magazine/archive/2018/09/trump-ice/565772/.

33. Lucy Rodgers and Dominic Bailey, "Trump Wall: How Much Has He Actually Built," *BBC News*, October 31, 2020, https://www.bbc.com/news/world-us-canada-46824649.

34. McCarty, "How Congressional Polarization is Transforming the Separation of Powers," 433.

35. The final bill passed the House with just six no votes and it passed the Senate unanimously. It is true that Republicans were less enthusiastic about the impoundment control provisions of the Budget Act, but they agreed to them as part of a broader package of reforms that included congressional mechanisms to limit spending and deficits (see Eric Schickler, "Institutional Development, 1937–1989: A Return to Party Government or the Triumph of Individualism?" chap. 5 in *Disjointed Pluralism: Institutional Innovation and the Development of the US Congress* [Princeton: Princeton University Press, 2001]).

36. By weaking the Senate's confirmation role President Trump's heavy reliance on acting officials to lead agencies added a further obstacle to serious congressional scrutiny.

37. There also may be a cost when it comes to policy quality when each branch is no longer playing its constitutional role. The broad coalitions generally necessary to enact legislation lend the resulting policies a degree of buy-in and durability that may be absent when the president acts unilaterally (see McCarty, "How Congressional Polarization is Transforming the Separation of Powers").

38. McCarty, "How Congressional Polarization is Transforming the Separation of Powers," 449–53; and Lee, "How Party Polarization Affects Governance," 271–72.

39. Lee, "How Party Polarization Affects Governance," 271.

40. Lee, *Insecure Majorities*.

41. Andy Barr, "The GOP's No-Compromise Pledge," *Politico*, October 28, 2010, https://www
.politico.com/story/2010/10/the-gops-no-compromise-pledge-044311.

42. Frances E. Lee, *Beyond Ideology: Politics, Principles, and Partisanship in the US Senate*
(Chicago: University of Chicago Press, 2009), 76–79.

43. Jonathan S. Gould and David E. Pozen, "Structural Biases in Structural Constitutional
Law," *New York Law Review* 97 (2022): 59–136.

44. Elinson and Gould, "The Politics of Deference," 539.

45. Elinson and Gould, "The Politics of Deference," 524.

46. Stacy Cowley, "How Millions of Borrowers Got $127 Billion in Student Loans Canceled,"
New York Times, November 11, 2023, https://www.nytimes.com/2023/11/11/business/student-loans
-debt-cancellation.html.

47. Elinson and Gould, "The Politics of Deference."

48. Jackie Calmes, "How Republicans Have Packed the Courts for Years." *Time*, June 22,
2021, https://time.com/6074707/republicans-courts-congress-mcconnell/.

49. Steven M. Teles, *The Rise of the Conservative Legal Movement: The Battle for Control of
the Law* (Princeton: Princeton University Press, 2008).

50. Coral Davenport, "Republican Drive to Tilt Courts against Climate Action Reaches a
Crucial Moment," *New York Times*, June 19, 2022, https://www.nytimes.com/2022/06/19/climate
/supreme-court-climate-epa.html.

51. Peter Baker and Shailagh Murray, "Bush Defends Supreme Court Pick," *Washington
Post*, October 5, 2005, https://www.washingtonpost.com/archive/politics/2005/10/05/bush-defends
-supreme-court-pick/9f289349-6825-4d85-a158-cb164e076937/.

52. "ABA Ratings During the Trump Administration," *Ballotpedia*, https://ballotpedia.org
/ABA_ratings_during_the_Trump_administration, accessed November 11, 2023.

53. Calmes, "How Republicans Have Packed the Courts for Years."

54. Through September 2023, Biden appointed thirty-six circuit court judges (compared to
forty-three for Trump and nineteen for Obama during the same time span during their administrations) and 103 district court judges (compared to 101 for Trump and 74 for Obama). See Rus-
sell Wheeler, "Biden Judicial Appointment Status Report—Topping Trump Seems Impossible,"
Brookings, October 5, 2023, https://www.brookings.edu/articles/biden-judicial-appointment-status
-report-topping-trump-seems-impossible/.

55. Mark Joseph Stern, "Believe Mitch McConnell: Republicans Will Never Confirm Another Democrat-Appointed Supreme Court Justice," *Slate*, June 14, 2021, https://slate.com/news
-and-politics/2021/06/mcconnell-biden-breyer-supreme-court.html.

56. Davenport, "Republican Drive to Tilt Courts against Climate Action Reaches a Crucial
Moment."

57. Elinson and Gould, "The Politics of Deference," 525–30.

58. Amanda Hollis-Brusky, "Can Congress Resurrect Roe If It's Overturned? Well, It Could
Try," *Washington Post*, May 4, 2022, https://www.washingtonpost.com/politics/2022/05/04/roe
-overturned-congress-abortion-law.

59. Elinson and Gould, "The Politics of Deference."

60. On the predominance of liberal enactments, see Matthew Grossmann, *Artists of the Possible: Governing Networks and American Policy Change since 1945* (New York: Oxford University
Press, 2014).

61. Daniel J. Hopkins, *The Increasingly United States: How and Why American Political Behavior Nationalized* (Chicago: University of Chicago Press, 2018); and Grumbach, *Laboratories against Democracy*.

62. Boris Shor and Nolan McCarty, "The Ideological Mapping of American Legislatures," *American Political Science Review* 105 (2011): 530–51; and Boris Shor and Nolan McCarty, "Two Decades of Polarization in American State Legislatures," *Journal of Political Institutions and Political Economy* 3 (2022): 343–70.

63. See Cassandra Handan-Nader, Andrew C. W. Myers, and Andrew B. Hall, "Polarization and State Legislative Elections," Working paper, Stanford University, 2022. Changes in campaign finance laws have also contributed. Recent studies have shown that the *Citizens United* decision has especially helped more conservative Republican state legislative candidates. See Anna Harvey and Taylor Mattia, "Does Money Have a Conservative Bias? Estimating the Causal Impact of Citizens United on State Legislative Preferences," *Public Choice* 191 (2022): 417–41.

64. "Historical and Potential Changes in Trifectas," *Ballotpedia*, https://ballotpedia.org/Historical_and_potential_changes_in_trifectas. The *Ballotpedia* data goes back to 1992; we thank Devin Caughey for providing information on unified party control in the states going back to 1948. See also Caughey and Warshaw, *Dynamic Democracy*, 71–75.

65. Alexander Hertel-Fernandez, *State Capture: How Conservative Activists, Big Businesses, and Wealthy Donors Reshaped the American States—and the Nation* (New York: Oxford University Press, 2019).

66. The Act was repealed in a referendum in November 2011, with 62 percent voting to overturn the restrictions on unions. A similar law, however, survived a repeal effort in Wisconsin.

67. See Grumbach, *Laboratories against Democracy*, xiii; and Samuel Trachtman, "When State Policy Makes National Politics: The Case of 'Obamacare' Marketplace Implementation," *Journal of Health Politics, Policy and Law* 45 (2020): 111–41.

68. Nick Corasaniti, "How a Little-Known Group Helped Resurgent Democrats Wield Power," *New York Times*, September 25, 2023, https://www.nytimes.com/2023/09/25/us/politics/states-project-democrats.html?searchResultPosition=1.

69. See Grumbach, *Laboratories against Democracy*, xiii.

70. Caroline Cummings, "2023 Minnesota Legislative Session ends. See What Bills Passed," *CBS News*, May 22, 2023, https://www.cbsnews.com/minnesota/news/session-nears-end-a-look-at-what-bills-have-passed-and-whats-still-left-on-the-table/.

71. Grumbach, *Laboratories against Democracy*, 47, 51, figure 3.3.

72. Caughey and Warshaw, *Dynamic Democracy*.

73. Calculations by the authors from the data in "Historical and Potential Changes in Trifectas," *Ballotpedia*. Democrats narrowed the gap to just twenty-two to seventeen following the 2022 elections.

74. Emma Pettit, "'Cynical and Illegitimate': Higher-Ed Groups Assail Legislative Efforts to Restrict Teaching of Racism," *Chronicle of Higher Education*, June 16, 2021; Rick Seltzer, "Restrictions Threaten 'Integrity of Our System of Higher Education,' Groups Say," *Higher Ed Dive*, June 8, 2022, https://www.highereddive.com/news/restrictions-threaten-integrity-of-our-system-of-higher-education-groups/625159/; and Desmond King and Rogers Smith, *America's New Racial Battle Lines: Protect versus Repair* (Chicago: University of Chicago Press, 2024).

75. Skyler Swisher, "DeSantis Targets Tenure and 'Politicized' Classes," *Daytona Times*, June 10, 2022, https://www.daytonatimes.com/community/education/desantis-targets-tenure-and-politicized-classes/article_a6aabb1a-e8de-11ec-af90-3bfc81be8390.html. DeSantis's "Don't Say Gay"

Act, restricting discussions of sexual orientation and gender identity in public schools also gar-nered considerable national attention for the Florida Governor.

76. Grumbach, *Laboratories against Democracy*.

77. The Massachustts GOP was chaired by pro-Trump conservative Jim Lyons from 2018–22. Lyons referred to Donald Trump as "the greatest president in my lifetime." Michael P. Norton, "Trump Spirit, Fighting Theme Runs Through Mass. GOP Convention," *NBC Boston*, May 23, 2022, https://www.nbcboston.com/news/politics/trump-spirit-fighting-theme-runs-through-mass -gop-convention/2728081/.

Chapter Seven

1. Clark would resurface in an alarming 2023 report on a seventy-five–group effort, Proj-ect 2025, organized by the Heritage Foundation. The report suggests the project is intended to ensure that the next Republican administration's Justice Department would be far less inde-pendent of the president. According to the report Clark was leading work on the Insurrection Act, which could be invoked to deploy federal troops in response to popular protests. Isaac Arnsdorf, Josh Darsey and Devlin Barrett, "Trump and Allies Plot Revenge, Justice Department Control in a Second Term," *Washington Post*, November 5, 2023, https://www.washingtonpost.com /politics/2023/11/05/trump-revenge-second-term/.

2. Eric Tucker and Farnoush Amiri, "Hearing: Trump Told Justice Department to Call Elec-tion 'Corrupt,'" Associated Press, June 23, 2022, https://apnews.com/article/capitol-siege-elec tions-donald-trump-campaigns-presidential-4e7e68e2ff57aadd96d09c873a43a317.

3. See, e.g., Robert C. Lieberman et al., "The Trump Presidency and American Democracy: A Historical and Comparative Analysis," *Perspectives on Politics* 17, no. 2 (2019): 470–79. The Bright Line Watch project, which included students of American political behavior as well as specialists on global politics, was also an early and important source of insight. See John M. Carey et al., "Searching for a Bright Line in the Trump Presidency," *Perspectives on Politics* 17 (2019): 699–718, http://dx.doi.org/10.2139/ssrn.3142310.

4. Tom Ginsburg and Aziz Z. Huq, *How to Save a Constitutional Democracy* (Chicago: Uni-versity of Chicago Press, 2018).

5. See Juan J. Linz and Alfred Stepan, eds., *The Breakdown of Democratic Regimes* (Balti-more: Johns Hopkins University Press, 1978).

6. Steven Levitsky and Daniel Ziblatt, *Tyranny of the Minority: Why American Democracy Reached the Breaking Point* (New York: Crown, 2023), 50.

7. Nick Corasaniti, Karen Yourish, and Keith Collins, "How Trump's 2020 Election Lies Have Gripped State Legislatures," *New York Times*, May 22, 2023, https://www.nytimes.com/interactive /2022/05/22/us/politics/state-legislators-election-denial.html.

8. McKay Coppins, *Romney: A Reckoning* (New York: Scribner, 2023), 9, 243.

9. Mead Grover, "Wyoming GOP Censures Rep. Liz Cheney over Impeachment Vote," Associated Press, February 6, 2021, https://apnews.com/article/donald-trump-capitol-siege -censures-rawlins-wyoming-3d2a5ad3377bb748c22f632642ba23f1; Sam Metz, "GOP Censures Cheney, Kinzinger as it Assails Jan 6. Probe," Associated Press, February 4, 2022, https://apnews .com/article/donald-trump-salt-lake-city-election-2020-campaign-2016-liz-cheney-cca6e ba133e2edee7987cac10e86d5c7.

10. As we discuss in chapter 1, this perspective has always had important blind spots. Indeed, federalism enabled a form of subnational authoritarianism to thrive in the South for generations.

Robert Mickey, *Paths Out of Dixie: The Democratization of Authoritarian Enclaves in America's Deep South, 1944–1972* (Princeton: Princeton University Press, 2015).

11. Guillermo O'Donnell, "Delegative Democracy," *Journal of Democracy* 5 (1994): 61.

12. Jenna Bednar, "Polarization, Diversity, and Democratic Robustness." *Proceedings of the National Academy of Sciences* 118, no. 50 (2021), https://doi.org/10.1073/pnas.2113843118.

13. Jennifer Agiesta and Ariel Edwards-Levy, "CNN Poll: Percentage of Republicans Who Think Biden's 2020 Win Was Illegitimate Ticks Back Up near 70%," *CNN*, August 3, 2023, https://www.cnn.com/2023/08/03/politics/cnn-poll-republicans-think-2020-election-illegitimate/index.html.

14. Because of our focus on domestic politics we do not explore here another vulnerability: the growing risk that foreign actors will successfully intervene in American elections. The growing divergence between the parties has increased the stakes of American elections for foreign governments as well as American citizens. They too can attempt to hack the system, supporting the efforts of whichever team they favor. Because tilting a few votes in a few states can be decisive this possibility should not be underestimated. What would be the impact, for instance, if Saudi Arabia chose to raise oil prices a few months before a presidential election? And, of course, the possibility is not merely hypothetical. Russia already engaged in such efforts in 2016.

15. John Sides, Michael Tesler, and Lynn Vavreck, *Identity Crisis: The 2016 Presidential Campaign and the Battle for the Meaning of America* (Princeton: Princeton University Press, 2018); Robert Mickey, Steve Levitsky, and Lucan Way, "Is America Still Safe for Democracy?" *Foreign Affairs*, May/June 2017,

16. Arlie R. Hochschild, *Strangers in Their Own Land: Anger and Mourning on the American Right* (New York: New Press, 2016); Katherine J. Cramer, *The Politics of Resentment: Rural Consciousness in Wisconsin and the Rise of Scott Walker* (Chicago: University of Chicago Press, 2016).

17. Trevor Brown, Suzanne Mettler, and Samantha Puzzi, "When Rural and Urban Become 'Us' versus 'Them': How a Growing Divide is Reshaping American Politics," *Forum* 29, no. 3 (2021): 365–93, https://doi.org/10.1515/for-2021-2029.

18. Levitsky and Ziblatt, *Tyranny of the Minority*.

19. Unlike legislation to counter the president—which requires a veto-proof margin to succeed—either chamber of Congress can independently launch investigations with few limitations on their scope.

20. Douglas L. Kriner and Eric Schickler, *Investigating the President: Congressional Checks on Presidential Power* (Princeton: Princeton University Press, 2016); Josh Chafetz, *Congress's Constitution: Legislative Authority and the Separation of Powers* (New Haven: Yale University Press, 2017).

21. Chafetz, *Congress's Constitution*; David R. Mayhew, *America's Congress: Actions in the Public Sphere* (New Haven: Yale University Press, 2002).

22. Ari Rabin-Havt, "How Much Money Can Republicans Raise Off Benghazi? Ask Darrell Issa," *New Republic*, May 11, 2014, https://newrepublic.com/article/117713/darrell-issas-benghazi-fundraising-how-his-campaign-grew-rich.

23. Kriner and Schickler, *Investigating the President*.

24. See Eric Schickler, "Institutional Development, 1937–1952: The Conservative Coalition, Congress against the Executive, and Committee Government," chap. 4 in *Disjointed Pluralism: Institutional Innovation and the Development of the US Congress* (Princeton: Princeton University Press, 2001).

25. Schickler, *Disjointed Pluralism*, 159.

26. Ruth Bloch Rubin, "Organizing for Insurgency: Intraparty Organization and the Development of the House Insurgency, 1908–1910," *Studies in American Political Development* 27 (2013): 86–110. For example, President Taft's decision to fire Land Office Director Gifford Pinchot—following Pinchot's refusal to abide by a gag order preventing him from going to Congress with complaints about administration policy—sparked an investigation by the Republican Congress. Notably, progressive Republicans—mostly from the Midwest and West—deprived Speaker Joseph Cannon of the power to appoint committee members in order to prevent the investigation from being a whitewash. Meanwhile, progressive Republican Senator La Follette led an investigation of Taft's effort to purge Theodore Roosevelt's allies from the post office, exposing corruption and highlighting the plight of workers gagged by executive restrictions. This effort led to passage of the Lloyd–La Follette Act of 1912, which affirmed federal workers' right to provide information to Congress. See Stephen Skowronek, *Building a New American State: The Expansion of National Administrative Capacities, 1877–1920* (Cambridge, MA: Harvard University Press, 1982), 191.

27. Telford Taylor, *Grand Inquest: The Story of Congressional Investigations* (New York: Simon and Schuster, 1954), 55–56.

28. On World War II investigations, see Roland A. Young, *Congressional Politics in the Second World War* (New York: Columbia University Press, 1956); on Iraq, see Kriner and Schickler, *Investigating the President*, 62–65.

29. John Herbers, "Subpoena Scored by White House," *New York Times*, December 22, 1973, 23; George Lardner Jr., "GOP Minority Denounces Panel Findings as 'Hysterical,'" *Washington Post*, November 19, 1987, A25; Dylan Scott and Tara Isabella Burton, "'Witch hunt!': The History of Donald Trump's Favorite Impeachment Defense, Explained," vox.com, December 17, 2019, https://www.vox.com/policy-and-politics/2018/4/17/17235546/donald-trump-impeachment -witch-hunt-salem.

30. Louise Hutchinson, "Percy introduces resolution: Senate asks Nixon for Watergate prosecutor," *Chicago Tribune*, May 2, 1973, 5.

31. Richard L. Madden, "Brooke Appeals to Nixon to Resign for Nation's Sake," *New York Times*, November 5, 1973, 1.

32. Charles Franklin, "Nixon, Watergate, and Partisan Opinion," *Medium*, August 12, 2018, https://medium.com/@PollsAndVotes/nixon-watergate-and-partisan-opinion-524c4314d530.

33. Several Republicans expressed concern that Democrats would use the investigation to tarnish the Reagan administration, but the 416–2 House vote and eighty-eight to four Senate vote reflected broad agreement that an investigation was justified. David Rosenbaum, "Senate to Set up Iran Inquiry Panel," *New York Times*, January 7, 1987, https://www.nytimes.com/1987/01/07/world /senate-to-set-up-iran-inquiry-panel.html; and Helen Dewar and Edward Walsh, "House Creates Iran-Contra Probe Unit; Senate May Query Foreign Leaders," *Washington Post*, January 8, 1987, A7.

34. Dan Morgan, *Washington Post*, "Iran Report Accuses Administration of 'Disdain for Law,'" November 19, 1987), 1, 28. Although some Republican colleagues were not pleased with Rudman's stance, he was by no means read out of the party. Indeed, Rudman later served as cochair of John McCain's 2000 presidential run.

35. Pew Research Center, "Presidential Approval by Party, From Eisenhower to Obama," January 10, 2017, https://www.pewresearch.org/interactives/presidential-approval-by-party-from -eisenhower-to-obama/.

36. Jen Kirby, "Trump's Purge of Inspectors General, Explained," Vox.com, May 28, 2020, https://www.vox.com/2020/5/28/21265799/inspectors-general-trump-linick-atkinson.

37. David Weigel, "House Republicans Are Already Preparing for 'Years' of Investigations of Clinton," *Washington Post*, October 26, 2016; and Amber Phillips, "Why Is Jason Chaffetz Suddenly Retiring from Congress? One Word: Ambition." *Washington Post*, April 19, 2017.

38. Ashley Parker, Rosalind Helderman, Josh Dawsey, and Carol Leonnig, "Trump Sought Release of Classified Russia Memo, Putting Him at Odds with Justice Department," *Washington Post*, January 27, 2018, https://www.washingtonpost.com/politics/trump-sought-release-of-classified-russia-memo-putting-him-at-odds-with-justice-department/2018/01/27/a00f2a4c-02bb-11e8-9d31-d72cf78dbeee_story.html.

39. Matthew Rozsa, "Devin Nunes Finds that Shilling for Donald Trump Is Paying Off—Literally," *Salon*, May 25, 2018, https://www.salon.com/2018/05/25/devin-nunes-finds-that-shilling-for-donald-trump-is-paying-off-literally/.

40. Charlie Savage, "Trump Vows Stonewall of 'All' House Subpoenas, Setting Up Fight over Powers," *New York Times*, April 24, 2019, https://www.nytimes.com/2019/04/24/us/politics/donald-trump-subpoenas.html.

41. As recently as June 2012, when House Republicans voted to hold President Obama's Attorney General Eric Holder in contempt of Congress for his refusal to turn over specific documents related to the Department of Justice's failed "Fast and Furious" gun operation, seventeen Democrats crossed the aisle and voted for contempt, and twenty-one Democrats voted to allow the House Oversight and Government Reform Committee to sue the Justice Department for additional documents. The Holder case—like most other battles over executive privilege prior to the Trump administration—featured negotiations between the administration and Congress that resulted in at least some documents being turned over without requiring a court order. See Douglas L. Kriner and Eric Schickler, "Congressional Investigations in a Polarized Era or Has Polarization (and Trump?) Broken the Investigative Check," in *Congress Reconsidered*, 12th ed., ed. Lawrence C. Dodd, Bruce Oppenheimer and C. Lawrence Evans (Washington, DC: CQ Press, 2021).

42. Quinta Jurecic, "White House Letter to Congress on Impeachment Inquiry," *Lawfare*, October 8, 2019, https://www.lawfareblog.com/white-house-letter-congress-impeachment-inquiry.

43. Peter Baker, "The Impeachment Witnesses Not Heard," *New York Times*, November 21, 2019, https://www.nytimes.com/2019/11/21/us/politics/impeachment-witnesses.html.

44. Mike Lillis et al., "Republicans Storm Closed-Door Hearing to Protest Impeachment Inquiry," *The Hill*, October 23, 2019, https://thehill.com/homenews/house/467092-republicans-storm-into-house-hearing-to-break-up-trump-impeachment-testimony.

45. Michael Shear and Nicholas Fandos, "Republicans Block Impeachment Witnesses, Clearing Path for Trump Acquittal," *New York Times*, January 31, 2020, https://www.nytimes.com/2020/01/31/us/politics/trump-impeachment-trial.html.

46. Jeffrey M. Jones, "Trump Job Approval at Personal Best 49%," *Gallup*, February 4, 2020, https://news.gallup.com/poll/284156/trump-job-approval-personal-best.aspx.

47. *US News & World Report*, "Mitch McConnell's Statement to the Senate on the Storming of the Capitol," January 6, 2021, https://www.usnews.com/news/elections/articles/2021-01-06/read-mitch-mcconnells-statement-to-the-senate-on-the-storming-of-the-capitol.

48. Jonathan Martin, Maggie Haberman, and Nicholas Fandos, "McConnell Privately Backs Impeachment as House Moves to Charge Trump," *New York Times*, January 12, 2021, https://www.nytimes.com/2021/01/12/us/politics/mcconnell-backs-trump-impeachment.html.

49. The Clinton impeachment battle was also highly partisan, with Democrats nearly unified in opposition. However, many congressional Democrats were harshly critical of the presi-

dent and favored censuring him. It is noteworthy that one of Clinton's sharpest Democratic critics, Sen. Joseph Lieberman (D-CT) was the party's nominee for vice president in the next election.

50. Nancy Bermeo, "On Democratic Backsliding," *Journal of Democracy* 27 (2016): 5–19.

51. Bednar, "Polarization, Diversity, and Democratic Robustness."

52. Dan Slater, "Threats or Gains: The Battle over Participation in America's Careening Democracy," *Annals of the Academy of Political and Social Sciences*, 699 (2022): 90–100; Robert Mickey, "Challenges to Subnational Democracy in the United States, Past and Present," *Annals of the Academy of Political and Social Sciences*, 699 (2022): 118–29.

53. Gretchen Helmke, Mary Kroeger, and Jack Paine, "Democracy by Deterrence: Norms, Constitutions, and Electoral Tilting," *American Journal of Political Science* 66 (2022): 434–50, https://doi.org/10.1111/ajps.12668.

54. Grumbach, *Laboratories against Democracy*.

55. See Steve Bickerstaff, *Lines in the Sand: Congressional Redistricting in Texas and the Downfall of Tom DeLay* (Austin: University of Texas Press, 2007). The old map inherited a pro-Democratic bias because of a stalemate induced by divided government following the 2000 election. The new, GOP-drawn map, however, had a significant Republican tilt.

56. Christopher Warshaw, Eric McGhee, and Michal Migurski, "Districts for a New Decade—Partisan Outcomes and Racial Representation in the 2021–22 Redistricting Cycle," *Publius: The Journal of Federalism* 52 (2022): 430, https://doi.org/10.1093/publius/pjac020.

57. David A. Lieb, "Census Data Spurred GOP's Largest Partisan Edge in Decades," Associated Press, August 10, 2021, https://apnews.com/article/joe-biden-census-2020-redistricting-house -elections-04f3d29cbc4441705922dbc40ba61961.

58. Edward-Isaac Dovere, "Obama, Holder to lead post-Trump redistricting campaign," *Politico*, October 17, 2016, https://www.politico.com/story/2016/10/obama-holder-redistricting -gerrymandering-229868.

59. Jonathan A. Rodden, *Why Cities Lose: The Deep Roots of the Urban-Rural Political Divide* (New York: Basic Books, 2018).

60. Craig Gilbert, "New Election Data Highlights the Ongoing Impact of 2011 GOP Redistricting in Wisconsin," *Milwaukee Journal Sentinel*, December 6, 2018, https://www.jsonline.com /story/news/blogs/wisconsin-voter/2018/12/06/wisconsin-gerrymandering-data-shows-stark -impact-redistricting/2219092002/.

61. Rob Yablon, "Explainer: Wisconsin's New State Legislative Maps Compare Unfavorably to Other Court-Adopted Maps on Partisan Equity," *State Democracy Research Initiative*, April 18, 2022, https://statedemocracy.law.wisc.edu/featured/2022/explainer-wisconsins-new-state-legislative -maps-compare-unfavorably-to-other-court-adopted-maps-on-partisan-equity/.

62. Julie Bosman, "Justices in Wisconsin Order New Legislative Maps," *New York Times*, December 23, 2023, https://www.nytimes.com/2023/12/22/us/wisconsin-redistricting-maps-gerry mander.html.

63. Michigan, which had split control of government, also used an independent commission for its thirteen seats. See Chris Leaverton, "Who Controlled Redistricting in Every State," Brennan Center, October 5, 2022, https://www.brennancenter.org/our-work/research-reports/who -controlled-redistricting-every-state.

64. Nathaniel Rakich, "The New National Congressional Map is Biased Toward Republicans," *Fivethirtyeight.com*, June 15, 2022, https://fivethirtyeight.com/features/the-new-national -congressional-map-is-biased-toward-republicans/.

65. Nicholas Fandos, "Top Court Clears Path for Democrats to Redraw House Map in New York," *New York Times*, December 12, 2023, https://www.nytimes.com/2023/12/12/nyregion/new-york-redistricting-democrats.html.

66. Chris Leaverton, "Who Controlled Redistricting in Every State"; on North Carolina, see Patrick Marley and Robert Barnes, "NC Supreme Court Reverses Redistricting Ruling in a Win for Republicans," *Washington Post*, April 28, 2023, https://www.washingtonpost.com/politics/2023/04/28/north-carolina-courts-redistricting-voter-id/.

67. Warshaw, McGhee, and Migurski, "Districts for a New Decade," 428.

68. Rakich, "The New National Congressional Map is Biased Toward Republicans." It is worth noting that even with Republicans' gerrymandering advantage, the party's popular vote share outpaced its seat share in the 2022 House midterm. This outcome was in part due to differences in candidate quality in closely contested races, with the GOP failing to nominate candidates well-positioned to compete in several swing districts. The GOP's continued gains in rural areas have also led to greater wasted votes for the party as it becomes more challenging to draw efficient districts in some states; indeed, twenty-four Republicans had no Democratic opponent in 2022, as compared to six Democrats with no GOP opponent. See Darragh Roche, "Democrats Allowed 24 Republican House Candidates to Run Unopposed," *Newsweek*, November 17, 2022, https://www.newsweek.com/democrats-allowed-24-republican-house-candidates-run-unopposed-1760345.

69. See Nate Cohn, "Why Republicans Could Prevail in the Popular Vote but Lose in the House," *New York Times*, October 11, 2022, https://www.nytimes.com/2022/10/11/upshot/republicans-midterms-house-analysis.html.

70. Mickey, "Challenges to Subnational Democracy," 123.

71. Mickey, "Challenges to Subnational Democracy," 121.

72. Grumbach, *Laboratories against Democracy*; Hertel-Fernandez, *State Capture: How Conservative Activists, Big Businesses, and Wealthy Donors Reshaped the American States—and the Nation* (New York: Oxford University Press, 2019); and Mickey, "Challenges to Subnational Democracy."

73. Hertel-Fernandez, *State Capture*.

74. "Voter ID Laws," *National Council of State Legislatures*, https://www.ncsl.org/research/elections-and-campaigns/voter-id.aspx, accessed June 24, 2022.

75. Brennan Center for Justice, "Voting Laws Roundup: October 2021," https://www.brennancenter.org/our-work/research-reports/voting-laws-roundup-october-2021. Mickey notes that since *Shelby County*, twenty-three states have enacted laws restricting voting; twenty of the states had unified GOP control of the legislature and governor's mansion ("Challenges to Subnational Democracy," 122).

76. Enrico Cantoni and Vincent Pons, "Strict ID Laws Don't Stop Voters: Evidence from a US Nationwide Panel, 2008–2018," *Quarterly Journal of Economics*, 136 (2021): 2615–60.

77. Corasaniti, Yourish, and Colins, "How Trump's 2020 Election Lies Have Gripped State Legislatures."

78. Zach Schonfeld, "Texas GOP Approves Measure Declaring Biden 'Was Not Legitimately Elected,'" *The Hill*, June 20, 2022, https://thehill.com/homenews/3529666-texas-gop-adopts-measure-declaring-biden-was-not-legitimately-elected/.

79. Richard L. Hasen, "Identifying and Minimizing the Risk of Election Subversion and Stolen Elections in the Contemporary United States," *Harvard Law Review Forum*, April 2022, https://harvardlawreview.org/forum/no-volume/identifying-and-minimizing-the-risk-of-election-subversion-and-stolen-elections-in-the-contemporary-united-states/; and Amy Gard-

ner, "A Majority of GOP Nominees Deny or Question the 2020 Election Results," *Washington Post*, October 12, 2022, https://www.washingtonpost.com/nation/2022/10/06/elections-deniers -midterm-elections-2022/.

80. On Marchant and Mastriano, see Zach Montellaro, "Trump Backers Unbowed in Push to Overtake State Election Offices," *Politico*, June 13, 2022, https://www.politico.com /news/2022/06/13/trump-state-election-offices-00038956.

81. Adrian Blanco, Daniel Wolfe, and Amy Gardner, "Tracking which 2020 election deniers are winning, losing in the midterms," *Washington Post*, December 18, 2022, https://www.washing-tonpost.com/politics/interactive/2022/election-deniers-midterms/?itid=sf_elections_Election %20deniers_p007_f002.

82. Heidi Przybyla, " 'It's Going to Be an Army': Tapes Reveal GOP Plan to Contest Elections," *Politico*, June 1, 2022, https://www.politico.com/news/2022/06/01/gop-contest-elections -tapes-00035758.

83. Hasen, "Identifying and Minimizing the Risk of Election Subversion."

84. Aziz Huq, "The Supreme Court and the Dynamics of Democratic Backsliding," *The Annals of the American Academy of Political and Social Science*, 699 (2022): 51, https://doi.org /10.1177/00027162211061124.

85. Nicholas Riccardi, "Supreme Court to Hear Case on State Authority over Elections," Associated Press, June 30, 2022, https://apnews.com/article/2022-midterm-elections-us-supreme -court-north-carolina-election-2020-state-courts-712d5aa719884bab9652d3c132ee56c6.

86. Karen Yourish, Larry Buchanan, and Denise Lu, "The 147 Republicans Who Voted to Overturn Election Results," *New York Times*, January 7, 2021, https://www.nytimes.com/interac tive/2021/01/07/us/elections/electoral-college-biden-objectors.html.

87. See, e.g., Linda Soo, Joseph Tanfani, and Jason Szep, "Pro-Trump Conspiracy Theorists Hound Election Officials Out of Office," *Reuters Investigates*, October 19, 2022, https://www.reu ters.com/investigates/special-report/usa-election-nevada-washoe/; and *Reuters*, "Campaign of Fear: The Trump World's Assault on US Election Workers," 2021, https://www.reuters.com /investigates/section/campaign-of-fear/.

88. Grumbach, *Laboratories against Democracy*.

89. Mac Brower, "Why Texas Republicans Want a State Electoral College," *Democracy Docket*, August 3, 2022, https://www.democracydocket.com/analysis/why-texas-republicans-want-a-state -electoral-college/; Whitney Downard, "Republic vs. Democracy: Does the Indiana platform word change hold greater significance," *Indiana Capital Chronicle*, July 5, 2022, https://indianacap italchronicle.com/2022/07/05/republic-vs-democracy-does-it-mean-anything/. See also Robert Draper, "The Arizona Republican Party's Anti-Democracy Experiment," *New York Times Magazine*, August 15, 2022, https://www.nytimes.com/2022/08/15/magazine/arizona-republicans-demo cracy.html.

90. Again, the case of Reconstruction underscores that reactionary forces at the state level were fully capable of undermining democracy, abetted by a supportive court majority and largely silent Congress.

Chapter Eight

1. Anthony Downs, *An Economic Theory of Democracy* (New York: Harper, 1957); Morris P. Fiorina and Samuel J. Abrams, *Disconnect: The Breakdown of Representation in American Politics* (Norman: University of Oklahoma Press, 2009), xvii.

2. Although the public's views of immigration are complicated and depend heavily on how issues are framed, there is little doubt that Democrats have moved to the left on immigration policy and that a majority of voters express more conservative views on at least some key border policies (see, e.g., Asma Khalid, "Democrats Used to Talk about 'Criminal Immigrants,' So What Changed the Party?" *NPR*, February 19, 2019, https://www.npr.org/2019/02/19/694804917 /democrats-used-to-talk-about-criminal-immigrants-so-what-changed-the-party; Amina Dunn, "Americans Remain Critical of Government's Handling of Situation at US–Mexico Border," Pew Research Center, June 21, 2023, https://www.pewresearch.org/short-reads/2023/06/21/americans -remain-critical-of-governments-handling-of-situation-at-us-mexico-border/.

3. Downs's own account pointed to a number of factors that can lead parties to take non-centrist positions. Nonetheless, as Fiorina makes clear, the "master theory" associated with Downs emphasizes the strong pull exerted by the median voter.

4. Pippa Norris, " 'Things Fall Apart, the Center Cannot Hold': Fractionalized and Polarized Party Systems in Western Democracies" (unpublished manuscript, 2023).

5. On identity-inflected issues, see John Sides, Chris Tausanovitch, and Lynn Vavreck, *The Bitter End: The 2020 Presidential Campaign and the Challenge to American Democracy* (Princeton: Princeton University Press, 2022).

6. Rosalind Heiderman and Jonathan Cohen, "As Republican Convention Emphasizes Diversity, Racial Incidents Intrude," *Washington Post*, August 29, 2012, https://www.washingtonpost .com/politics/2012/08/29/b9023a52-f1ec-11e1-892d-bc92fee603a7_story.html.

7. See Bernard Fraga, Yamil Velez, and Emily West, "Reversion to the Mean, or their Version of the Dream? An Analysis of Latino Voting in 2020" (unpublished working paper, August 2023), https://preprints.apsanet.org/engage/apsa/article-details/64c9451d9ed5166e93de2210. See also Hannah Hartig et al., "Voting Patterns in the 2022 Elections," Pew Research Center Reports, July 12, 2023, https://www.pewresearch.org/politics/2023/07/12/voting-patterns-in-the -2022-elections/.

8. C. Lawrence Evans, "The Counter-Majoritarian Senate" (unpublished working paper, March 2023); and Suzanne Mettler and Trevor Brown, "The Growing Rural–Urban Political Divide and Democratic Vulnerability," *The Annals of the American Academy of Political and Social Science* 99 (2022): 130–42, https://doi.org/10.1177/00027162211070061.

9. Janet Malzahn and Andrew B. Hall, "Election-Denying Republican Candidates Under-performed in the 2022 Midterms" (unpublished manuscript, February 2023), https://andrew benjaminhall.com/Malzahn_Hall_Election_Denying_Candidates_2022.pdf.

10. Marianne Levine, "Trump Calls Political Enemies 'Vermin,' Echoing Dictators Hitler, Mussolini," *Washington Post*, November 13, 2023, https://www.washingtonpost.com/politics/2023 /11/12/trump-rally-vermin-political-opponents/; Julia Johnson, "DeSantis and Haley forced into balancing act as they hold fire against Trump," *Washington Examiner*, December 12, 2023, https:// www.washingtonexaminer.com/news/campaigns/desantis-haley-trump-criticism-republicans.

11. Jonathan Swan, Maggie Haberman, and Charlie Savage, "How Trump and His Allies Plan to Wield Power in 2025," *New York Times*, November 15, 2023, https://www.nytimes.com/article /trump-2025-second-term.html.

12. Sides, Tausanovitch, and Vavreck, *Bitter End*.

13. Lee Drutman, *Breaking the Two-Party Doom Loop: The Case for Multiparty Democracy in America* (New York: Oxford University Press, 2009).

14. Jacob S. Hacker et al., "Bridging the Blue Divide: The Democrats' New Metro Coalition and the Unexpected Prominence of Redistribution," *Perspectives on Politics*, forthcoming.

15. Jacob Hacker, Paul Pierson, and Sam Zacher, "Why So Little Sectionalism in the United States? The Under-Representation of Place-Based Interests," in *Unequal Democracies*, ed. Noam Lupu and Jonas Pontusson (Cambridge, UK: Cambridge University Press, 2024).

16. William S. Becker, "Red States Win with Inflation Reduction Act—GOP Wants to Kill It Anyway," *The Hill*, April 11, 2023, https://thehill.com/opinion/campaign/3944108-red-states-win -with-inflation-reduction-act-gop-wants-to-kill-it-anyway.

17. Mary L. Dudziak, *Cold War Civil Rights: Race and the Image of American Democracy* (Princeton: Princeton University Press, 2001).

18. Democrats had begun to centralize control of the legislative process in the 1980s, with Jim Wright's speakership representing a departure from the more restrained partisanship that had characterized the House. These changes helped persuade House Republicans that Gingrich's strategy of all-out opposition was their best option to gain power. See David W. Rohde, *Parties and Leaders in the Postreform House* (Chicago: University of Chicago Press, 1991); and John M. Barry, *The Ambition and the Power* (New York: Penguin Books, 1989).

19. Yuval Levin, *The Fractured Republic: Renewing America's Social Contract in an Era of Individualism* (New York: Basic Books, 2017).

20. Robert Mickey, *Paths Out of Dixie : The Democratization of Authoritarian Enclaves in America's Deep South, 1944–1972* (Princeton: Princeton University Press, 2015).

21. Grumbach, *Laboratories against Democracy*.

22. Steven Levitsky and Daniel Ziblatt, *Tyranny of the Minority: Why American Democracy Reached the Breaking Point* (New York: Crown, 2023).

23. See also Robert A. Dahl, *How Democratic is the American Constitution?* (New Haven: Yale University Press, 2001).

24. A more generous standard might treat the two-term limit for presidents, the ban on the poll tax for federal elections, and the lowering of the voting age to eighteen as "fundamental reforms." By that looser standard the reform drought is fifty-one years.

25. Although some have argued that there are constitutional strategies that would get around the Article 5 provision that "no state, without its consent, shall be deprived of its equal suffrage in the Senate," these strategies would still require ratification from three-quarters of the states, a very high bar. See George Mader, "Binding Authority: Unamendability in the United States Constitution—A Textual and Historical Analysis," *Marquette Law Review* 99 (2016): 841–91.

26. This does not rule out the important possibility of workarounds that seek to modify constitutional features without amending the Constitution itself, such as the proposed "interstate compact" that would use state legislation to ensure the popular vote winner for president is also the victor in the Electoral College.

27. See, e.g., Bruce E. Cain and Cody Gray, "Parties by Design: Pluralist Party Reform in a Polarized Era," *New York University Law Review* 93 (2018): 621–46; Raymond J. La Raja and Jonathan Rauch, "Voters Need Help: How Party Insiders Can Make Presidential Primaries Safer, Fairer, and More Democratic," *Brookings*, January 31, 2020, https://www.brookings.edu/articles /voters-need-help-how-party-insiders-can-make-presidential-primaries-safer-fairer-and -more-democratic/; Richard Pildes, "How to Fix Our Polarized Politics? Strengthen Political Parties," *Washington Post*, February 6, 2014; Frances M. Rosenbluth and Ian Shapiro, *Responsible Parties: Saving Democracy from Itself* (New Haven: Yale University Press, 2018); and Daniel Schlozman and Sam Rosenfeld, *The Hollow Parties: The Many Pasts and Disordered Present of American Party Politics* (Princeton: Princeton University Press, 2024).

28. Ruth Bloch Rubin, *Building the Bloc: Intraparty Organization in the US Congress* (New York: Cambridge University Press, 2017).

29. Initial empirical evidence suggests that nonpartisan "top two" primaries have only modest effects on legislators' ideology. One problem is that voters, at least in House and state legislative races, often lack information about the relative ideological placement of candidates within a party (Douglas Ahler, Jack Citrin, and Gabriel Lenz, "Do Open Primaries Improve Representation? An Experimental Test of California's 2012 Top-Two Primary," *Legislative Studies Quarterly* 41 [2016]: 237–68). On the other hand, if the goal is to make it viable for a faction of more centrist candidates to win (rather than shifting the ideology of the *typical* legislator), it may be that even modest effects that are concentrated in a handful of races would help foster potentially beneficial centrist factions.

30. Seth E. Masket, "It Takes an Outsider: Extralegislative Organization and Partisanship in the California Assembly, 1849–2006," *American Journal of Political Science* 51 (2007): 482–97.

31. In his book *Breaking the Two-Party Doom Loop*, Lee Drutman recommends reforms that would bolster the opportunities for third parties and move the US toward a multiparty framework. He argues that this could be done by adopting an ambitious package of electoral reforms: abolishing primaries, moving to multimember districts for the House, and introducing ranked-choice voting for the Senate. Such an agenda would require support from party leaders who were willing and able to work against the immediate political interests of many members of their coalition in the pursuit of goals that would probably have limited popular appeal.

Index